CHINA'S SENT-DOWN GENERATION

Public Management and Change Series
Beryl A. Radin, Series Editor

Editorial Board

Robert Agranoff   William Gormley
Michael Barzelay   Rosemary O'Leary
Ann O'M. Bowman   Norma Riccucci
H. George Frederickson David H. Rosenbloom

Titles in the Series

Challenging the Performance Movement: Accountability, Complexity, and Democratic Values
Beryl A. Radin

Charitable Choice at Work: Evaluating Faith-Based Job Programs in the States
Sheila Suess Kennedy and Wolfgang Bielefeld

Collaborating to Manage: A Primer for the Public Sector
Robert Agranoff

The Collaborative Public Manager: New Ideas for the Twenty-first Century
Rosemary O'Leary and Lisa Blomgren Bingham, Editors

The Dynamics of Performance Management: Constructing Information and Reform
Donald P. Moynihan

Federal Management Reform in a World of Contradictions
Beryl A. Radin

The Future of Public Administration around the World: The Minnowbrook Perspective
Rosemary O'Leary, David M. Van Slyke, and Soonhee Kim, Editors

The Greening of the US Military: Environmental Policy, National Security, and Organizational Change
Robert F. Durant

High-Stakes Reform: The Politics of Educational Accountability
Kathryn A. McDermott

How Information Matters: Networks and Public Policy Innovation
Kathleen Hale

How Management Matters: Street-Level Bureaucrats and Welfare Reform
Norma M. Riccucci

Implementing Innovation: Fostering Enduring Change in Environmental and Natural Resource Governance
Toddi A. Steelman

Managing within Networks: Adding Value to Public Organizations
Robert Agranoff

Measuring the Performance of the Hollow State
David G. Frederickson and H. George Frederickson

Organizational Learning at NASA: The Challenger *and* Columbia *Accidents*
Julianne G. Mahler with Maureen Hogan Casamayou

Program Budgeting and the Performance Movement: The Elusive Quest for Efficiency in Government
William F. West

Public Administration: Traditions of Inquiry and Philosophies of Knowledge
Norma M. Riccucci

Public Values and Public Interest: Counterbalancing Economic Individualism
Barry Bozeman

The Responsible Contract Manager: Protecting the Public Interest in an Outsourced World
Steven Cohen and William Eimicke

Revisiting Waldo's Administrative State: Constancy and Change in Public Administration
David H. Rosenbloom and Howard E. McCurdy, Editors

CHINA'S SENT-DOWN GENERATION

Public Administration and the Legacies of Mao's Rustication Program

HELENA K. RENE

Georgetown University Press
Washington, DC

© 2013 Georgetown University Press. All rights reserved. No part of this book may be reproduced or utilized in any form or by any means, electronic or mechanical, including photocopying and recording, or by any information storage and retrieval system, without permission in writing from the publisher.

Library of Congress Cataloging-in-Publication Data

Rene, Helena K.
  China's sent-down generation : public administration and the legacies of Mao's rustication program / Helena K. Rene.
       p. cm.
  Includes bibliographical references and index.
  ISBN 978-1-58901-987-4 (pbk. : alk. paper)
 1. Urban youth—Government policy—China—History—20th century. 2. Forced migration—China—History—20th century. 3. Urban-rural migration—Government policy—China—History—20th century. 4. Administrative agencies—China—Evaluation. I. Title.
 HQ799.C55R37 2012
  305.2350951'091732—dc23
  2012038648

♾ This book is printed on acid-free paper meeting the requirements of the American National Standard for Permanence in Paper for Printed Library Materials.

20 19 18 17 16 15 14 13   9 8 7 6 5 4 3 2

First printing

This book is dedicated

To my father, Mark A. Rene, who taught me, age thirteen, my first words in English when we first immigrated to the United States;

To my mother, Zhang Wei, who taught me to always dare to dream the impossible;

To all the first-generation Chinese immigrants who aspire to achieve the American dream;

To the people of China whose resilience and spirit will always live on;

To China, a nation of 1.3 billion, once ravaged by wars and decades of political turbulence but that now stands tall and thrives on the world stage;

And to the United States, a land of opportunities that has given me so much, a nation indivisible, with liberty and justice for all.

Contents

	List of Illustrations	ix
	Preface	xi
	Acknowledgments	xv
	List of Abbreviations	xvii
1	The Problem: How Was China Able to Send Seventeen Million Urban Youth to the Countryside during the Cultural Revolution?	1
2	Administering Economic Development: A Prelude to the Cultural Revolution and Rustication	15
3	The Politics of the Cultural Revolution (1965–67): Toppling Bureaucrats, Perduring Bureaucracy	37
4	Rustication: Policy and Administrative Implementation	75
5	Public Administration and the Sent-Down Experience	103
6	Conclusion: Rustication as Public Administration	163
	Appendix A: Interviewee Profiles	181
	Appendix B: Interview Schedule	211
	Glossary	215
	References	217
	Index	223

Illustrations

Tables

1.1	Interviewee Characteristics: Sent-Downs	10
1.2	Interviewee Characteristics: Controls	11
3.1	Deposed CCP Bureaucrats by 1966	57

Figures

2.1	Timeline of Administering Economic Development: A Prelude to the Cultural Revolution and Rustication	17
3.1	Timeline of the Politics of the Cultural Revolution (1965–67): Toppling Bureaucrats, Perduring Bureaucracy	39
4.1	Timeline of Rustication: Policy and Administrative Implementation	77

Photographs

4.1	Two young women in Tiananmen Square	79
4.2	A youth propaganda team	80
4.3	Two young men who were sent down to a military farm	83
4.4 and 4.5	Young women in the rustication program	88
5.1	Transportation of sent-down men on a flatbed truck to rustication destinations	129
6.1	Three sent-down women happily studying Mao's Thought for the camera	166

Boxes

1.1	Sent-Down Destinations	9
2.1	Mao in the Eyes of My Interviewees	20

Preface

This book is about the public administration of the 1968–78 Chinese Cultural Revolution "Up to the Mountains and Down to the Countryside" program for socialist reeducation that sent seventeen million urban Chinese youth to rural communes, state and military farms, and the Inner Mongolian grasslands for periods ranging from a few years to life—or death. These youth, known as sent-downs, typically labored for long hours under harsh conditions, frequently suffered constant hunger, and were vulnerable to injury and disease. Physical abuse was common, and many women were subject to sexual harassment, predation, and rape. Collectively, the sent-downs are now referred to as China's "lost generation" because their adolescence and life courses were thoroughly disrupted as their social, educational, and economic opportunities were severely truncated. For many, four words encapsulated their experience: "We were the oxen." Nevertheless, many of China's current leaders, including president Xi Jinping and prime minister Li Keqiang, were tempered by the program and thrived after completing it.

The Up to the Mountains and Down to the Countryside campaign, also known as the rustication program, was a large-scale socioeconomic policy intervention that, overall, produced downward mobility for the sent-down youth. In 1978 China scholar Susan Shirk observed that "one is struck with the lack of constituencies for the transfer program: the city teenagers and their parents don't like it; the peasants don't like it; the scientific-intellectual establishment doesn't like it; the [Chinese Communist] Party and Army cadres who are parents don't like it" and asked "what explains the government's capacity to carry out the program despite the lack of support?"

Based largely on extensive interviews with fifty-four former sent-downs and others whose lives were affected by the rustication program or parallel policies, the book provides a surprising answer. In the midst of the turmoil of the Cultural Revolution, the highly efficient design, organization, and implementation of the program cast a wide net from the central government to the front doors of the individual apartments in which the urban youth lived and from the national capital in Beijing down to very remote rural areas. The public administration of the Up to the Mountains and Down to the Countryside campaign left eligible urban youth with virtually no viable means of elusion or circumvention, except for the limited number who were able to join the military, generally based on their parents' personal connections. In fact, due to the program's design, which publicized it as a great adventure to promote revolutionary socialism, many urban youth were anxious to be sent down. While highly efficient on the sending side, the program more frequently fell short on the receiving end in the rural communes, state and military farms, and, to a lesser extent, on the grasslands of Inner Mongolia. The rustication bureaucracy did not always perform well in protecting the sent-downs from abuse and misfortune, providing socialist reeducation, and, for those sent to rural villages, settling the youth into their new locations and integrating them with the peasantry.

In public administration, program objectives and design are often critical to effective implementation. Chapters 2 and 3 demonstrate that the rustication program, which can be viewed as the capstone of the Cultural Revolution, was the outcome of a long-term, ongoing struggle between Communist Party chairman Mao Zedong and Chinese Communist Party members who believed that economic development required rational—essentially Weberian—bureaucratic organization, technical expertise, and technology to a greater extent than revolutionary socialist consciousness alone. With respect to the rustication policy and administrative design, Mao prevailed, which explains a great deal about how the program was organized and implemented. Although it may have had other impacts, such as reducing urban unemployment and promoting rural development, it was first and foremost a program to promote socialist reeducation of urban youth through connection to the peasantry, soldiers, and workers, hard labor under harsh conditions, and the study of Mao's Thought. A major purpose of socialist reeducation was to create a generation of urban youth who were not corrupted by privilege relative to the peasantry, damaged by an educational system Mao detested, and counterrevolutionarily tainted by the social, educational, and economic advantages their parents might pass on to them.

Chapters 4 and 5 present an overview and analysis of the rustication policy and its structural organization, along with the most detailed account of the administration of the program yet produced. The detail comes from my interviewees, whose recollections of their experiences remain vivid and compelling in terms of human interest as well as the general and technical aspects of public administration. The book's conclusion considers several ironies of the program—the bureaucratization of China that Mao hoped to slow or reverse, grew instead; socialist reeducation in rural villages and Inner Mongolia was often pro forma or even nonexistent; and exposure to the peasantry could be ineffectual or counterproductive in terms of building revolutionary consciousness. Based on my interviewees' accounts, the sent-downs were "tempered in the revolutionary furnace," as a revolutionary song touted, but at a high personal cost and without necessarily promoting their revolutionary socialist commitment. In short, the administration of the program was better at technique than achieving purpose.

Because what happened to the sent-downs was a human event as well as an administrative one, the book should be of interest to many who study China or wish to know more about it as well as individuals who are primarily interested in public administration and policy. Some of my interviewees feel that the rustication program robbed them of their youth and wreaked havoc on their opportunities for achieving the life they had hoped for in terms of education, marriage, family, and financial success. By contrast, a few had some of the happiest experiences of their lives. All were assured anonymity and given pseudonyms to protect their privacy and identities and to enable them to speak about their sent-down years as openly as they wished. With this assurance in mind, many clearly wanted to describe their experiences in detail so that their voices—some silent for many years until now—could be heard. I very much hope readers find the book as interesting to read as I did to write, and that it does provide a compelling answer to Shirk's question by explaining the what, why, and how of this troubling chapter in China's long and sometimes cataclysmic history.

Acknowledgments

A research project of this magnitude creates a debt of gratitude to the many individuals who provided help, guidance, and assistance along the way. I could not have undertaken the research without generous financial aid from the Ann and Neil Kerwin PhD Fellowship at American University (Washington, DC). Neither could it have been completed without the willingness of my fifty-four interviewees to spend hours upon hours with me and provide candid, detailed descriptions of their experiences—often very painful—during the Chinese Cultural Revolution and Up to the Mountains and Down to the Countryside rustication program. Several people who wish to remain anonymous also provided photographs from their personal collections for the book. In many respects the final product is theirs as much as mine. The book builds on the excellent pioneering research on the rustication program by previous scholars who are too numerous to name here but who are quoted and cited in the text and listed in the references. I am also thankful to Beryl Radin, editor of Georgetown University Press's series Public Management and Change, for superb and essential direction for strengthening the focus of the manuscript on the rustication program as public administration. My thanks also go to Hon Chan of City University of Hong Kong and Samuel Krislov, David Rosenbloom, and Robert Durant, all at American University, for their careful attention to the manuscript, insights, and invaluable suggestions for improving the study as well as to Zhang Jing and Shan Sanya for their assistance. Additional thanks go to Ting Gong of City University of Hong Kong and to an anonymous reader, who reviewed the manuscript for Georgetown University Press and provided strong recommendations for its publication and helpful advice for making revisions. I am also very grateful to Donald Jacobs of Georgetown University Press for his decision to pursue the manuscript and his support and guidance in finalizing it. My greatest debt and thanks go to my parents, Zhang Wei and Mark Rene, for their unflagging dedication and encouragement for my education and well-being, which made everything else possible.

Abbreviations

CCP: Chinese Communist Party
MAC: Military Affairs Commission; also referred to as Central Military (Affairs) Commission of the Chinese Communist Party; leads China's armed forces
PLA: People's Liberation Army
PRC: People's Republic of China, established on October 1, 1949

Chapter 1

The Problem

How Was China Able to Send Seventeen Million Urban Youth to the Countryside during the Cultural Revolution?

> "[Bureaucrats] sit with full stomachs, dozing in the office . . . [and] are eight-sided and slippery as eels."
>
> Mao Zedong[1]

> "I think Mao felt that the bureaucracy had been a lifelong enemy to him."
>
> Ning Lan (I24, 12)[2]

> "We will be forgotten individually but at least we left our mark in history and even though no one would know who we are, at least they would know that in history, a large-scale Up to the Mountains and Down to the Countryside movement occurred."
>
> Yun Wu (I48, 13)

The Rustication Puzzle: Organization among Chaos

In 1978 Susan Shirk, a noted China scholar, asked a probing question about the Chinese Cultural Revolution program that ultimately produced a "lost generation" by sending seventeen million urban youth to live on rural communes, military and state farms, and the Inner Mongolian grasslands. These youth, who were "sent-down to the countryside" for indefinite periods, including life, typically faced very harsh living conditions, hard labor, hunger, potential injury, including sexual abuse, and a variety of deprivations.[3] In Shirk's words: "One is struck with the lack of constituencies for the transfer program: the city teenagers and their parents don't like it; the peasants don't like it; the scientific-intellectual establishment doesn't like it; the [Chinese Communist] Party and Army cadres who are parents don't like it. . . . What explains the government's capacity to carry out the program despite the lack of support?" (Shirk 1978, 151). This book provides the first systematic answer, and one that comes as a surprise: highly effective public administration.[4] Alternatively known as "rustication" or the "Up to the Mountains and Down to the Countryside" campaign, the program was exceedingly well organized in strict bureaucratic fashion from the national level in Beijing, to the street level in the nation's major cities, and to the local levels that received the youth.[5] What makes this a surprise is that the rustication administration's efficiency in moving millions of teenagers to their destinations from 1968 to 1978 partially coincided with the Cultural Revolution (1966–76), which was one of the most chaotic periods in China's long history.[6]

This multilevel public administrative efficiency persisted even though the Cultural Revolution itself was partly an effort by Communist Party chairman Mao Zedong to purge China's public administrative system of technocrats and replace them with functionaries who had a high degree of socialist revolutionary consciousness. The turbulent decade witnessed widespread collapse of the educational system, social dislocation, economic disruption, governmental disintegration, family dissolution, tremendous violence, and the premature death of three million Chinese citizens (Chang and Halliday 2005, 569). Yet the rustication bureaucracy persisted and reached the front door of virtually every urban building with a teenager living in it, ultimately engulfing "10.5 percent of China's non-farming population in 1979" (Pan 2003, 1).

To find out how high-level administrative performance was achieved amid chaos, I interviewed fifty-four rustication survivors in 2009 and quickly found that their perspectives differed substantially from those presented in much of the English-language academic and journalistic literature on the Cultural Revolution. Jian Zhang (I52, 3), a professional social science researcher, maintained that the Cultural Revolution remains poorly understood because "for Chinese researchers, it is hard not to be censored so they still can't say too much, but as for Westerners, who don't have this problem, they are too creative" in "overemphasizing one aspect" or another and forcing "rationality upon the development and the events of the Cultural Revolution." His understanding, shared by several other interviewees (see chapter 3), is that "even when it was chaotic in society, even at its worst, the administrative machine—the national public administrative system—was always operating and never collapsed. People changed but the machine was always working . . . throughout the Cultural Revolution" (I52, 2).

More direct evidence of this came from Yun Wu (I48, 5), an administrator in a sports organization, who noted that there were "still moral and legal boundaries. For example, when we were Red Guards, we raided the homes of political suspects, but there were procedures to turn in valuable things that we found." This was confirmed by Jia Li (I25, 5), a researcher in a think tank:

> What I remember most on that day was that the Red Guard dug a very deep hole in the middle of our courtyard facing our living room and set a fire in that hole and burned everything made of paper, which included my parents' books, my father's cut-out sec-

tions from old newspapers, any editorials or magazines he kept, just anything that was cultured was burned there in that hole on that day. . . . The only things left were Chairman Mao's books. . . . They also raided many other things such as pictures for public display to support the charges against my parents' crimes of revisionism and capitalism. For example, they took my parents' wedding photos as proof of their capitalist ways because my parents were dressed in Western-style wedding outfits.

However, she went on to note that some of the "precious photos from our family album . . . were returned to us after my parents were rehabilitated" (I25, 5). Consequently, some public administrative bureau must have identified, classified, and safely stored these personal treasures even during the most chaotic years of the Cultural Revolution, 1966–68.

Several interviewees noted how efficient Chinese national administration was during the Cultural Revolution. Bin Ding, a now retired municipal official said,

> Of course the efficiency was much higher then [during the Cultural Revolution] both in its effectiveness and coordination among the governmental agencies because the implementers had absolutely no doubt regarding their implementation and there was no compromise, resistance, and only unadulterated implementation at every level, and therefore the whole process of policy implementation was highly efficient, effective, and fast. Back then, it was straight top-down administration so whatever the top orders, the lower level implements to the tee, unlike today [when] the power is decentralized and differentiated by multiple government bureaus or departments and so the implementation requires much more effort and coordination because the administrators may have different opinions in regards to the desirability of the general policy and may drag their feet or do selective implementation. This was simply not the case back then. It was total full, unadulterated enforcement. (I6, 12)

The persistence of this degree of administrative order in such turbulent times is all the more striking because the rustication program was the capstone of a long struggle by Mao against the growth of bureaucracy and technocracy, which he believed threatened the success of communism. Rustication was part of a broader reeducation effort and was specifically intended to thoroughly integrate urban youth with peasants, workers, and soldiers in order to instill them with socialist, nonbureaucratic/nontechnocratic values. Rustication policy was partly designed to save China from bureaucratization, and its attendant "technocratization," but it relied heavily on bureaucracy to transfer and relocate millions of sent-downs, generally aged fifteen to twenty years old, to rural areas. Ironically, it resulted in bureaucratic growth in size and power as well as the kind of administrative behavior about which Mao bitterly complained. Putting rustication into its context of entwinement with the Cultural Revolution helps to explain the high levels of its efficiency that are documented in chapters 4 and 5.

A Framework for Analyzing Rustication and Bureaucracy

As one would expect of an event of its magnitude, scholars have studied the Cultural Revolution from several different perspectives and have highlighted many of its complex dimensions. All analyses place Mao at the center of the Cultural Revolution. This inevitably poses analytic difficulties because Mao was complex, and his private persona was often at odds with the moral tone of his public leadership (see Snow 1973). Apart from Mao, studies explore the role of ideological divisions, group politics, intraparty power struggles, and structural factors such as urbanization, overpopulation, and unemployment in fostering the Cultural Revolution. To place the rustication policy into a conceptual framework that emphasizes its public administrative and bureaucratic dimensions—largely unexplored in other research—this book focuses on yet another central feature of the buildup to and unleashing of the Cultural Revolution: the conflict between Mao's vision of what a socialist society should be and the rise of bureaucratic power and privileged administrative elites within the Chinese Communist Party (CCP).

The conflict over Marxian and bureaucratic organization of China's polity, society, and economy has been touched on by others, most extensively in the work by Maurice Meisner (1971a, 1971b, 1977, 1999) on the increasing bureaucratization of the CCP and government and by Ezra Vogel (1967), who analyzed China's internal administrative transformations "from revolutionary to semibureaucrat." Emphasizing the same themes, Hong Yung Lee (1978, 2) explains that Western scholars have interpreted the Cultural Revolution as "a confrontation between a charismatic leader and a bureaucratic organization," among other roots. Building on these excellent works, this book develops the revolutionary versus bureaucratic framework much more fully. Using this framework as a lens adds a comprehensive dimension to contemporary interpretation of the Cultural Revolution and places the rustication program in a historical context that highlights the central roles of public administration, particularly bureaucracy, in implementing large-scale public policies. In emphasizing the importance of Mao's opposition to increasing bureaucratization as a cause of the Cultural Revolution and an important factor in determining its path, this book does not deny or disparage other dimensions. Rather, it seeks to augment them in order to promote a fuller understanding of a highly complex political and administrative phenomenon—one that cannot reasonably be attributed to a single factor, event, or cause.

Using this framework, the Cultural Revolution can be understood partly as the culmination of a prolonged political struggle between Mao and a number of highly influential CCP leaders. Mao and his allies envisioned a Marxist society that incorporated radical egalitarianism and viewed the peasantry as central to change. They were opposed by CCP functionaries who believed that economic development required governance based on technical rationality and rationally organized public administration. For Mao, bureaucratization was antithetical to equality and communism itself because it would make technical specialists rather than peasants the central force in society. The advocates of technical rationality, who in this framework are referred to as "Chinese Weberians," believed that the inequality associated with bureaucratized public administration was a necessary price for China's national development. Although the CCP was politically founded on Marxist-Leninist principles, in practice, Leninist public management bears a striking resemblance to the key principles of Weberian bureaucracy: it emphasizes rational organization, procedures, and process; hierarchical authority and discipline; and the promotion of experts who possess technical and specialized knowledge. Indeed, Lenin himself was an advocate of rational management.

This is not to say that Marxist-Leninism can be equated to Weberianism but only to emphasize that one of its key dimensions is strongly to promote bureaucratic organization. Moreover, Max Weber's ideal or pure type theory of bureaucracy has considerable explanatory power in the Chinese political context from the founding of the party-state in 1949 through the rustication period under study here.[7] However, the term "Chinese Weberians" must be used advisedly and with caution. For Weber, bureaucratic organization was the ideal type organizational structure for exercising rational-legal authority. In the ideal type model, which is not intended to describe real-life public bureaucracies empirically, strong adherence to the rule of law is a precondition for full bureaucratization, and clearly established lines of administrative authority are required to implement rational-legal authority. These conditions were not priorities for the Chinese Weberians, at least in terms of binding the CCP to the rule of law and establishing fixed lines of authority from the national government down to the local levels. Even today, well after China opted for technorational and highly bureaucratized economic and military development, neither the rule of law nor clear and stable lines of administrative authority or responsibility are defining characteristics of the regime. The CCP leadership has never been willing to relinquish substantial authority based on merit or expertise to lower-level bureaucrats collectively.

In some respects, the term "Chinese Weberians," recalls the phenomenon analyzed by Robert Michels in *Political Parties* (1949): Political parties externally oriented toward mass democratization were nevertheless organized oligarchically internally. Yet they might still be referred to as "social democrats." Similarly, the

Chinese Weberians' Weberianism was aimed largely at rational economic developmental policy and administration rather than internal CCP and governmental organization. However, as with much else in the party-state, categories tend to be fuzzy, and it is important to note that the Chinese Weberians were committed to placing technically competent personnel in key CCP positions. In the balance between "red" and "expert," the Maoist Marxians strongly favored the red whereas the Chinese Weberians emphasized the need for technical expertise.

Past scholars focus extensively on the political processes of the Cultural Revolution while largely overlooking its public administrative and bureaucratic organizational dimensions. In studying the Cultural Revolution, scholars have labeled the CCP leaders in opposition to Maoist radicalism as Leninists in terms of political ideology or expediency. Emphasizing the contest between Maoist Marxians and Chinese Weberians provides another dimension that shows how this conflict was also grounded in public administration. Highlighting the conflict between the Maoist Marxians and, rather than Leninists, the Chinese Weberians underscores the administrative, structural, and behavioral changes advanced by bureaucratization from 1951 to 1966 that generated a series of events culminating in an epic confrontation between the two factions regarding China's development preceding the Cultural Revolution.

The struggle took the form of action by one side and counteraction by the other from the advent of the "Three Antis-Campaign" in 1951 to the rustication program in the late 1960s. Despite Mao's intent, the Cultural Revolution and the rustication program failed to extinguish bureaucratic authority. Public administration and public administrators remained central to the experiences of sent-down youth, especially their recruitment, assignment, management on military farms, and return to urban areas. Furthermore, rustication not only contributed to growth in bureaucratic size, power, and discretion, it also gave rise to practices that dramatically and fundamentally changed China's pre–Cultural Revolution administrative culture. These included self-serving behavior by public administrators and far greater reliance on "*guanxi*" (relationships formed by personal connections, gifts, hospitality, bribes, and sexual favors) to obtain favorable use of administrative discretion and desired outcomes. As discussed in chapter 5, the rise of contemporary *guanxi* was particularly associated with the processes for enabling rusticated youth to return to the cities.

Learning Systematically from Survivors

Studying the administration of the rustication program presents several challenges. Official documents, when they exist, are not accessible to independent (nongovernmental) researchers and have not been the basis of any comprehensive study in either Chinese or English.[8] Studies providing broad overviews of rustication tend not to focus on its public administrative aspects and in any case face the same data and archival limitations. Memoirs by former sent-downs are detailed and gripping. Although they often include information on administration, even collectively they do not provide systematic analyses of the structure, operation, behavior, and culture of the rustication bureaucracy. Because memoirs do not necessarily address the same features of rustication administration, or even any of them in detail, they do not provide a basis for meta-analysis. Despite several limitations, this leaves interviewing as the most viable research strategy available. Thomas Bernstein's *Up to the Mountains and Down to the Villages* (1977a) demonstrates the efficacy of interviewing sent-downs or former sent-downs. However, Bernstein's findings are limited because they are based on only eleven interviewees who were all drawn from Guangdong, one of China's more temperate and less remote provinces, in the early days of the program when speaking freely about rustication experiences could be politically risky. The present study follows Bernstein's lead and seeks to provide a comprehensive analysis of rustication as public administration based on interviews.

Interviewing survivors, of course, also has limitations. By definition, the experiences of survivors were different from those of the many sent-downs who died of injury, suicide, disease, or execution for transgressions. Execution aside, however, it is unlikely that their deaths were related to their treatment by the by the rustication bureaucracy. Survivors and nonsurvivors alike received inadequate medical care and had to deal with deep depression and despair. The interviews were deliberately limited to those who returned to the cities—excluding those who stayed in the countryside—in order to learn how the administrative process worked as the rustication program was terminated. This turned out to be fortuitous because it was during the return phase that administrators on the communes and military farms had the greatest opportunity to use and abuse discretion. Although there are many historical precedents, it was during the termination phase that China's contemporary administrative culture became characterized by the use of relationships, gift-giving, bribery, and sexual favors (i.e., *guanxi*) to obtain favorable administrative treatment. As a practical matter, locating a sufficient number of surviving sent-downs who remained in different areas of the countryside would be difficult and expensive, if not impossible.

In order to tap a wide variety of experiences, semistructured interviews were conducted with fifty-four individuals who personally experienced transfer to rural areas and eventual relocation in Beijing and Shenzhen. These cities were chosen for the interviews because their populations are drawn from China as a whole, which increased the likelihood of capturing geographic diversity within the rustication program. The interviewees included forty-four former sent-downs who were under the authority of the rustication administration (Knowledgeable

Youth Up to the Mountains and Down to the Countryside Resettlement Office), one administrator, and nine additional individuals who were under parallel policies for socialist reeducation that were administered through other programs. The experiences of the latter group serve as "controls" that help to clarify what may have been intrinsic to implementation by the rustication administration rather than due to transfer from the cities alone. The group included three college students, three who were sent to factories, two youths who returned to their ancestral villages, and one who worked as a street-level administrator. Overall, they were more mature and older than the sent-downs. During their socialist reeducation, these youths worked in areas related to their educational specialization or, in the case of the returning youth of peasant background, agriculture. Except for the returning youths, they were considered state workers, received a regular wage, had more comfortable living arrangements, and faced less physical hardship than the sent-down interviewees. The returning youth had the advantages of having intact families, already living in the general locale of their villages, being familiar with agricultural work, and being easily integrated into the local community.[9] The lone rustication period administrator worked as a military representative in the Beijing schools when they were under army control. He was able to provide firsthand accounts of the experiences and roles of military personnel assigned to the Beijing schools during the initial organization of the rustication program in 1967–68. Forty-six interviews were conducted in Beijing and eight in Shenzhen.

In the total group, thirty-four interviewees are male and twenty are female; of those sent down as part of the rustication program, twenty-six are male and eighteen are female. On average, the sent-downs in the rustication program did not return to the cities for 6.3 years, and the others remained in the countryside for only about 1–2 years. (See appendix A.) The interviewees came from the full variety of the family class designations used during the Cultural Revolution, ranging from the top (revolutionary martyr, revolutionary soldier [military personnel], revolutionary cadre [military officer], worker, and poor and middle peasant) to the bottom five bad classes (landlord, rich peasant, counterrevolutionary, bad element, and rightist). They were also sent down from a broad variety of places: Beijing, Hangzhou, Harbin, Longchuan county town, Meixian county town (both in Guangdong), Shanghai, Shenyang, and Yongding county town (Fujian).

The forty-four sent-downs were relocated to the following variety of destinations, as shown in box 1.1. This diversity of destinations is important because much of the literature on sent-down youth, including memoirs, is based on life in one jurisdiction, or even one village, and fails to capture the full range and variety of the rusticated youths' experiences (see tables 1.1 and 1.2).

Box 1.1: Sent-Down Destinations

Rural villages:
    Guangdong: 1
    Heilongjiang: 1
    Inner Mongolia: 1
    Outskirts of Beijing: 3
    Shanxi: 10
    Shaanxi: 1

State and military farms:[a]
    Heilongjiang: 17
    Inner Mongolia: 1
    Yunnan: 4

Inner Mongolian grasslands: 4
Factory: Shanxi: 1

[a] State farms had civilian administration whereas military farms were under the PLA. During the period under study, the state farms were transitioning to military control. The military farm in Inner Mongolia was the only pure one with all personnel on active military duty.

Interviews lasted from one and a half hours to six hours. All but four of the interviewees sent down as part of the rustication program who answered the question of whether they believed their experience was representative asserted it was representative of sent-downs in their family class and at their destinations, or of a substantial component of the sent-down population. The four exceptions said they were not representative because they spent less time in the countryside than most, returned home under atypical circumstances, or received exceptional treatment for idiosyncratic reasons. However, they all believed that their experiences while in the countryside were representative.

The interviewees were located through snowball sampling facilitated by the fact that many sent-downs remain in touch with one another. Due to their dwindling numbers and age, no former bureaucrats who were directly involved in the rustication process were located or interviewed.

All but two of the interviews were conducted in Chinese and recorded electronically.[10] I translated and transcribed them in English in their entirety. Some transcriptions run fifty single-spaced pages or more. Citations to the transcriptions identify the interviewee by pseudonym and number, followed by the page number on which the quoted or cited material appears. The interviewees were

Table 1.1: Interviewee Characteristics: Sent-Downs[a]

Interviewee Characteristics	Male	Female	All (%)
Gender	26 (59.1%)	18 (40.1%)	44 (99.2[b])
Average age when sent down	17.1	17.4	17.2
Average years sent down	5.7	7.2	6.3
Average age when interviewed	58.1	57.8	58.0
Education: average grade when sent down	9.0	8.3	8.7
Current education:[c]			
Postgraduate	10	2	12 (27.9)
Bachelor	11	7	18 (41.8)
Technical/vocational	2	7	9 (20.9)
Associate degree	1	1	2 (4.7)
Grade school (average grade)	1 (8th)	1 (8th)	2 (8th) (4.7)
Family class background			
Good	10	3	13 (29.5)
Bad	13	14	27 (61.3)
Neutral	3	1	4 (9.1)
Destination and average stay (years)			
Military/state farm	14 (6.7)[d]	7 (8.1)	21 (7.2) (47.7)
Rural commune/village	9 (4.0)	7 (5.3)	16 (4.6) (36.4)
Inner Mongolia (all locations)	3 (6.3)	3 (6.0)	6 (6.2) (13.6)
Factory	0	1 (17)	1 (17.0) (2.3)
Returning youth	0	0	0
Chinese Communist Party Member	18	8	26 (59.1)

[a] Includes sent-downs; excludes military representative and controls.
[b] Less than 100% due to rounding.
[c] One value missing.
[d] Three males left military farms to join the People's Liberation Army after one, two, and four years.

guaranteed anonymity and given pseudonyms to protect their privacy and to encourage them to speak freely about their experiences. Trusting that their identities would not be revealed, several said that they were able to discuss for the first time ordeals that they had never even mentioned to their spouses or children. Appendix B presents the English translation of the interview schedule. The interviews were held during June–August 2009.[11]

The interviewees' responses included a great deal of storytelling.[12] Steven Maynard-Moody and Michael Musheno (2003, 27) point out that "no clear line separates the open-ended interview from the story" because "interviewees often make points by telling stories." That was certainly true of many interviewees

The Problem

Table 1.2: Interviewee Characteristics: Controls

Interviewee Characteristics	Male	Female	All (%)
Gender	7 (77.8%)	2 (22.2%)	9 (100)
Average age when sent down	20.0	18.5	19.7
Average years sent down	5.1	20.5	8.6
Average age when interviewed	64.1	59.0	63.0
Education: when sent down			
Bachelor	1	0	1 (11.1)
Some college	3	0	3 (33.3)
Technical/vocational	0	2	2 (22.2)
Grade school (average grade)	3 (9.0)	0	3 (9.0) (33.3)
Current education:			
Postgraduate	0	0	0 (0)
Bachelor	6	0	6 (66.7)
Technical/vocational	0	2	2 (22.2)
Associate degree	1	0	1 (11.1)
Grade school	0	0	0 (0)
Family class background			
Good	3	1	4 (44.4)
Bad	3	1	4 (44.4)
Neutral	1	0	1 (11.1)
Destination and average stay (years)			
Military/state farm	3 (1.0)	0	3 (1.0) (33.3)
Rural commune/village	0	0	0 (0)
Inner Mongolia (all locations)	0	0	0 (0)
Factory	2 (7.0)	2 (20.5)	4 (13.8) (44.4)
Returning youth	2 (8.5)	0	2 (8.5) (22.2)
Chinese Communist Party Member	3	2	5 (55.6)

here. Some illustrated their responses to questions with long narratives about events and incidents that happened to them or that they directly observed. Their stories provide a relatively full understanding of their sent-down and return experiences as they interpreted them. Rustication as a teenager was a life-altering event. In many of the longer interviews, it was evident that the interviewees wanted their stories heard and retold because it would make their experiences known and understood. In the Chinese context, Jan Myrdal's *Report from a Chinese Village* (1965) serves as the archetypal model for eliciting stories and benefiting from them.

Stories are not necessarily accurate historical accounts. Nevertheless, to the extent that the stories of forty-four interviewees, who consider their experiences largely representative, converge, it is safe to conclude that their stories are one version of how past events are understood by those who experienced them.[13] In three cases, the interviewees were interviewed in pairs, which served to enhance their recall.[14] One important benefit gained from the interviewees' stories is recognition of how widely the sent-downs' experiences varied depending on whether they were rusticated in rural villages, on military farms, or in the grasslands of Inner Mongolia. For some it was the best time of their lives; for others, the worst. The experiences of males and females also differed significantly in some, but not all, respects. The variegated nature of these experiences is rarely, if ever, explored or evident in sent-down memoires and the extant literature on the rustication program. The personal photos of former sent-downs inserted throughout the text confirm much of what the interviewees described.

In closing this section, it should be emphasized that although the remaining official administrative records on the rustication program may one day become available if they are not destroyed as time elapses, the opportunity to study rustication through the recounted personal experiences of sent-down survivors is narrowing. Those who were sent down in the early stages of the program are now in or approaching their sixties and their numbers are likely to dwindle significantly in the coming years. In a real sense, this may have been the last best chance to interview them and learn from their stories.

The Plan of the Book

The book has five additional chapters. Chapter 2 shows how central public administration, and especially bureaucratization, was to the conflict between Mao and the Chinese Weberians presaging the Cultural Revolution. Chapter 3 analyzes the Cultural Revolution through the lens of the contest between rational public administration and Mao's Marxian vision of revolutionary socialism as means of promoting national development. These chapters are distinctive in the literature in demonstrating the full importance of bureaucratization as an antecedent of the Cultural Revolution and the rustication program. Chapter 4 focuses on the rustication policy and provides an overview of its public administrative aspects. Relying primarily on interviews with former sent-down youth, chapter 5 documents the roles of public administration and bureaucracy in the dynamics of the rustication program. It also explains how the program affected China's administrative culture, particularly as sent-downs returned to the cities. The chapter points out the ironies associated with Mao's reliance on rustication, which was highly bureaucratized, as a means of counteracting the very ills he perceived as associated with bureaucracy. The chapter contains a great deal of oral history. Chapter 6, "Rustication as Public Administration," concludes the study with consideration of whether, despite its bureaucratic administration, rustication may have served Mao's wider Cultural Revolutionary goal of promoting the socialist reeducation of urban youth.

Notes

1. See Meisner (1971a, 24–25).

2. My interviewees are profiled in appendix A, which lists them in alphabetic order by pseudonym (the surname is in full capital letters) and also numbers each profile. For consistency with how authors are introduced in the text, names follow the US English practice of putting the given name first and surname last, instead of the Chinese practice of putting the surname first. The first mention of an interviewee includes the full name in the text; citations include the code number only. The family names are capitalized in appendix A for clarity. References include the interviewee's surname, "I" followed by the interviewee's number, and the page number of the transcription on which the quoted material appears. In this reference, the interviewee's pseudonym is Ning Lan; I24 stands for interviewee 24; 12 is the page of the quoted material.

3. The sent-downs in this program are referred to as *zhiqing* in Chinese. *Zhiqing* is shorthand for *zhishi qingnian*, meaning "knowledgeable youth." It comes from the first two syllables of *zhishi qingnian*. *Zhiqing* constituted only one group among several who were sent away for socialist reeducation during the Cultural Revolution, such as cadres and university students.

4. A few other works pay limited attention to the role of bureaucracy in rustication but do not analyze the administration of the program comprehensively or in depth or focus on how it directly affected the sent-downs' experiences in the countryside. Among these are Bernstein (1977a) and Meisner (1999).

5. Throughout this study, the terms "rustication" and "rusticants" refer to individuals sent down under the authority of the national Knowledgeable Youth Up to the Mountains and Down to the Countryside Resettlement Office in Beijing.

6. In 1969 Chinese Communist Party chairman Mao Zedong declared that the Cultural Revolution was over. However, most researchers of the period date it from 1966 to 1976, when Mao died.

7. The term "party-state" is intended to capture the indistinct separation of party and state in the People's Republic of China. See Laliberté and Lanteigne 2008.

8. Jian Zhang's research comes closest to providing a general overview. He noted his frustration with trying to gain access to archival material. "The *Zhiqing* Resettlement Offices were the street-level bureaucracies, so from the national level to the county level, there were corresponding offices that had their records kept in the archival offices. And there are a lot of records kept but they don't grant you access. I went to all the national and local recordkeeping bureaus and offices. I really tried to find connections and *guanxi* [relationships for "back door" access] to get in but I was told to get out everywhere" (I52, 6).

9. For fuller analysis of the differences between returning youth and sent-down youth, see Bernstein 1977a, 22–24.

10. Kang Lin (I28) and Lijun Yang (I49) declined to be recorded but permitted me to take extensive notes.

11. Pan (2003, 6) interviewed "over sixty" rusticated youth as part of her broad overview of rustication, which also relies heavily on published work. She does not provide detailed information on the characteristics of these interviewees or report in depth on their individual experiences. Her research speaks only tangentially to the public administrative and organizational behavioral aspects of the rustication program and bureaucracy.

12. For a discussion of using storytelling in research, see Maynard-Moody and Musheno (2003, especially 25–27). They consider storytelling to be a "powerful research instrument" (26).

13. Manning (2005, 2008) illustrates the viability of interviewing survivors of past events such as the Great Leap Forward.

14. Chao Duan (I8) and Tao Fan (I9); Jing Tan (I42) and Bo Tang (I43); Jie Tian (I44) and Yanli Wan (I45).

Chapter 2

Administering Economic Development

A Prelude to the Cultural Revolution and Rustication

> "In a very fundamental sense, what happened to the organisation of cadres since 1949 corresponds more closely to the visions of Max Weber than to the visions of Chairman Mao."
>
> Ezra Vogel (1967, 59)

The People's Republic of China (PRC), founded on October 1, 1949, is often referred to as a "party-state" because the ruling Chinese Communist Party (CCP) and the formal governmental (state) units, at both the national and local levels, are fused and indistinct. In large part, the party's domination of the state is maintained by staffing the organizations that compose the government with CCP members who are subject to the party's personnel and disciplinary systems (Chan 2004). The CCP was founded on Marxist principles and CCP chairman Mao Zedong was committed to realizing the communist utopian state in the PRC.

Maoist Marxians interpreted socialism as elimination of the bourgeoisie elite, capitalist enterprises and the abolition of private property. In addition to restructuring the means of production and division of labor, Mao emphasized a policy of radical egalitarianism. In Mao's view, both the revolutionary cadres and the masses should have equal access to education, employment, health care, and housing. Unlike Marx, Mao believed that the human will, in proper consciousness, can change history as mankind pleases if it possesses the "revolutionary spirit" to surmount material impediments. In this sense, the subjective can change the objective if mankind is so dedicated in its spiritual quest. Mao advanced this theory in terms of the "mass line," which was central to his political outlook and, ultimately, his decision to initiate the Cultural Revolution. According to him, "The people, and the people alone, are the motivating force in the making of world history" (Mao 1966, ch. 11). The CCP defines the "mass line" in the following terms:

The mass line means everything for the masses, reliance on the masses in everything, and "from the masses, to the masses." The party's mass line in all its work has come into being through the systematic application in all its activities of the Marxist-Leninist principle that the people are the makers of history. . . . Comrade Mao Zedong stressed time and again that as long as we rely on the people, believe firmly in the inexhaustible creative power of the masses and hence trust and identify ourselves with them, no enemy can crush us while we can eventually crush every enemy and overcome every difficulty. He also pointed out that in leading the masses in all practical work, the leadership can form its correct ideas only by adopting the method of "from the masses, to the masses" and by combining the leadership with the masses and the general call with particular guidance. This means concentrating the ideas of the masses and turning them into systematic ideas, then going to the masses so that the ideas are preserved and carried through, and testing the correctness of those ideas in the practice of the masses. And this process goes on, over and over again, so that the understanding of the leadership becomes more correct, keener and richer each time. This is how Comrade Mao Zedong united the Marxist theory of knowledge with the party's mass line. As the vanguard of the proletariat, the party exists and fights for the interests of the people. But it always constitutes only a small part of the people, so that isolation from the people will render all the Party's struggles and ideals devoid of content as well as impossible of success. To persevere in the revolution and advance the socialist cause, our Party must uphold the mass line (CCP, 2006).

Mao's Antibureaucratic Ethos

In the context of the CCP's efforts to develop China economically, commitment to the mass line opposes top-down decision making by educated public administrators and technocrats in isolation from the masses. Rather, the economists, engineers, agronomists, enterprise managers, and other technically trained government and party personnel must be highly responsive to the masses, essentially merge with them, and be completely in their service. The mass line "envisions the opinions, needs and ideas of ordinary people being communicated up the party structure to the central level, where policy is formulated" and is then, in turn, communicated downward through all levels for administrative implementation (Latham 2007, 36). The role of the media is central to mass line public administration for "dissemination of information, instruction on policy implementation, explanation of policy rationales and principles, and, most importantly encouraging the active participation of the people" (ibid.). Bureaucrats and technocrats who are separated from the masses by political, economic, and social privileges and advantages are antithetical to mass line theory and administrative implementation and, consequently, the CCP's revolutionary goals. This

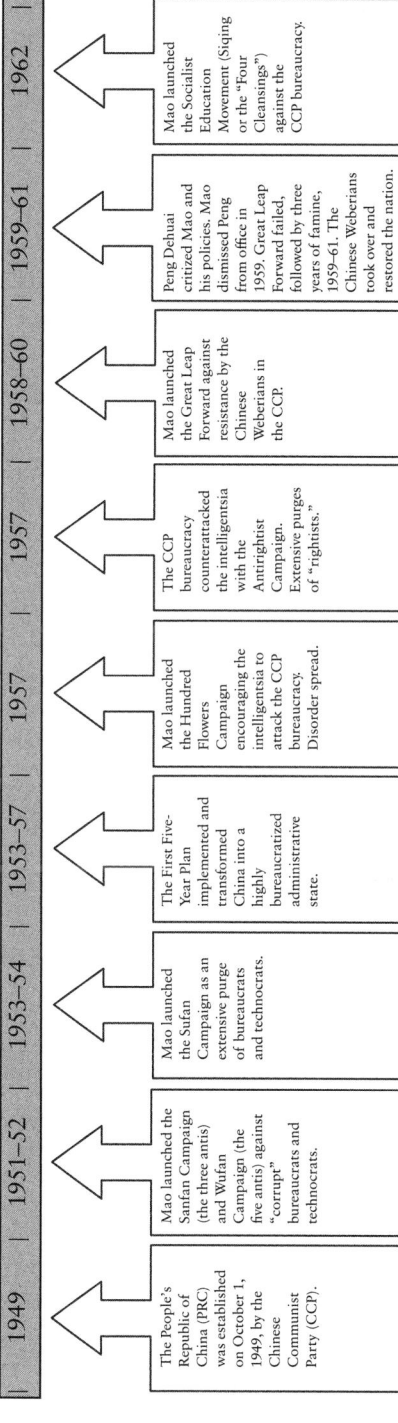

Figure 2.1: Timeline of Administering Economic Development: A Prelude to the Cultural Revolution and Rustication

set up a conflict between those who sought to develop China according to the mass line and those who would do so by relying on rationally organized public administration and technical expertise in developing and implementing new economic and social policies.

The Sanfan and Wufan Campaigns

Mao's long struggle to prevent perversion of the communist revolution by bureaucratization began almost immediately after the People's Republic was born. Following the mass line, between 1951 and 1952, two campaigns were launched against public administrative bureaucracies and the technocrats in leadership positions. The Sanfan (the three antis) focused on eliminating "corruption, waste and the bureaucratic spirit," whereas the Wufan (the five antis) was directed against "bribery, tax evasion, fraud, theft of governmental property, and stealing of state economic secrets" (Meisner 1999, 87). Mao saw the older party cadres as corrupt because bureaucratism and detachment from the masses had eroded their revolutionary spirit. The two campaigns purged thousands of cadres, leading to an ominous path as Mao's distrust grew deeper against the new bureaucratic structure, organization, and personnel system (Vohra 2000).

The First Five-Year Plan (1953–57)

The CCP introduced the First Five-Year Plan (1953–57) to guide the national economy toward rapid development of heavy industry and greater urbanization. The Maoist Marxians believed economic growth was a necessary step to socialism. Mao stressed the importance of urban development and "build[ing] a powerful country with a high degree of socialist industrialization" (Meisner 1999, 111). Accordingly, economic planners in the State Planning Commission imported a wholesale approach from the Soviet Union emphasizing urban enterprises at the expense and exploitation of the rural sector. By 1957 China's industry grew more rapidly than the anticipated 14.7 percent per annum. Chinese official statistics and Western estimates placed growth between 16 and 18 percent. China had doubled its total industrial output by producing vast quantities of steel, pig iron, cement, coal, and electricity. It also began producing jet planes, trucks, farm equipment, and ships (Meisner 1999, 113).

The growth of industry led to rapid urbanization. In 1944 there were five cities with large populations. Toward the end of the First Five-Year Plan, the total urban population had increased from fifty-seven to ninety-nine million (Jowett 1984). By 1957 thirteen cities had populations that exceeded one million. Although Mao supported and promoted urbanization, eventually he would regard the economic, educational, and social advancement of urbanites relative to rural peasants as undercutting the mass line and displacing the Chinese communist revolution from its grounding in the peasantry. A decade after the First Five-Year Plan ended, Mao viewed the rustication of urban youth—that is, sending them up to the mountains and down to the countryside to be merged into rural and peasant life—as a partial solution to this problem.

Administrative Transformation

The development of industry and urbanization transformed China's society and its administrative bureaucracy in ways that Mao failed to anticipate and ultimately opposed. Development caused national public administration to become an increasingly fundamental, powerful, and complex feature of the Chinese formula for economic development. Having ruled out market mechanisms for coordinating economic activity in accordance with Marxist principles, policy planning for the economy and society required high levels of expertise, rationalized rules, hierarchical authority, fixed procedures, discipline, and social stability. All of these properties promoted bureaucratization and were in tension with the mass line approach. The bureaucracy expanded in size and power because greater administrative capacity was necessary to accommodate China's aspirations for economic development and its attendant societal changes. Public administration now needed bureaucrats with specialized knowledge and expertise. Technocrats who were more expert than red, selected through technical qualifications, meritocracy, and scientific management instead of political background and ideology, supplanted Maoist Marxians in leadership positions. In these respects, with the formulation and implementation of the First Five-Year Plan, the CCP bureaucracy was reorganizing into a Weberian administrative model and becoming distanced from Mao's mass line.

Bureaucratization fostered by the First Five-Year Plan followed Max Weber's theory of bureaucracy almost as if it were a roadmap. In China's case, from 1953–57, Weber's ideal type theory of bureaucracy and bureaucratization had great explanatory power. As noted earlier, Weber theorized that bureaucracy was the ideal type administrative structure for exercising rational-legal authority (Weber 1958, ch. 8). Such rational-legal authority stands in stark contrast not only to the mass line approach but also to charismatic authority on which much of Mao's leadership was based (see box 2.1). Weber described rational-legal authority as based "on a belief in the 'legality' of patterns of normative rules and the right of those elevated to authority under such rules to issue commands" (Weber 1964, 328). The First Five-Year Plan propelled into positions of authority technical specialists more imbued with expertise in economics, engineering, and management than socialist ideology. The party needed a new type of leaders who were knowledgeable "professional[s] with specialized . . . administrative

> **Box 2.1:** Mao in the Eyes of My Interviewees
>
> **Bin Ding (I6, 2):** "At the time, Mao's Thought was the guiding light for all Chinese citizens, then after being processed through the public media, radio broadcasting, newspapers, magazines, novels, literature, and theatrical drama, which all served to deify Mao, it was clear that the chairman was God, not a mortal. Chairman Mao's Thought was treated as the foundation of all understanding of reality for the Chinese people. Lin Biao said it best, 'Every sentence uttered by the Chairman was absolute truth, and one sentence of the Chairman's words is more important than 10,000 sentences from elsewhere.' In the minds and hearts of all Chinese people, Chairman Mao was God Almighty himself."
>
> **Ningli Gan (I12, 6),** a retired bookkeeper: "We were all so fanatic about Chairman Mao. It was beyond a cult of personality. Even though I was from a bad family background, I was still completely, from the bottom of my heart, supportive of anything and everything that Chairman Mao said."
>
> **Jun Liang (I26, 13),** now a university professor of international relations: One reason for public participation in the Cultural Revolution was "the hero worshipping and total adulation of Mao's cult of personality. The total, unflinching trust people placed in Mao and the exaggeration of Mao as a person, who was given a status close to, if not God Almighty himself. It was complete blind trust in Mao; whatever Chairman Mao said, that's what I will do."
>
> **Jian Zhang (I52, 1):** "Mao was God." The Cultural Revolution "was made possible by the blind following of Mao who was considered to be a God."

skills" instead of uneducated peasant guerilla fighters "dedicated to the cause" (Lee 1991, 46). As Meisner observed, the First Five-Year Plan witnessed the replacement of the "old revolutionaries" by "new cadres" who, as technicians and engineers, presented a "new social model" (1999, 119).[1]

Once in place, as Weber predicted, bureaucracy would be very difficult to dislodge. Economic development depended on its expertise, specialization, and formalization. Its use of hierarchy for coordination violated Mao's socialist egalitarianism and mass line. However, it was highly effective and seemingly necessary. The "old revolutionaries" may have complained that "the bureaucratization of political and economic life was a repudiation of the revolutionary heritage and a betrayal of socialist ideals," but it was also a fact of life (Meisner 1999, 119). As Weber (1958, 214) theorized, bureaucracy expands because it is technically superior to other forms of organization due to its precision, speed, clarity, specialized knowledge, discretion, unity, hierarchical authority system, and impersonality.[2] It has a tendency to take on more and more tasks as societies and economies become more complex and require greater coordination. Eventually, its power position becomes "overtowering" as "the 'political master' finds himself in the position of the 'dilettante' who stands opposite the 'expert,' facing the trained official who stands within the management of administration" (Weber 1958, 232).

Meisner's analysis of the First Five-Year Plan leaves no doubt that it promoted Weberian-style bureaucratization. A review of his detailed analysis is unnecessary. It is enough to underscore that he observes that industrialization promoted "authoritarian discipline, social stability, and economic rationality," "bureaucratic centralization," a high degree of specialization, "Party members" serving "as economic managers first and as political leaders second," and "the erosion of [the CCP's] revolutionary spirit." "'Rationalize,' 'systematize,' and 'regularize' were the slogans of the day and they reflected . . . an implicit repudiation of the Maoist revolutionary heritage." "Economic rationality and administrative efficiency" were the "actual governing values" in place (see Meisner 1999, 114–20).

As Weber foresaw, bureaucratization in a rapidly modernizing society is almost certain. Industrialization and its attendant urbanization reduce social structures of ascription and entrenched privilege based on inherited status and wealth. In feudalistic and quasi-feudalistic economies, modernization frees labor from the land. In China "the long deferred antifeudal revolution in the countryside" did not come until land reform was completed in 1952 (Meisner 1977, 1019). Urbanization weakens traditional social controls as people retain anonymity while interacting with one another, and these restraints are partly replaced by bureaucratically administered governmental restrictions on individuals' behavior (Mayo 1945). According to Weber, bureaucratization accompanies modernization in part because "every process of social leveling creates a favorable situation for the development of bureaucracy" (1964, 340). The First Five-Year Plan fundamentally altered the CCP's organizational structure and process on the road toward a Weberian bureaucracy.

The Rise of the Bureaucratized Chinese Communist State

Weber theorized that "bureaucratization is occasioned more by intensive and qualitative enlargement and internal deployment of the scope of administrative tasks than by their extensive and quantitative increase" (1958, 212). The First Five-Year Plan required more and better trained cadres for implementation and measuring progress. As Weber epitomizes this, "the bureaucratic structure goes hand in hand with the concentration of the material means of management in the hands of the master"—the CCP, in this case (1958, 221). Furthermore, the division between modernizing towns and traditional country life expanded at the end of the First Five-Year Plan, which further contributed to bureaucratization. Rapid industrialization succeeded in part because the plan exploited the countryside, extracting its economic surplus and reinvesting it in urban development. After paying for grain and other taxes, there was little food or cash left for the peasants (see chapter 4). Consequently, the agrarian sectors stagnated and the already subsistent peasant life worsened as rural income dwindled further (Pan 2003; Bernstein 1977a). The delineation between town and country also extended to the cultural realm. Social stratification supposedly abolished by the CCP returned within the educational system and public administrative employment. Even though official policies emphasized the preferences for children of peasants and workers, admission to formal education disproportionately favored students from the higher strata: children of the party cadres and the technological intelligentsia. Similarly, higher education focused on science and technology in both methods and curricula, thereby upholding the privileges of the technical elite (Meisner 1999).

As Mao charged, Weberian bureaucracy has a tendency toward elitism because expertise and meritocracy are requisites for entering and advancing within its administrative system. This requires access to higher education, which overwhelmingly favors the technological intelligentsia.[3] In this respect, Weberian bureaucratization directly fostered the rise of the new elite whose position violated the mass line and Marxian revolutionary ideal of egalitarianism. Additionally, bureaucracy was the "sole channel of upward mobility for ambitious individuals" and their "official position in the bureaucratic system is what define[d] elite status" (Lee 1991, 4). Accordingly, Mao "saw the new bureaucracy following the ancient pattern of autocratic government from the top down," which "would leave the peasant masses where they had always been, at the bottom of society, being exploited by a new elite" (Fairbank and Goldman 2006, 386). For example, the higher-level bureaucrats enjoyed a variety of material benefits inconsistent with socialist egalitarianism. These included their substantially greater wages than the average worker or peasant received; free meals, furniture, and compensation for various expenses; and "for high-level leaders, houses, servants, chauffeur-driven cars, access to special stores and goods, and vacations at official resorts" (Meisner 1999, 371; see also chapter 5, this volume).[4]

From Mao's perspective, the only cure was to reform "corrupted bureaucratism," and to purge the revisionism that he "defined as an abandonment of the goals of the revolution and acceptance of the evils of special status and special accumulation of worldly goods, which could be called a restoration of capitalism" (Fairbank and Goldman 2006, 386). In Mao's view, socialism required enabling the masses to take power or, short of that, to participate directly in the operations of the state institutions and bureaucracy. This would finally break the Chinese tradition of top-down government and create a true socialist state dedicated to the mass line through mass participation (Vohra 2000, 236–39).

The expansion of bureaucracy and the rise of the technocratic class thoroughly challenged Mao's Marixan socialism (see Djlas 1957). Moreover, bureaucratization strongly enhanced control over the population for communist China had become an "intensely bureaucratic managerial state" in which "political authority penetrated all levels of the life of the people" (Yan and Gao 1996, 2). As Mar-

Administering Economic Development

tin Whyte observed, "For urban residents, then, access to housing, jobs, food and clothing, and even aid in dealing with family problems or approval for having more children require[d] that they confront the bureaucratic structures the Chinese Communists introduced" (Whyte 1980, 126). Street-level bureaucrats in the urban street offices were responsible for watching the goings-on in individual apartment buildings and units and for correcting undesirable or antisocial behavior (see chapter 5). In addition, the *hukou* system of household registration permits drastically limited individuals' geographic mobility and "rationalized" this set of controls that were "regarded as unavoidable . . . under . . . [the] heavy industry oriented development strategy" of the First Five-Year Plan (Chan and Zhang 1999, 820). Whyte succinctly conveys the scope of public administrative regulation and involvement in individuals lives:[5] "Most housing in large cities has come under the control of city housing allocation offices, or work units, and jobs are assigned by city labor offices. Individuals are forbidden to come to the city to live unless specifically recruited for jobs or schooling; even marriage to an urban resident does not entitle a villager to move in. Grain, cotton cloth, and many other [major] necessities of life are rationed, and individuals not properly registered are not entitled to such rations" (1980, 125). As Lee sums it up, "the party-state imposed its bureaucratic structure on every functional field of society" (1991, 4).

By the end of the First Five-Year Plan, both the CCP bureaucracy and the Chinese state had undergone substantial transformation. The effects of administrative and technical rationality percolated from the bureaucratic apparatus throughout the organization of society. Given the scarce economic resources and the responsibility for centralized policy planning in every arena, the Chinese Weberians had to manage the state with efficiency and rationalized strategy, procedure, and process.

However, bureaucratization has foreseeable consequences that even Weber came to deplore. Bureaucracy's technical superiority and efficiency invite expansion not only into economic organization but also into areas previously dominated by social action such as marriage, procreation, family structure, and geographical mobility. The bureaucratization of society comes at the cost of human freedom. Weber likened bureaucracy to an "iron cage" that traps individuals as well as bureaucrats and deprives them of independent action (Weber 1994, xvi). Ralph Hummel, an expert on Weber and bureaucracy, explains that "society imposes general rules for proper social behavior, but personal discretion is allowed, providing plenty of room for actions based on mutual understanding. As society becomes more bureaucratic, however, rationally organized action finally collapses that room" (1994, 50).

Weber referred to this characteristic of bureaucracy as the "parceling-out of the soul," meaning that dependence on bureaucracy forces conformity to bureaucratic rules and criteria for action (Kalberg 2003, 188). As Hummel notes:

"Bureaucracy is a tool for ferreting out what is relevant to the task for which the bureaucracy was established. As a result, only those facts in the complex lives of individuals that are relevant to that task need be communicated between the individual and the bureaucracy" (1994, 33–34). To facilitate this, bureaucratic criteria transform individuals into cases: "Only if a person can qualify as a case is he or she allowed treatment" (ibid., 34). Bureaucracy typically deals with cases, not persons; consequently, as bureaucratization expands, social norms are replaced by bureaucratic norms. Weber viewed this "dehumanization" as the "special virtue" of bureaucracy because in his ideal type formulation, it guarantees performance without "personal, irrational, and emotional elements" (Weber 1958, 216). But freedom is also lost because "being a cog in such machinery, the individual [as well as the bureaucrat] has lost much of the control over his own destiny" (Thompson 1961, 4). The net result is that bureaucratization forces a trade-off between efficiency and material advancement on the one hand and "a societal-wide passivity in which people are 'led like sheep'" on the other (Kalberg 2003, 188).

As the "iron cage" encloses more and more aspects of political, economic, and social life, there is no escape: "The ruled, for their part, cannot dispense with or replace the bureaucratic apparatus of authority once it exists" because "if the official stops working, or if his work is forcefully interrupted, chaos results, and it is difficult to improvise replacements from among the governed who are fit to master such chaos" (Weber 1958, 229). A bureaucratized society along such Weberian lines is perhaps nobody's ideal. However, the CCP Weberians, imbued with the desire to bring technical rationality to China's economic development, implicitly or explicitly favored efficiency in the trade-off with personal freedom and equality. This was understandable because the vast majority of Chinese were already deprived of freedom by the nation's grinding poverty and social and economic backwardness in the wake of the brutal Japanese invasion and protracted civil war with the Kuomintang. The Chinese Weberians, much like China's leaders today, were pragmatic in choosing economic development over extended human freedom based on the assumption that only when people have a "full stomach" can they "afford to pursue the more esoteric aspects of self-fulfillment" (Ake 1987, 84).

In stark contrast, Mao and his supporters viewed the conformity and loss of independent social action associated with bureaucratization as a threat to socialist transformation based on the peasantry. If the peasants were controlled by bureaucracies with elites at the top, they would never be equal regardless of material advances. Mao's solution to the problem of generating economic development without bureaucratization was communalism (and communism), which in theory would preserve social action. As with other aspects of his romanticized vision of the peasantry, including the expected benefits of the rustication program during the Cultural Revolution, his version of communalization—

collectivization of agriculture through the Great Leap Forward—fell far short of its goals.

Maoist Marxians versus Chinese Weberians: The Struggle over Administering Development

The struggle between the Maoist Marxians and the Chinese Weberians was protracted and bitter. It took several twists and turns as action by each side spurred reaction by the other.

The Sufan and Purge of Gao Gang (1953–55)

The sociopolitical implications of the First Five-Year Plan (1953–57) derailed Mao's vision for the postrevolutionary China. In Mao's view, the Weberian ethos now prominent in the CCP bureaucracy and Chinese society corrupted the "revolutionary spirit," and the rise of the technocrats formed a new elite class as "functional bourgeoisie," deriving power from their bureaucratic positions instead of private property (Meisner 1997, 370). The inequality between the upper-level bureaucratic cadres and the masses belied Mao's proclamation of Marxian socialism and mass line egalitarianism. Increasingly alarmed, Mao mobilized the Sufan movement, the "Campaign to Wipe Out Hidden Counterrevolutionaries," as an extensive bureaucratic purge. It featured the ouster of a major technocrat leader, Gao Gang, the first of many to follow in Mao's foreboding move.

A pro-Soviet professional, Gao was an expert in developing policies on heavy industry. He was the appointed chair of the State Planning Commission and the chief engineer of the First Five-Year Plan. Gao's revolutionary background was impeccable, first as a leader of peasant guerrilla warfare and later as a founder of the Communist Party base to which Mao retreated at the end of the Long March (Meisner 1999).[6] During the planning phase, Gao was the head of the Manchurian region, which became the capital for heavy industrialization. He embraced the "Soviet methods of industrial organization" and pursued the rationalized system with vigor (Meisner 1999, 121). Gao, however, was charged with being tainted by the Soviet influences of professionalization and conspiring to run "an independent kingdom" (Meisner 1999, 121). The Sufan campaign ended with Gao's suicide and purges of a number of bureaucrats.[7] Although the circumstances of Gao's downfall were complex, his demise clearly signaled that Mao was willing to sacrifice an accomplished technical expert for political reasons.[8] Nevertheless, it was a Band-Aid approach that failed fully to engage the tensions between socialism and bureaucratization. Indeed, in Mao's view, "the evil of bureaucracy" grew "nowhere more than within the Party that [he] headed" (Meisner 1999, 123).

Mao's Agrarian Socialism

In July 1957 Mao overrode the CCP Central Committee and forced the party's approval for his own policy of land collectivization, which was subsequently launched in October. The party's gradualist approach of agricultural cooperativization had become intolerable to Mao because "land redistribution and the resulting private ownership" revived the "evils that had marred life in the countryside" before the revolution (Vohra 2000, 196). Mao justified his "agrarian socialism" on the basis that "what exists in the countryside today is capitalist ownership by the rich peasants and a vast sea of private ownership by the individual peasants. As it is clear to everyone, the spontaneous forces of capitalism have been growing steadily in the countryside in recent years. . . . There is no solution to this problem except . . . the socialist transformation of the whole agriculture" (ibid.).

Following his commitment to the mass line, Mao insisted on a bottom-up approach for the implementation of national policies. Leaders had to learn from the masses as a form of self-education to reaffirm revolutionary objectives. Urban cadres were sent down to the rural villages to (re)connect with the peasantry and organize cooperatives (Meisner 1999, 139).[9] As the program rapidly unfolded, party officials questioned Mao's wisdom in forcing drastic social change to advance his own utopian vision. To Mao, the party's response and its bureaucratic resistance were proof that the party had grown conservative and lost its revolutionary edge. He perceived that the CCP was no longer dedicated to Marxian ideals and had become a handicap to his increasingly radical policies. By now Mao's conflicts with the CCP bureaucracy extended far beyond the policies regarding the rural economy and his challenges to it generated retaliatory confrontations.

The Hundred Flowers Campaign

By 1957 the CCP had nationalized China's industrial, commercial, and agricultural economies. The party considered China as having successfully transitioned to a socialist state, and the Second Five-Year Plan was ready to begin. However, for Mao and his followers, the price of China's modernization was massive bureaucratization and growing elitism within the CCP and public administrative organizations. The cost of such progress was unacceptable to Mao and to those committed to the mass line and Marxian ideology. Instead of the Second Five-Year Plan, Mao proffered an alternative proposal promoting the communalization of the agrarian economy and the decentralization of government. The CCP disregarded Mao's demands and formally approved the Second Five-Year Plan, scheduled to proceed in 1958. Mao, once the most prominent leader, could no longer rely on his charismatic authority to steer the party organization as he wished. The Weberian development of the CCP had diffused Mao's power with bureaucratically organized, rational-legal authority resting on trained expertise exerted through a functional division of labor and specialized jurisdictions. Consequently, bureaucratic officials were no longer obedient to an individual but to the organizational system. In Weberian terms, the former "political master," Mao, now was ill-equipped to override the bureaucrats' technical expertise.

Moreover, Liu Shaoqi and Deng Xiaoping presided over the CCP and exerted considerable amount of control over the party apparatus. Liu, a military hero during the Japanese invasion, was generally credited with rationally reorganizing China's post-1949 armed forces. Deng Xiaoping would later emerge as China's paramount leader and would replace Marxian ideologues with technocrats while changing China's history with his reform policies after Mao's death in 1976.[10] Both men were Chinese Weberians who preferred economic pragmatism to ideological radicalism. At the time there was "a growing gulf between Mao Zedong and Liu Shaoqi" over economic production and distribution (Yan and Gao 1996, 3). A majority of the CCP cadres endorsed Liu and Deng's policies while Mao's populist plans failed to garner support from the Politburo. Mao's ideas met with resistance because they were antagonistic to rational administration by the CCP's increasingly bureaucratized organizations (Meisner 1999, 162).

Mao's conflict with the party crystallized as he launched the Hundred Flowers Campaign, mobilizing intellectuals to discredit the CCP bureaucracy. Mao had never been a champion of the intelligentsia for whom his distrust had been widely noted. He was less interested in intellectual freedom than in using the Hundred Flowers as a "rectification campaign" to generate criticism of the party as a means of correcting the "evil of bureaucratism, sectarianism, and subjectivisms that [had] marred the party's work style" (Vohra 2000, 202). Mao underlined the delicate balance between "democracy" and "centralism" or "modesty and prudence on the part of [CCP] leaders" and "reliance on the mass line." He encouraged the party to "let a hundred flowers bloom together, let the hundred schools of thought contend" (Fairbank and Goldman 2006, 364).

Initially reluctant to "bloom" and "contend," intellectuals were nevertheless impelled to voice their views by May 1957. Soon thousands of big-character posters appeared on the walls of universities, colleges, and public buildings everywhere. Hundreds of letters poured into the press. Debates, rallies, and demonstrations surged as people scathingly vented their frustration and anger. They condemned the CCP as a despotic government in violation of civil rights. They denounced the party's political structure and its social policies. They resented the emergence of the privileged elite. They questioned the single-party system, the lack of free elections, and whether China could be a true socialist state without democracy (Vohra 2000; Meisner 1999). One letter in particular captured their indignation: "China belongs to the six hundred million people.... It does not belong to the Communist party alone.... The masses may knock you down, kill the Communists, overthrow you. This cannot be called unpatriotic as the Communists no longer serve the people" (Vohra 2000, 203).

Within a month, university students began to mobilize, seizing government buildings and holding the party officials hostage. Domestic disorder coupled with knowledge of the International Hungarian Revolution thoroughly disquieted the CCP.[11] The party quickly repressed the movement and retaliated with the Antirightist Campaign as it sought to eradicate the "poisonous weeds" among the "fragrant flowers" that were "blooming" and "contending."

The Antirightist Campaign

Mao's Hundred Flowers Campaign was implemented against the party's opposition, and it threatened the very existence of the CCP's administrative organization. When Mao was caught off guard by the momentum of the movement, the Chinese Weberians fought back to preserve the bureaucratic structure. Liu Shaoqi, the head of the state, cleverly spun Mao's Hundred Flowers Campaign into an initiative intended to protect the bureaucracy from "poisonous weeds." Deng Xiaoping, the party's secretary-general, led a witch hunt against intellectuals who had "bloomed" earlier. They presented the Hundred Flowers Campaign as a party strategy for a class struggle to smoke out antisocialist enemies and bourgeoisie rightists. In the next two years, the CCP carried out an extensive antirightist campaign, and over a million were purged from the party (Meisner 1999, 188). Not only were intellectuals targeted, so were technocrats, administrators, and party officials. Some were publicly humiliated or driven to suicide while others were executed for their alleged crimes (Vohra 2000) The use of *xiafang* (downward transfer) also intensified as more cadres were sent down to hard labor camps for reeducation and "thought reform" in the countryside.[12] Liu and Deng's efforts notwithstanding, Mao repossessed the control of the party apparatus as he had taken advantage of the Antirightist Campaign to purge his own adversaries. By 1958 the Second Five-Year Plan was on hold. Mao reintroduced his economic policies, later formally approved by the Central Committee of the CCP. These policies signaled the onset of the Great Leap Forward.

The Great Leap Forward (1958–60)

Mao formulated the policies of the Great Leap Forward partly to cleanse the "corruption" of the Weberian bureaucracy and the bureaucratized administrative state brought forth by the First Five-Year Plan. He successfully circumvented the execution of the Second Five-Year Plan in preference for an agrarian revolution. Between 1958 and 1960 the whole country was under fanatic zeal, "leaping" toward Mao's vision of the communist utopia. Based on the theories of Marxist-Leninism and permanent revolution, Mao offered no specifics for his program but only emphasized mankind's commitment and proper will in overcoming material impediments toward a historical revolution. However, his economic strategy was the "very antithesis of the rational planning and calculating mentality that went into the making of five year plans of economic development" and it "was profoundly unsettling" to the Chinese Weberians and other CCP officials (Meisner 1999, 195).

Mao's policies promoted decentralization of the government bureaucracy, industrialization of the countryside, a shift toward labor-intensive commerce, and the collective communalization of rural land. People's brigades, modeled on the Marxist Paris Commune, were formed to replace bureaucratic administration in the countryside. The new organizations were responsible for local economies, food distribution, health care, education, and even military training for their members. The red led the expert in local cooperatives. Every man and woman was put to work to increase industrial and agricultural output in futile efforts to fulfill the unrealistic quotas set by local officials in compliance with the command to leap forward in production. However, the lack of planning led to gross inefficiency, and Mao's experiment was met with total physical exhaustion, wasted resources, broken machinery, and overproduction of useless low-quality steel (Vohra 2000). The Great Leap Forward was a shocking disaster and a blow to Maoist myths of infallibility or even competency.

In 1958 China's economy deteriorated as popular support waned for the Great Leap Forward. Facing mounting pressure, the CCP met at Wuhan in late November to formulate strategies for economic restoration. Party cadres questioned Mao's judgment regarding the prospect of radical transformation of society. Couching their objections in Marxian theories, they rejected Mao's assertion that it was possible to achieve communism despite bypassing the necessary historical stage of material accumulation and economic development. After a series of meetings following the Wuhan retreat, Liu and other pragmatists regained control of the party. They effectively reversed Mao's economic policies, halting communalization and instituting *sanzi yibao*, or the "three freedom" policy permitting the personal use of small plots of land, small-scale commerce in nongrain produce, and cooking in individual homes (Thaxton 2008, 215–16). In December Mao agreed to step down from his long-held political position as president of the PRC. Liu succeeded him, becoming the second president of the PRC. While Mao remained as the CCP chairman, he was no longer fully in charge of governmental administration. Mao later expressed his personal contempt for the Wuhan decisions; nonetheless, the Chinese Weberians emerged victoriously as Mao failed to revive support for the Great Leap Forward. In the following months, the Liu-led Weberians and Maoist Marxians would resume their political battle for control of the CCP bureaucracy. It had become apparent that custody of the bureaucratic apparatus was instrumental for policymaking and implementation, which in turn would define the future of China.

The Dismissal of Peng Dehuai and the Lushan Plenum

By 1959 even Peng Dehuai, a long-time loyalist to Mao since the late 1930s, recognized the gravity of China's economic plight. Peng, along with other party officials, threw his support to the Chinese Weberians. He publicly criticized Mao's policies of the Great Leap Forward during his visit to the Soviet Union and Eastern Europe in his official capacity as minister of the Department of Defense. He argued that Mao's campaign had jeopardized China's national security because military defense requires rational economic planning and development as a prerequisite to the modernization of the armed forces and weaponry. Peng also charged that Mao's populist ideas took a toll on military professionalism. Later Peng penned a personal letter to Mao condemning the Maoist Marxians as responsible for the economic catastrophes brought forth by the Great Leap Forward.

In July the Peng–Mao confrontation proceeded into the Eighth Plenum of the Central Committee in Lushan where Mao accused Peng of engaging in a conspiracy with Soviet general secretary Nikita Khrushchev. Mao also retaliated against his critics by threatening to form and lead a new peasant-based army to take control of the party-state if his policies were dismantled (Meisner 1999, 232). The Chinese Weberians, guided by their rational-legal pragmatism, opted not to further provoke Mao or to escalate the political-economic crisis into a possible military coup d'état. They compromised with Mao and acquiesced in purging Peng from the party, evoking the fall of Gao Gang during the Sufan. When the plenum concluded, Peng was officially denounced and dismissed from office. The Maoist Lin Biao succeeded him as the minister of defense and took control of the People's Liberation Army (PLA).

The Bitter Years of Great Famine (1959–61)

Mao's political victory was cut short by the aftermath of the Great Leap Forward. The Bitter Years soon arrived between 1959 and 1961 with an onslaught of natural calamities and man-made disasters. Typhoons flooded southern regions and drought plagued northern provinces, affecting more than 60 percent of China's arable land. Grossly exaggerated figures of harvest and livestock produc-

Administering Economic Development

tion claimed by local officials created a nationwide impression that there was an immense food surplus and, consequently, that it was unnecessary to maintain agricultural productivity. Food production plunged and shortages of supply became rampant (Bernstein 1984). In 1958 China produced 200 million tons of grain. Over the next three years, 1959–61, production dropped successively by 12 percent, 26 percent, and 24 percent (Peng 1987, 650). Meanwhile, China's urban population grew from 107.2 million in 1957 to 130.7 million in 1960 (ibid., 655). At the end of the three Bitter Years, 35 million to 50 million had died from starvation and other unnatural deaths, particularly in the countryside (Shapiro 2001, 89). Wang Zhaojun, a writer of the "wound literature" and survivor of the Great Leap Forward remembers:[13]

> My experience of hunger after the Great Leap Forward is unforgettable. . . . In the beginning, we smelted scrap iron. . . . Almost anything containing any metal was confiscated . . . [even] cooking utensils. . . . The woks were smashed to make raw iron [to meet the industrial quota]. . . . In fact, our district had an excellent harvest in 1958. But it all rotted in the fields because every able man was mobilized to make steel. . . . In the spring of 1960, people began to die of starvation. Usually it started with the old people's developing swollen bodies; their eyes sometimes became so swollen that they could not see. . . . Every day I took a stick, flipping and turning over the soil for food. I ate insects in the fields, earthworms, and straw roots. . . . After birds became scarce, we stripped tree leaves. . . . When there was almost nothing left, many people starved to death. Those who didn't die had dropsy. (Wang, quoted in Leung 1994, 200–202)

By 1960 even Mao understood that a widespread famine had ravaged the Chinese people, and the experiment of the Great Leap Forward had come to a disgraceful end. Mao's good intentions paved the road to hell for those who suffered and perished during the Bitter Years. The Great Leap Forward was thoroughly discredited and Mao's political grip weakened. Later Mao withdrew entirely from the day-to-day operation of the CCP administration. Liu Shaoqi and Deng Xiaoping regained dominance in the party bureaucracy.

Bureaucratic Restoration and Weberian Reorganization

After the First Five-Year Plan (1953–57), the CCP and the communist bureaucracy grew expansively and a new elite class, the technocrats, rose to prominence. For Marx, states and bureaucracies were enslaving institutions and socialism and human emancipation could not be realized without their abolition. Mao, a Marxian idealist, and his supporters sought to realize Marx's teachings with the Great Leap Forward by decentralizing state government, redistributing political powers to the people, and installing communes. The Great Leap

Forward ended in an unprecedented disaster and left the CCP organization in shambles, particularly in the countryside where the administrative bureaucracy had been superseded by the local communes. By 1960 the party cadres were demoralized as the Chinese people lay dying of starvation and disease throughout much of the nation. China's political and economic chaos further impelled public administrative rationality, reorganization, and centralized planning and control. Liu Shaoqi reprised the Weberian ethos in the politically correct terms of Leninism, emphasizing the need for bureaucratic attributes within the CCP and Chinese public administration. The red were dismissed and the expert returned to dominance. The Liu administration stocked the bureaucracy with technocratic specialists and professionals. At the end of 1961 the Chinese Weberians were showing success stabilizing the society, restoring China's economic and agricultural sectors, and reinstating the party's political functions. Liu Shaoqi and Deng Xiaoping emerged as the top leaders during the restoration period, and Mao was relegated to a relatively minor role within the CCP. Mao famously complained that he was being treated like a "dead ancestor" while Deng Xiaoping was strutting like an emperor (Tyler 1997, 7).

The cost of stabilization was an increasing disparity between the urban and rural populations and especially between the technocrats and the rest of the society. China had reverted to the pre–Great Leap Forward years with the rise of a privileged class of higher-level bureaucrats. With their primary focus on economic development, administrative regularity and performance, and political order, Liu and Deng were inattentive to Maoist concerns with egalitarianism and Marxian ideology. The educational system also placed heavy emphasis on the technological skills in demand for China's restoration, further promoting social inequality. Medical care in the rural areas drastically declined as economic resources were shifted back to the urban sectors. As the gap between urban and rural health care grew, Mao complained that China's health care system should be renamed the "Ministry of Urban Gentlemen's Health" (Mao 1965). Mao increasingly found the growing inequality repugnant and contemplated regaining his former influence. His endeavor relied on Lin Biao, the Maoist successor to Peng Dehuai as minister of defense. Having lost much of his influence in the party, Mao sought to rely on the army to obtain his objectives. This strategy reflected Mao's belief that "political power grows out of the barrel of a gun" or at least victory requires strong military backing (Mao 1967, 224).

The Socialist Education Movement

In 1962 Mao launched the Socialist Education Movement (also known as Siqing) just as China recovered from the pandemonium of the Great Leap Forward. According to Mao, the Siqing, or the "four cleansings" movement, was necessary to cleanse politics, economics, organization, and ideology as another rectification program against the bureaucracy (Meisner 1999, 277). Mao called for a renewed class struggle against "revisionists" and "capitalist-roaders" within the bureaucracy, the restoration of collectivized communes, and mass mobilization of peasants. Mao believed that party cadres had been once again corrupted by bureaucratic power and separated from the masses. Consequently, officials should work in the fields with the peasants and reeducate themselves through their personal labor to become both red and expert. Mao's campaign was met with immediate bureaucratic resistance. Liu and Deng, forewarned by the radical tones of Mao's rhetoric and recalling the onset of the Great Leap Forward, sought to blunt the Siqing movement. They appointed "work teams" (task force teams) of party cadres to various administrative agencies to supervise and oversee the implementation of the Siqing at local levels. The work teams, of course, were an instrument of control for the party apparatus and served to guard against radical action. Mao became dissatisfied as he saw the purification campaign diverted by the Liu-led Weberians who duly followed Mao's instructions on the surface but changed its form in practice.

Disillusioned by the party's "conservatism," Mao looked to the military as a solution. During Peng Dehuai's tenure, the PLA was transforming into a professionalized armed force. When Peng was deposed, Mao, with Lin Biao, sought to reorganize the PLA army thorough ideological reeducation. Lin in turn cultivated Mao's "cult of personality" to reinvigorate an army demoralized by Peng's purge and to increase the political influence of the PLA in China's civilian administration and public affairs. The Liuist Weberians nevertheless persisted in their dominance of the party apparatus though facing an increasingly hostile Maoist faction emboldened by the army's support. By 1965 it was a political stalemate between the pragmatic Chinese Weberians and ideological Maoist Marxians. The stage had been set for the inception of the Great Proletarian Cultural Revolution, Mao's final attempt to infuse the CCP bureaucracy with revolutionary socialism by eradicating and subjugating longstanding efforts to imbue it with administrative rationality and technical expertise.

Conclusion: Public Administration for Development

The struggle between the Maoist Marxians and the Chinese Weberians was very largely over how to best organize development administration—that is, "the process of formulating and implementing strategies involving policies, plans, programs, and projects aiming at achieving social improvement and inducing economic growth and social change" (Jreisat 2012, 154). With the benefit of hindsight and sixty years of public administrative analyses, it is clear that the

Chinese Weberians' approach had the greater potential for success. Although thinking regarding development administration has evolved from focusing on "rational techniques of planning and management" to "building institutional capacities" to "structural adjustment" and more market-oriented strategies (Jreisat 2012, 142; Rondinelli 1993, vii), all approaches emphasize the need for sufficient levels of administrative capacity. Jreisat notes that "despite diverse, sometimes incongruous, views on how to transform developing countries into modernity, one finds a reasonable fusion of core concepts and policies." These include the propositions that "genuine national development is not based on a priori economic assumptions, but on empirical understanding of local political, administrative, and economic realities" and "application of scientific and technological methods to achieve growth and increase production is unavoidable" (2012, 149).

The Maoist Marxian's faith in revolutionary socialism, the mass line, and the peasantry, coupled with their disdain for the perceived ills associated with the Chinese Weberians' approach to development administration, ultimately hampered Chinese economic growth, led to environmental degradation, and created great human suffering. The Great Leap Forward followed by the three Bitter Years of Great Famine claimed more than ten times the number of lives believed lost in the construction of the Great Wall over several centuries. As noted earlier, the famine was partly the product of irrational public administration. Ding lived through the famine and explained its origins as an administrative failure of massive proportions:

> At the time [of the Great Leap Forward], people were always singing about "small blast burning out steel everywhere, and in three years China would surpass Great Britain, and in ten the United States.". . . Meanwhile, all levels of government responded to Mao's new economic policies, people ignored agricultural production and foodstuff production declined across the board. The provincial commune leader in every region over-reported the predicted grain harvest, and the lower-level cadres competed in their gross exaggerations. In reality, you could probably produce 300 *jin* [about 136 pounds] of wheat at most in the best conditions, and even then probably only half of it could be put to good use, but the commune leaders simply lied and boasted that their district made 1,000 *jin*, the more unscrupulous regional leaders reported that they produced 10,000 *jin* of wheat, some said they produced 100,000 and finally . . . one commune leader claimed that they had produced 520,000 *jin* in one harvest season alone. When you add up all those figures . . . this would take [the population of 650 million] ten years and they still would not be able to finish all this food. Upon hearing such news, everyone participated in backyard steel production and stopped their agricultural work. . . . No one did any farming for about a year and so this campaign began in 1957 and no one farmed in 1958. In fact, people did farm in 1957, but after they learned there was so much food for everyone for the next ten years, they didn't

Administering Economic Development

even bother to harvest the crop that was ready to be picked up in the field and all that foodstuff simply rotted in the field. . . .

When people were totally involved in backyard steel production, which in the end made completely unusable crude steel—what happened in this process was the massive destruction of the ecological environment. They cleared trees everywhere and there were no trees left, so later when storms came, the lack of trees caused major mudslides and flooding. It was all about "if there's a will, there's a way." If we "will it, it will happen and be made." "If we will the grain production to reach the sky then toward heaven our harvest will stack." At that time, every organ of government at every level, every factory, every school, every street office had a backyard steel production unit and it was advocated that "small furnaces blasting everywhere across the nation and we are getting ready for the new stage of China."

. . . We ate leaves, roots and everything you can think of. (I6, 2–4)

The Great Leap Forward was perhaps a great leap of faith as well as an attempt to spur economic development. Mao also placed unwarranted faith in the grain figures reported by local officials, even though Defense Minister Peng Dehuai alerted him to the fact that crops were rotting in the fields (I6, 3). Mao also had an amazing ability to mobilize the entire nation. However, rational development administration demands rational policy and program design as well as accurate reporting (which continues to be an issue in China; FAO 2006; Yu and Sisci 2002). It is tempting to engage in the counterfactual, "what if China had implemented the Second Five-Year Plan instead of taking the Great Leap Forward, how much faster might it have developed?" However, the onslaught of the Cultural Revolution in 1966 makes the question even more moot.

Notes

1. The term "cadre" includes political functionaries as well as government bureaucrats. Zhou (2004, 155–56) explains: "Until recent years, administrators, managers, and professionals were all labeled 'cadres' in China, and the distinction between [administrative and political cadres] was not strictly maintained." The text here follows Zhou (2004, 156) in using "the notion of '*bureaucrats*' to refer to both administrators and political cadres in the public domain (e.g., heads of Communist Party branches in work organizations) and professionals, because professionals are also an integral part of the Chinese 'cadre' system." Cadres could also be termed "functionaries."

2. The popular tendency to equate bureaucracy with inefficiency notwithstanding, the twentieth century witnessed "the bureaucratization of the world." See Jacoby 1973.

3. In the Chinese context, meritocracy was modified by politics. For example, the offspring of rightists may have faced barriers to higher education in some fields.

4. By contrast, among my interviewees, a majority of those whose parents were cadres reported that, unlike higher-level cadres, ordinary cadres were not substantially better off materially than urban workers (see chapter 5, this volume). Perhaps Mao's concept of privilege was more expansive than that of my interviewees.

5. Although dated in 1980, this description was just as accurate earlier; see chapter 5, this volume.

6. The Long March, from Jiangxi to Shaanxi, took place from October 1934 to October 1935 and covered roughly seven thousand to eight thousand miles, during which a force of eighty-seven thousand shrunk to ten thousand.

7. Among them, the most significant was Rao Shushi, another technocrat who served on the State Planning Commission. Rao was purged from his position as the head of the State Bureau in Shanghai. Imprisoned for ten years, he was later released for mental illness and confined to a state farm until his death in 1975.

8. For a fuller analysis, see Teiwes 1993, 130–65.

9. A similar approach would be adopted later as a national policy for China's seventeen million urban youth during the rustication movement.

10. See Lee 1991, 163–374, for fuller analysis.

11. The Hungarian Revolution began on October 23 and ended on November 4, 1956.

12. *Xiafang* (also spelled as *hsia-fang*, prior to the standardization of pinyin) is different than *xiaxiang*. *Xiafang* refers to a system of "downward transfer," which "requires all the personnel of government and party, armed services, enterprises and industries, students as well as teachers, except for those too old or too sick, to spend at least one month a year at a lower or basic level of their respective units or in rural villages where they participate in manual labor in order to transform their world outlook" or reform their thoughts. See Chen 1972, 365. *Xiaxiang* is the shorthand for *shangshan xiaxiang*, which refers to the national policy of sending urban youth "up to the mountains and down to the countryside."

13. *Shanghen wenxue*, variously translated as "scar" or "wound literature." In August 1978 Lu Xinhua (b. 1953), a former rusticated youth, published a short story, "The Wound" or *Shanghen*. This story was "considered the first piece of *zhiqing* (rusticated youth) fiction in the post-Mao era" and "of great historical significance" (Leung 1994, xxxvii, 249). The term is now used for the entire body of rustication literature.

Chapter 3

The Politics of the Cultural Revolution (1965–67)

Toppling Bureaucrats, Perduring Bureaucracy

> "He [Mao] wanted to use the tactic of a mass movement to overthrow the entrenched, corrupt bureaucratic class that ruled Chinese society."
>
> Chen Jiangong (as told to Leung 1994, 17)

> "Mao had made a litany of complaints . . . about all major departments of the national bureaucracy as being dominated by effeminate scholar beauties and the little emperors and their underlings, [to him] the whole national bureaucracy was like a castle of demons with their bureaucracy from hell."
>
> Ning Lan (I24, 10)

This chapter focuses on the continuing struggles between the Maoist Marxians and the Liu-led Chinese Weberians that partly defined the Cultural Revolution. It follows chapter 2 in showing that the movement toward rational public administration, and bureaucratization in particular, was a central facet of Chinese politics in the Mao era. In so doing, the chapter adds another dimension to the voluminous literature on the Cultural Revolution, much of which is highly detailed and examines the period in terms of personalities as opposed to underlying structural factors. Examining the frenetic years and events of the Cultural Revolution in terms of Mao's struggle against public administration characterized by hierarchy and human resources management based on expertise and technical specialization sets the stage for gaining a more comprehensive understanding of the rustication policy and its administrative organization and implementation, which is the focus of the next three chapters.

Mao's opposition to bureaucratization was a defining aspect of the Cultural Revolution that led to purges of bureaucrats from the highest ranks in the central government to the lowest local levels. Bureaucrats were a major target of "struggle sessions" at which they were publicly degraded, humiliated, beaten, maimed, and often killed or driven to suicide.

Jing Tan, now a medical doctor in the United States recalls,

I remember that, even though I was very young, I often heard news of people [of bad family background] committing suicide. Today I may hear Mrs. so-and-so hanged herself in the bathroom, and tomorrow I would hear that Mr. someone-else was paraded on the street, so all those things that you always hear about the Cultural Revolution really did happen. It was such terror and everyone was scared. . . . I was so afraid that my family would be similarly affected. (Tan I42,4)

As Maoist Marxians mobilized the masses, the political conflicts spilled over into the Red Guard. Some of the Red Guards who were the sons and daughters of higher-level cadres sought to redirect the Cultural Revolution toward intellectuals, educators, and the education system in order to deflect it from focusing on their parents. Other Red Guards of working-class backgrounds were more radical and aggrieved by the inequalities they faced as bureaucratization bred more privileges for high-level cadres, bureaucrats, and technocrats. The radicals followed Mao in believing that bureaucratized public administration posed an impediment to further socialist development and saw no benefit in preserving the stability and order that bureaucrats prized. Unlike the children of cadres, the radicals were anxious to take out their grievances on bureaucrats, experts, intellectuals, and technocrats.

Mao's supporters directly incited the radical Red Guards to follow his lead in seeking to annihilate the Liu-led Chinese Weberians and their adherents within the administrative system along with their bureaucratic practices. Mao's "war on bureaucracy" was woven into the major events, developments, and turning points of the Cultural Revolution. As the deep schism between the top echelons transformed into a mass conflict, the conservative forces and their radical counterparts engaged in an armed struggle that later threatened to escalate into civil war. This chapter proceeds chronologically in analyzing the saliency of public administration to the Cultural Revolution. It focuses on the key actors and the events of the Cultural Revolution to demonstrate how the contest between Maoist Marxians and Chinese Weberians penetrated every aspect of the Cultural Revolution.

The Cultural Revolution proved to be Mao's last attempt to end what he perceived as the Chinese Communist Party (CCP) bureaucracy's perversion of communist revolutionary ideals and to restore the party to its former glory—an institution dedicated to the promotion of Marxian values. Mao sought radically to reform the CCP organization to excise the twin ills of social inequality and declining socialist values associated with China's economic and bureaucratized development administration. Ironically, bureaucracy increased in size and scope during the Cultural Revolution.

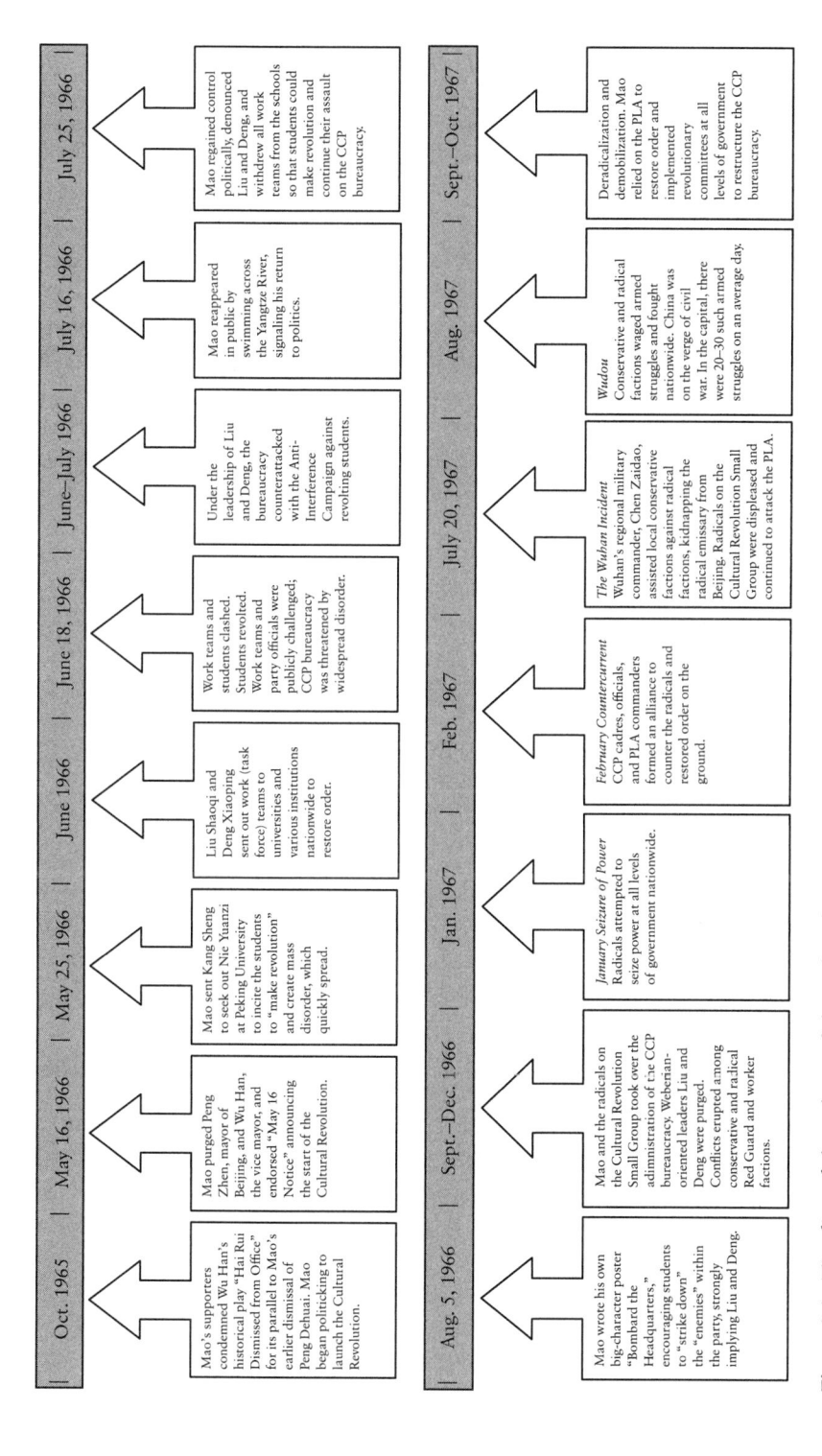

| Oct. 1965 | May 16, 1966 | May 25, 1966 | June 1966 | June 18, 1966 | June–July 1966 | July 16, 1966 | July 25, 1966 |

- **Oct. 1965:** Mao's supporters condemned Wu Han's historical play "Hai Rui Dismissed from Office" for its parallel to Mao's earlier dismissal of Peng Dehuai. Mao began politicking to launch the Cultural Revolution.
- **May 16, 1966:** Mao purged Peng Zhen, mayor of Beijing, and Wu Han, the vice mayor, and endorsed "May 16 Notice" announcing the start of the Cultural Revolution.
- **May 25, 1966:** Mao sent Kang Sheng to seek out Nie Yuanzi at Peking University to incite the students to "make revolution" and create mass disorder, which quickly spread.
- **June 1966:** Liu Shaoqi and Deng Xiaoping sent out work (task force) teams to universities and various institutions nationwide to restore order.
- **June 18, 1966:** Work teams and students clashed. Students revolted. Work teams and party officials were publicly challenged; CCP bureaucracy was threatened by widespread disorder.
- **June–July 1966:** Under the leadership of Liu and Deng, the bureaucracy counterattacked with the Anti-Interference Campaign against revolting students.
- **July 16, 1966:** Mao reappeared in public by swimming across the Yangtze River, signaling his return to politics.
- **July 25, 1966:** Mao regained control politically, denounced Liu and Deng, and withdrew all work teams from the schools so that students could make revolution and continue their assault on the CCP bureaucracy.

| Aug. 5, 1966 | Sept.–Dec. 1966 | Jan. 1967 | Feb. 1967 | July 20, 1967 | Aug. 1967 | Sept.–Oct. 1967 |

- **Aug. 5, 1966:** Mao wrote his own big-character poster "Bombard the Headquarters," encouraging students to "strike down" the "enemies" within the party, strongly implying Liu and Deng.
- **Sept.–Dec. 1966:** Mao and the radicals on the Cultural Revolution Small Group took over the administration of the CCP bureaucracy. Weberian-oriented leaders Liu and Deng were purged. Conflicts erupted among conservative and radical Red Guard and worker factions.
- **Jan. 1967:** *January Seizure of Power* Radicals attempted to seize power at all levels of government nationwide.
- **Feb. 1967:** *February Countercurrent* CCP cadres, officials, and PLA commanders formed an alliance to counter the radicals and restored order on the ground.
- **July 20, 1967:** *The Wuhan Incident* Wuhan's regional military commander, Chen Zaidao, assisted local conservative factions against radical factions, kidnapping the radical emissary from Beijing. Radicals on the Cultural Revolution Small Group were displeased and continued to attack the PLA.
- **Aug. 1967:** *Wudou* Conservative and radical armed factions waged armed struggles and fought nationwide. China was on the verge of civil war. In the capital, there were 20–30 such armed struggles on an average day.
- **Sept.–Oct. 1967:** Deradicalization and demobilization. Mao relied on the PLA to restore order and implemented revolutionary committees at all levels of government to restructure the CCP bureaucracy.

Figure 3.1: Timeline of the Politics of the Cultural Revolution (1965–67): Toppling Bureaucrats, Perduring Bureaucracy

Conception of the Cultural Revolution (1965–66)

Mao triggered the Cultural Revolution in a campaign against Wu Han and his historical play "Hai Rui Dismissed from Office." Wu, the vice mayor of Beijing, was an accomplished historian and scholar who specialized on the Ming Dynasty. Inspired by true events, Wu's play praised Hai Rui, a bureaucrat during the Ming period who disobeyed corrupt higher officials and returned unjustly seized land to peasants. Subsequently, Hai Rui was imprisoned for criticizing the emperor and later dismissed from office. While Wu had conscientiously explained that his play was apolitical, few could miss its allegorical significance. Just few years earlier, in 1959, Mao had publicly dismissed from office in similar fashion the immensely popular minister of defense, Peng Dehuai. At this time, although still revered, Mao's political power and credibility had been weakened by the disastrous Great Leap Forward and the Three Bitter Years of Famine that followed. If Mao was contemplating his comeback, Wu Han's play provided an excellent opportunity.

In October 1965 Mao asked Peng Zhen, the mayor of Beijing and director of the arts and literature community, to officially condemn Wu Han's play. Peng Zhen did not fully comply; instead he protected Wu, his vice mayor and close friend, by organizing a team of writers to counter the attack on Wu. Meanwhile, Mao sent his wife, Jiang Qing, to Shanghai to enlist a writer to pen a critique of Wu's play. Jiang summoned an old friend, Zhang Chunqiao, a Marxian ideologue known for his radical egalitarian views (MacFarquhar and Schoenhals 2006, 14–16). Zhang subsequently chose Yao Wenyuan to write the critique of the play. After nine drafts and three personal revisions by Mao the polemic was ready for publication. In the essay Yao criticized Wu's play as "a poisonous weed and a reactionary intervention in the great class struggle between the bourgeoisie and the proletariat" (ibid., 17). Yao further insisted that Wu had committed "grave ideological errors, such as idealizing a feudal personality while ignoring the main class struggle against . . . the bureaucrats, and . . . [consequently, Wu] safeguard[ed] the stability of 'the system'" (Snow 1973, 87).

Much to Mao's frustration, the once supreme leader who had mobilized the entire nation during the Great Leap Forward could not secure a publisher for Yao's article through regular official channels in Beijing. Liu Shaoqi, president of the CCP; Peng Zheng, mayor of the capital and CCP Central Committee Secretariat; Lu Dingyi, chief of the CCP Department of Propaganda; and Lu's deputy director, Zhou Yang, all opposed its publication (MacFarquhar and Schoenhals 2006, 18; Snow 1973, 25). Remarkably, Mao's power had so waned that he was unable to have his favored words published in the nation's capital.

Now Mao could only invoke his interpersonal relationships. He maneuvered to bypass official bureaucratic processes and had the critique published in a Shanghai newspaper, the *Wenhuibao*. The next day it was picked up by the Shanghai

Party Commission's official newspaper, the *Liberation Daily*. In Beijing Peng Zhen blocked publication in the party's mouthpiece, the *People's Daily*, and forbade its reprint in any other "national, provincial, and municipal papers" (MacFarquhar and Schoenhals 2006, 18). Peng was now under severe political pressure; nonetheless, he commissioned Deng Tuo, the municipal secretary of culture and education, to organize a team of writers to "prove" that Wu's errors, if any, were academic and not political, as Yao had charged. Enraged by Peng Zhen's open defiance, Mao called for a special meeting of the Central Committee. After the meeting Peng was labeled as public enemy number one, a "representative of the bourgeoisie," a "counterrevolutionary," and a leader in "taking the capitalist road" (Snow 1973, 87). Subsequently, misfortune befell all involved in the *Hai Rui* affair. Along with Peng Zhen and Wu Han, Lu Dingyi and Deng Tuo were also condemned for being antiparty and antisocialism (Lee 1978, 15). Clearly, for Mao and his supporters, making a bureaucrat the hero of a play was ideologically off limits.

On May 16, 1966, Mao endorsed an ominous directive alluding to the highest officials in the bureaucratized CCP (a thinly veiled reference to Liu Shaoqi and Deng Xiaoping). Later known as the "May 16 Notice," it defined the goals of the Cultural Revolution:

> The whole Party must . . . thoroughly expose the reactionary bourgeois stand of those so-called "academic authorities" who oppose the Party and socialism. . . . To achieve this, it is necessary at the same time to criticize and repudiate those representatives of the bourgeoisie who have sneaked into the Party, the government, the Army and all spheres of culture, to clear them out or to transfer some of them to other positions. Above all, we must not entrust them with the work of leading the Cultural Revolution . . . [because] this is extremely dangerous. . . . Some of them . . . we have already seen through, others we have not. Some are still trusted by us and are trained as our successors . . . still nestling beside us. . . . (Lee 1978, 16; quoting *Peking Review*, no. 21, May 19, 1967, 6–9.)

Having purged Peng Zhen and his colleagues in art and literature, Mao and Jiang effectively assumed control of the party's official media, convinced that "to overthrow a political power it is always necessary first of all to create public opinion, to do work in the ideological sphere" (Snow 1973, 90). This move would have a major impact on the development of the Cultural Revolution. The Department of Propaganda was restaffed with Marxian radicals and Mao's supporters. A Cultural Revolution committee, known as the Cultural Revolution Small Group, was formed. Its key members were Jiang Qing, Zhang Chunqiao, Yao Wenyuan, Guan Feng, Qi Benyu, Wang Li, and Mu Xin, led by Kang Sheng and Chen Boda (MacFarquhar and Schoenhals 2006, 45).

A Maoist Offensive

Mao instructed Kang Sheng, his ruthless former counterintelligence officer, to foment mass disorder and launch the Cultural Revolution. Kang sent his wife, Cao Yiou, to jump-start the Cultural Revolution on the campuses of Beijing's universities. Cao then called upon Nie Yuanzi at Peking University (also known as Beida[1]), a radical Marxian professor in the department of philosophy, to incite revolution among the students. Following Cao's directions, Nie put up a big-character poster on May 25, 1966, denouncing the Party Committee of Peking University in suppressing student participation in the Cultural Revolution. She insisted that it was necessary for the masses' demands to be recognized, and for them to hold rallies and to be led in the right direction (Lee 1978, 17; MacFarquhar and Schoenhals 2006, 57). Confusion and chaos immediately ensued as Nie instigated revolutionary fervor (MacFarquhar and Schoenhals 2006, 57).

More surprises followed. Mao preempted the Chinese Weberian leaders by ordering Xinhua News Agency, China's leading media outlet, to publish Nie's poster in its entirety in every newspaper throughout the nation. That very evening the poster's words were also broadcast nationally on China's official radio channel. Within a few days tens of thousands of big-character posters appeared on university campuses. The mass movement had been activated and students were mobilized. Everything went exactly as Mao had hoped, and there was no turning back. The Cultural Revolution was triggered and would be maintained throughout by Mao's personal connections, which enabled him to bypass the party's standard bureaucratic procedures and processes. Mao would later topple almost all legitimate leaders in order to elevate his own status as a classic charismatic leader, no longer bound by the rational-legal procedures of the CCP bureaucracy. His actions were similar to those of political leaders elsewhere who have relied on spoils systems to consolidate their own power.

By May 25, 1966, massive discord in Beijing universities had thoroughly unnerved the bureaucratic officials. Jiang Nanxiang, minister of higher education and president of Tsinghua University, urged his colleagues at the university to maintain order and "grab hold of the problems" (MacFarquhar and Schoenhals 2006, 58). Before the bureaucrats could react, the Maoist Marxians once again outfoxed them. With the Cultural Revolution Small Group in charge, the State Council suspended classes in China's schools nationwide so that 103 million primary, 13 million secondary, and 534,000 university students could leave their classes to participate actively in the Great Proletarian Cultural Revolution. As Beijing descended into widespread chaos and as turmoil prevailed everywhere else, Chairman Mao was nowhere to be found. Summering in Hangzhou and still in seclusion, not even Premier Zhou Enlai knew exactly where Mao was. Only Kang Sheng and a handful of confidantes in the Cultural Revolution Small

Group had access to Mao's whereabouts (ibid., 60). It would seem that Mao was plotting Liu's downfall from afar by masterminding a perfect political strategy. Creating mass disorder in absentia would force Liu and Deng to bear full responsibility. Predictably, these Chinese Weberians would follow standard bureaucratic procedure and do what the CCP had always routinely done—send down the "work teams" when troubles arise.

Bureaucratic Defense

In Mao's absence all eyes were on Liu Shaoqi, the CCP-elected president of the People's Republic, and Deng Xiaoping, the secretary general, who was in charge of China's day-to-day operations under Liu's leadership. The Weberian-oriented Liu and Deng naturally wanted to restore order as quickly as possible. First, however, they had to get Mao's permission. After learning about Mao's residence in Hangzhou, Liu flew to see Mao for guidance only to find his response equivocal and his position undecipherable. He neither opposed sending down the work teams nor gave explicit approval. Puzzled by Mao's reaction, Liu urged Mao to return to Beijing but "the Chairman laughed and refused" (MacFarquhar and Schoenhals 2006, 65). Liu could not afford to ponder Mao's intentions while anarchy was spreading nationwide. Under Liu's leadership, the Politburo Standing Committee held a special session and subsequently decided to send in the work teams—the favored method of placing cadre-led task forces in various organizations and agencies to assume top leadership.

In early June 1966, 7,239 cadre members on various work teams arrived at different institutions in Beijing, and provincial work teams soon followed in Shanghai, Hangzhou, and Hubei (MacFarquhar and Schoenhals 2006, 66). These work teams were composed of high- or mid-level officials and bureaucrats from superior governmental offices. Their mission was to direct the lower-level leadership in designated organizations. The work teams, representing and operating on behalf of the CCP, were vested with expansive powers as necessary to assume control. Work teams had authority ranging from rewriting workplace regulations to subjecting individuals to detention, isolation for self-examination, custody, labor, and even incarceration.

Moreover, the CCP mobilized participation from students whose interests were most aligned with the party's bureaucracy, primarily the children of cadres and the technological intelligentsia. As previously noted, China's bureaucratic expansion had been highly favorable to these two groups, which was also among Mao's chief reasons for starting the Cultural Revolution. Many of these children belonged to the Communist Youth League, and a number of cadres' children were enrolled in the very institutions that were at the epicenter of upheaval. For instance, Liu headed the work team at his daughter's middle school in Beijing and benefited from her assistance. Deng's daughter was enrolled in Peking University and later became a member of the work team there (MacFarquhar and Schoenhals 2006, 73).

The work teams, tasked with imposing control, immediately clashed with radical students who had kept themselves busy making revolution by hanging big-character posters and denouncing party officials. Students who were antagonistic to the work teams were put under surveillance. The pro–work team students, often cadres' own children, gained leadership positions, as in the case of Deng's daughter. Responding to what they perceived as unfair treatment, radical students responded with hostile resistance and complained that work teams came to obstruct revolution instead of facilitating it. On June 18 conflicts erupted into physical violence on the Peking University campus. Radical students who supported Nie Yuanzi tied up members of the work team and publicly humiliated and physically assaulted them. The "June 18 incident" soon expanded into a movement that engulfed "thirty-nine of the fifty institutes of higher learning in Peking" (Lee 1978, 28).

The Anti-Interference Campaign (1966)

Liu and Deng were unprepared for the students' violent confrontation, and the timing could not have been worse. In a letter addressed to Mao, Liu wrote that the Third Five-Year Plan had fallen far behind expected production levels. The Chinese Weberians' economic plans were again derailed by Mao's political movements. Still, their first priority was to reinstate order. Under Liu's leadership the CCP bureaucracy and its work teams retaliated with the Anti-Interference Campaign as its new official policy against the radical resistance on campuses everywhere. No longer lenient, the party organization characterized the revolting students as "monsters and freaks" who obstructed the revolutionary movement, and it vowed to get rid of the rebels who opposed the work teams. By mid-July widespread student revolt had been largely defeated and the party had gained the upper hand.

Mao Regains Control

On July 16 Mao suddenly reappeared in public. The seventy-two-year-old Mao joined some five thousand competitors to swim across the Yangtze River.[2] Mao's reappearance was widely speculated to be a calculated move to demonstrate his mental focus and physical virility, and perhaps to send a signal to all that he was reentering politics. Returning to Beijing three days later, Mao held a series of meetings condemning the implementation of work teams and calling for their immediate withdrawal. Echoing the same rhetoric of the anti–work team students, Mao claimed that the work teams had failed to adhere to the mass line

The Politics of the Cultural Revolution (1965–67)

and emphasized that the Cultural Revolution must be led by students themselves (Lee 1978, 31). Liu defended the work teams, asserting that they were critical to restoring order. He enjoyed the support of Deng and top party officials, including Bo Yibo, Ye Jianying, and Liu Zhijian from the People's Liberation Army (PLA), among others.

On July 25 Mao personally intervened and negated Liu's work team effort. He again condemned the "fifty days" during which the work teams took control of university and school campuses. On July 28 the Beijing Party Committee officially announced the decision to withdraw all work teams from the schools. Liu was never as upset and "vexed" as on that day (Lee 1978, 31). As Edgar Snow observed, Liu was unable to anticipate the full magnitude of what was to come: "Now this organizational man, Liu, the legalist and head of the Party Establishment, this firm believer in Party constitutionality, was probably temperamentally incapable of believing in the true extent of Mao's daring" (Snow 1973, 92).

Mao's intrusion stifled the efforts of the Chinese Weberians and shifted the Cultural Revolution toward a path of radicalism. Just as the Weberian-oriented Liu and Deng regained control, Mao intervened and redirected the course of events as in the past. Mao and his supporters would continue to contravene rational public administrative principles in order to promote Marxist objectives throughout the Cultural Revolution while the Chinese Weberians remained largely bound by the party's rational-legal bureaucratic processes (Lee 1978, 59). As Mao intensified the assault on the CCP bureaucracy, destroying its formal procedures and structure, he would increasingly rely on his personal networks and charismatic authority to circumvent the rational-legal authority of the CCP organization. He "invoke[d] his enormous personal prestige and popularity, using it as a major weapon in his struggle to recover full authority over the orientation of revolutionary power" (Snow 1973, 18).

Once the work teams had been withdrawn, Mao insisted that the masses should be free to mobilize themselves. On August 5, 1966, Mao wrote his own big-character poster encouraging the students at Peking University to "Bombard the Headquarters." It proclaimed that for about two months "some leading comrades from the central down to the local levels" implemented "a bourgeoisie dictatorship," suppressed the Cultural Revolution, and stifled the views of those with whom they disagreed. He referred to their actions as "a white terror" and expressed his contempt for their self-satisfaction, which he found "poisonous" (Lee 1978, 65).

Mao's words left little doubt that the "comrades" who erred were Liu and Deng. Not only did Liu's leadership suffer an extensive setback, Liu was himself in grave political danger. As Edgar Snow points out, "Liu recognized at last that he *was* 'headquarters'" (1973, 94). A political storm was raging, and it was becoming apparent that "Liu and Deng might not be able to survive" (MacFarquhar and Schoenhals 2006, 77).

Political and Practical Divisions: A New Class Struggle

Within days of Mao's intervention, the "monsters and freaks" emerged as heroes while the pro-work team students became "conservative" opponents of the great revolution. The students were divided both by political ideology and by the practical implications of their class origins.

Many of the rebel students were children of the lower social strata or those with undesirable backgrounds to whom Mao's vision of egalitarianism and lack of special privilege was particularly appealing.[3] By contrast, the conservative students who supported the work teams were often the children of cadres, bureaucrats, or the technological intelligentsia. Their interests were closely aligned with the survival of the CCP bureaucracy, the Weberian expansion of which favored them because their parents, especially those at higher ranks, enjoyed special privileges based on their bureaucratic power, technical expertise, or both. The latent conflicts between the social classes outwardly erupted when students had unprecedented freedom to mobilize in the name of the Cultural Revolution. Hu Ping, a writer who experienced the chaos of the Cultural Revolution as well as the hardships of the rustication policy, observed:

> When Chairman Mao launched the "Bombard the Headquarters" Campaign (*paoda siling bu*) against . . . the "bourgeois power holders" (*zichan jieji dangquan pai*) in the party, I was very happy. . . . My joy was in fact a reflection of a different kind of psychology. On a simple level, it can be interpreted as taking revenge. All along my classmates from high-ranking cadre families had been very proud and arrogant, always intimidating students like myself. Now overnight, they had become the sons and daughters of the "capitalist roaders." Suddenly we were all equal. To put it simply, I was a "son of a bitch," and so were they. In other words, we were not equal when we were normal human beings, but we were equal when we were the "sons of bitches.". . . Now Mao Zedong was doing something to fix the party itself. I was so happy. . . . I thought now I could become a rebel (quoted in Leung 1994, 57–58).

The division of class origins mirrored the students' ideological propensities during the Cultural Revolution and subsequently affected their political behavior and experience during the approaching rustication program.

Class Origins and Political Ideology

As one of the oldest civilizations, beginning as early as the Zhou Dynasty (1046–256 BCE), China traditionally organized its people into a hierarchy of social classes known as the four occupations.[4] Class origin is a familiar concept in Chinese culture. The duties and responsibilities prescribed by one's class and social relationships are the basis of Confucianism. Similarly, socioeconomic class is central to Marxist thought and communism. Inspired by Marx, Mao established the new China based on the ideals of classless egalitarianism. In this context, he initiated various political campaigns and finally activated the Cultural Revolution because he believed the Weberian bureaucratization of the CCP, government, and society was corrupting China by reverting it to a nation of class-based inequality.

The rise of the bureaucratized administrative state divided Chinese society and afforded high-ranking bureaucrats and the technological intelligentsia special privileges flowing from their knowledge and expertise. From Mao's perspective, this reversion to the old China was not only perverse but "counterrevolutionary" as Mao had led his peasant revolution to establish a new egalitarian state. Well before launching the Cultural Revolution, Mao believed it was necessary to counter the Chinese Weberians' influence. In 1965 Mao emphasized that "the bureaucratic class is a class sharply opposed to the working class and the poor and the lower-middle peasants. These people have become or are in the process of becoming bourgeois elements sucking the blood of workers" (Lee 1978, 70). The Cultural Revolution was Mao's last attempt to revert China to the "right" path that Mao had previously envisioned. As Snow observes, the struggle between the Maoists Marxian and Weberian-oriented Liu was a long-term difference over "two lines" that were, in Mao's words, "nonantagonistic contradictions [gradually] becoming antagonistic" (Snow 1973, 20; brackets in original). The struggle between Mao and Liu was less interpersonal than "mainly one of irreconcilable difference over means and ends affecting the fate" of the new China (ibid.). Throughout the Cultural Revolution, "class struggle" was used to emphasize political inequality as Maoist radicals claimed that "class is not only an economic concept; more important, it is a political concept" (Lee 1978, 70). Mao had much hope that his latest campaign, the Cultural Revolution, could correct the political consciousness of the Chinese population, particularly that of the younger generations, and free the country of the bourgeois tendencies brought about by bureaucratization (Snow 1973, 21). These youth, Mao's hope for a new China, would be known to the world as the Red Guards.

Red Guard Factionalism

The Cultural Revolution was a top-down political movement before mass mobilization. When the population became involved, the theoretical differences at the top levels between the Weberian-oriented pragmatists and Maoist Marxians seeped into lower-level conflicts among the masses. Class origin and the practical implications of ideology played an important role in the political behavior of students and their mobilization. Similar conflicts would later extend to the workers and even the military, thereby engulfing the whole society in the overarching conflicts between Weberian-oriented conservatives and Maoist radicals, now reconfigured in terms of privileged versus nonprivileged classes. When the Weberian-oriented CCP bureaucracy was intact, the latent conflicts were hidden from view. As the party establishment began to falter, the social conflicts among the classes resurfaced. Unlike what Mao had envisioned, a unity of youth becoming the bearers of a new revolution and rewriting the history of China, students almost immediately split into factions and subfactions, which coalesced into two major groups—privileged conservatives versus lower-class radicals. The rest of the society would soon follow suit.

Conservative Factionalism

Although the Maoist Marxians succeeded in recalling the work teams, the CCP bureaucracy retained its influence through its organizational structure on which the implementation of public policy depended. Before their withdrawal, the work teams transferred their authority to the Cultural Revolution committee in charge of managing the Red Guard organizations at each school. The Cultural Revolution committee was putatively the official representative body whereas the Red Guard formed a mass alliance without official status. However, only one Red Guard organization existed in each school, and those in charge held leadership positions in both organizations, which made the two affiliations indistinguishable in practice. Memberships in both organizations were drawn from the regional party committee, the Communist Youth League, and composed of children of party cadres or bureaucrats. In essence, CCP members and the previously pro-work team students were put in charge of both organizations. Additionally, the Cultural Revolution committees set strict standards of eligibility and screened the candidates for the Red Guard based on social class. Only those with social origins in the officially classified "five red categories" were accepted into the Red Guard, which was roughly 15 to 35 percent of the total student population (Lee 1978, 85).[5] In one school the eligibility was limited to only "children of high-ranking cadres above grade thirteen" in the CCP bureaucracy (ibid., 90). For example, at the middle school attached to Tsinghua University, only 256 out of 1,300 students (19.7 percent) were admitted into the Red Guard (ibid., 85). All Red Guard organizations drew most of their membership from elite schools where children of the CCP cadres and bureaucrats constituted about 70 percent of the total student body (ibid., 90).

Those who were selected became the original Red Guards, later known as the conservative faction. The vast majority of them were offspring of CCP cadres, bureaucrats, and PLA personnel, and many had access to military uniforms through their parents. They boastfully wore these uniforms to display their revolutionary family origins. The conservative Red Guards had a personal stake in

The Politics of the Cultural Revolution (1965–67)

preserving the status quo, as did the Chinese Weberians of the CCP who had previously deployed them to diffuse the campus revolts. The conservative Red Guards were disinclined to "bombard the headquarters" because that might jeopardize the privileges that they had enjoyed through their parents. Worse yet, it could topple their own parents, many of whom were higher-level bureaucrats in the CCP organization. Instead they followed the party's commands in redirecting the action away from the CCP bureaucracy and its personnel. Despite the extensive property damage commonly associated with these original Red Guards, such as destroying cultural relics, burning historical literary works, and even demolishing the Temple of Confucius, curiously enough, they never challenged the integrity of the CCP establishment.

The CCP promoted an alternative campaign to destroy the "four olds"—old ideas, cultures, habits, and customs—and the conservative Red Guards dutifully followed the party's initiative. By emphasizing that the Cultural Revolution was a comprehensive reformation of Chinese culture and a move to eradicate the four olds from society, the party deflected the Marxian radicals' attack on the CCP bureaucracy and its Weberian-oriented leaders. Therefore, rather than struggling against "power holders" within the CCP as Mao had demanded, the original Red Guards sought to identify the "social dregs" and the usual "bourgeoisie" scapegoats—the "stinking" intellectuals and academics who had always been an easy target of persecution in any past political movement. The conservative Red Guards enthusiastically raided houses of "teachers, professional people, capitalists, and rightists," but they "prohibited any raids on cadres' houses" (Lee 1978, 88). They physically abused "the sons of bitches" (literally, "dog bastards") from the undesirable social classes and tortured bourgeoisie "class enemies," but it did not occur to them to question the "structural legitimacy" of the party bureaucracy (ibid.). Moreover, they insisted that the CCP cadres and bureaucrats (such as their parents) should be exempt from the Cultural Revolution as "old cadres, old revolutionaries should not be tested by the masses, and should not be attacked" (ibid.). Hong Yung Lee notes that although the conservative Red Guards could enthusiastically oppose the four olds, they were conflicted "in the campaign against the [CCP] power holders," which forced them "to choose between following the Maoist leaders or protecting their own parents" (ibid., 89, 92). He also noted that their privileged position in Chinese society contributed to their arrogance and "authoritarian and coercive" behavior (ibid., 89).

Radical Factionalism

The political victory of the Maoist Marxians vindicated the rebel students when Liu was forced to withdraw the work teams. The radical students, previously disgraced by the work teams, expected to be fully rehabilitated and placed in important roles in the subsequent stages of the political movement. However, the conservatives soon outmaneuvered them and frustrated their expectations because rehabilitation of victims "persecuted" by the work teams was not automatic; it was at the discretion of the Cultural Revolution committees in the various schools. The conservatives reasoned that, excesses aside, some of those undermined by the work teams did in fact harbor antirevolutionary thought and should continue to be excluded from leadership positions in the Cultural Revolution. The conservatives now used the class line theory to assert their superiority, typically, at the expense of the radical students.[6] Many victims of the work teams were barred from the Cultural Revolution committees and found themselves as powerless and alienated as before. From the radicals' perspective, the demise of the work teams was a pyrrhic victory—at least in the short term.

The radicals' grievances remained and perhaps intensified as the Cultural Revolution committees did little to assuage them. The radicals were opposed to the CCP bureaucracy primarily for three reasons. First, they resented the privileges that CCP bureaucrats and their offspring enjoyed in what was supposed to be a classless society. This was also the chief complaint that the radical Maoist Marxians had lodged against the CCP, and it provided a justification for toppling bureaucrats and technocrats. Second, they were ill positioned to advance in a nation with an expanding public administrative bureaucracy that placed a heavy emphasis on technical expertise. Third, their opportunities would be severely curtailed and their lives would be extremely difficult in the absence of full political rehabilitation.

These grievances were central to the conflict between the radicals and the conservatives. For the radicals, the Cultural Revolution was potentially a rare opportunity to destroy and displace a power structure that seriously disadvantaged them. The conservatives, having no desire to lose their advantages, wanted to turn the Cultural Revolution into a campaign against the four olds. The conflict between these two groups was too deep to be resolved through compromise or incremental measures. Their objectives were diametrically opposed to each other regarding the fate of the CCP's rationally, rather than ideologically, oriented bureaucracy. The radicals continued to focus on the abuses of the work teams as a means of weakening the CCP and eliminating its privileges, whereas the conservatives relied on the "blood line" theory to demonstrate their own qualifications and the "natural unfitness" of the radicals.

Having been excluded from the Cultural Revolution committees, the radicals began to form their own Red Guard organizations, and the cleavage intensified. The division between the radicals and conservatives was replicated throughout the nation. These fundamental social differences would become the source of popular factionalism and subfactionalism that would continue to plague the Cultural Revolution movement. The radical students—many previously discriminated against by other social classes, scorned earlier by the work teams, and excluded from participation by the conservative Red Guards—would make it their core mission to topple the CCP bureaucracy and the "power holders" within the party when their fury was fully unleashed.

The Radicals' Rise: Deposing the Chinese Weberians

Mao activated the Cultural Revolution as a means of eliminating bureaucratic privilege and putting China back on the path to an egalitarian society guided by the mass line rather than technological and administrative expertise. So far mobilization for the Cultural Revolution put the children of privilege in control. The Red Guard, mostly composed of conservatives, managed to steer the Cultural Revolution and continue the pattern of elitism that Mao opposed. The CCP was also a roadblock. Its leaders were so bureaucratically oriented in outlook that they responded by trying to impose "unity, order, discipline, and majority rule in the Red Guard movement" (Lee 1978, 102). The conservatives could not be expected to yield their advantages and had thus far been able to retain them, much to Mao's frustration. Mao complained that they were "waving the Red Flag to oppose the Red Flag" (ibid., 103). Their success was partly due to the superiority of bureaucratic organization over charismatic leadership, as Weberian theory predicts. However, the routinization of Weberian bureaucracy is also a source of weakness. It can generate inflexibility and resistance to change. To the Maoist Marxians, bureaucracy was "characterized by conservatism, evasion, [and] inertia" (ibid.). Even if bureaucracies are top-down hierarchical organizations in which most functionaries are depersonalized "cogs," bureaucrats cannot easily be made to discard their "overtowering" power position, especially in the face of demands for a radical change in a nation's power structure (Weber 1958, 228, 232). Deng and Liu continued to defend the CCP central structure against Maoist demands for its demise. Liu's "main effort was to preserve the Organization, which he and Teng [Deng] had so painstakingly built up, from Mao's dangerously destructive course" (Snow 1973, 93). In a statement laden with ambiguity, Liu responded to the radicals' charge that the conservative Red Guards had "defended the emperor" by asking, "What emperor are you defending? How can it be said that you defended the emperor when you defended a Party general branch secretary or a Party committee member?" (Lee 1978, 101).

A bureaucracy that cannot adapt to, deflect, or defeat efforts at radical change may be displaced. With the bureaucracy's legitimate leadership out of favor and on the verge of being deposed, the Maoist Marxians on the Cultural Revolution Small Group were able to assert control. It is important to note that although the Chinese Weberians in the central government were largely immobilized by this stage, change throughout the provinces and local governments was not immediately as pronounced. Members of the Cultural Revolution Small Group, presumably with Mao's blessing, visited campuses daily to incite radical students to continue their "class struggle" against the "capitalist roaders" within the CCP. The Cultural Revolution Small Group eventually prevailed over the Chinese Weberians as the radical students gained the upper hand over the conservatives and the masses were persuaded to side with the Maoists against those taking the "capitalist road," a label launched against anyone who opposed Mao's vision.

The Radical Surge: Failing to Stop the Administrative Machine

By the fall of 1966 the thrust of the Cultural Revolution had shifted dramatically. The four olds were no longer the only enemies. The Cultural Revolution was redefined as a class struggle against capitalist roaders within the CCP bureaucracy. The Cultural Revolution Small Group effectively controlled the media, making it clear that the state and party organizations were subordinate to Mao's authority. Mao also enjoyed the support of Lin Biao, his appointee as the director of the PLA. In alliance with the Cultural Revolution Small Group radicals, Lin instructed the military to support the Cultural Revolution's new path. The Military Affairs Commission (often referred to as MAC) directed all military personnel to support "Mao Zedong Thought" and to oppose contrary ideas regardless of their source. Enjoying the broad backing of the Cultural Revolution Small Group, the top military leaders, and the radicals, Mao effectively succeeded in consolidating his control over the government, the formulation and implementation of public policy, and the direction of the Cultural Revolution. This emboldened the radical students to unify their organizations across the various universities. They were able to seize office space and supplies in each of the schools and to disband the original Red Guards or force them to surrender their positions as the vanguard of the Cultural Revolution. In a key shift, the radicals replaced class background with political commitment to Mao Zedong Thought as the marker for fitness to promote the Cultural Revolution.

The conservatives in the original Red Guard were severely undermined. Their organizations were disbanded, their members discredited, and their leaders imprisoned. Liu and Deng were forced to accept responsibility for what Mao labeled as the "fifty days of white terror" brought on by the work teams. They were denounced as latent bourgeoisies who would soon be deposed. With their top leaders isolated and powerless, the Chinese Weberians were unable to mount a defense or counterinitiative.

Still, bureaucratization could not be totally eliminated. First, as Weber theorized, there is an indispensability to bureaucracy that borders on inevitability. There is also an almost world-wide ubiquity of bureaucratized public administration. As noted briefly in chapter 1, when bureaucrats were toppled, others took their place. This point was emphasized again and again by my interviewees. Wu, a member of the original (conservative) Red Guard, explained:

The Politics of the Cultural Revolution (1965–67)

> The operators of the machine were toppled and replaced but the machine itself was never toppled and continued running throughout the Cultural Revolution. China was never in a state of real anarchy. . . . The machine continued to operate at a very high level of efficiency. Yes, the machine was affected in some ways, but it never stopped working. For example, you were the administrator, and you got toppled. I was selected by the rebels to take over your position. I replaced you, but essentially I'm still doing the same kind of work. The same administrative tasks and personnel stuff. I still have to take care of all the old administrative operations such as distributing people their salaries, wages, and benefits even though the leadership and other personnel have been replaced (I48, 5).

Chao Duan, a social science researcher, explained the continuity of bureaucracy in Weberian-like terms: "Although the old batch of operators were toppled, the administrative machine was never shut down. It never halted, never slowed down, never stopped functioning. . . . The bureaucratic machine goes on without missing a beat, without any problems, without any glitches or delays. The people, or the operators are always easily replaceable, but the machine goes on" (I8, 12). Ding agreed that

> the administrative machine never stopped operating and people continued to show up for work as per usual. The changes in the top leadership were really irrelevant to the continuous operation of the administrative machine. In fact, when the toppled old cadres were replaced by the new leadership—say, the rebels—this new leadership would actually work at a more fanatical pace than the old cadres because they wanted to outdo the past cadres to show their revolutionary forwardness and so they demanded stricter procedure, higher efficiency, and more effectiveness from their staff. They were political fanatics, gung-ho from the get-go, especially now that they assumed leadership positions. (I6, 19)

Kelin Yu, a businessman, concurred in similar words:

> Although cadres were toppled at different times or in various stages, the national operative machine was always churning. No matter who was in charge, whether it was the old cadres, or replaced by the rebels, there were always people in charge of this administrative machine. . . . In fact, the rebels who replaced the old administrators were even more diligent than the old cadres in their operation and implementation of new policies. . . . They were more thorough . . . to show their passion for and their commitment to the revolution. (I50, 12)

Not only did the administrative system persist, it expanded through patronage appointments to Maoist supporters of Cultural Revolution. Maurice Meisner found that "millions were added to the membership of the Communist Party and to the rolls of those holding bureaucratic posts" and noted that the bloating of the bureaucracy's "lower and middle levels" was an "ironic result" of the Cultural Revolution's antipathy toward "bureaucracy and bureaucratic privilege" (Meisner 1999, 371).

Second, in the particular setting of the Cultural Revolution, the military was a major force. Lin's personal self-interest lay in building his own power by purging Liu and Deng. However, within the PLA hierarchy were key elements that, being acculturated to military organization, strongly favored order and procedural regularity over the chaos that had already engulfed the universities and threatened to spread nationwide. Ultimately the structural integrity of the military would dictate maintaining the bureaucracy's ability to function.

A gulf developed between Lin, who depended on the military for his power, and Chen Boda, a leader of the Cultural Revolution Small Group. Chen emphasized the revolutionary part of the Cultural Revolution as an active struggle against power holders, whereas Lin focused on the cultural side. He would have been content if the Cultural Revolution were kept at the level of political studies as a means of improving the people's ideological consciousness in keeping with Mao Zedong Thought. Following self-interest (and, arguably, national interest as well), local and regional leaders tended to side with Lin. Although demonstrations, rallies, and parades held throughout the country denounced Liu and Deng, for Chen, who acted on behalf of Mao, the political demise of these Weberian-oriented leaders was insufficient. Chen wanted to reconfigure the national administrative system. Taking cues from the Cultural Revolution Small Group, the Red Guards turned increasingly violent. They invaded government offices, dragged out bureaucratic officials, held sit-ins, and threatened the remaining organizational structure. Conservatives who had tried similar tactics against the radicals and the Cultural Revolution Small Group were arrested and incapacitated as a political force.

The Cultural Revolution Small Group continued to mobilize the masses. Paralleling the conservatives' initial dominance of the Red Guard and in a counter-effort to maintain civil order, local, and regional officials sought to use workers' unions to control the radical Red Guards. They asserted that by limiting the movement to students on campuses, workers, peasants, and soldiers and were excluded from taking significant roles in the Cultural Revolution, which gave the workers a reason to participate in the movement (and blunt Red Guard radicalism). However, as the political movement progressed, more parties became spontaneously involved and disorder rapidly spread. Soon the workers were fully immersed in the Cultural Revolution and, like the students, they split into various factions. The radical workers allied with the rebel students as the conservative workers lent their support to the original Red Guards. In contrast to the students, the workers tended to be less idealistic, more practical, and generally more conservative, but their participation proved to be much more potent and forceful than that of the Red Guards. They had the capacity to delay production or shut down industry, and, of course, their sheer numbers could not be discounted.

Worker Factionalism

The First Five-Year Plan (1953–57) placed a heavy emphasis on economic and technological development. Consequently, the rapid growth of the economy and the increasing complexity of the society fostered the Weberian bureaucratization of the Chinese party-state based on specialized knowledge, skills, and technical expertise. The pragmatic Weberian-oriented leaders Liu and Deng favored economic development at the expense of political ideals, and they advocated meritocracy and professionalized management. Regarding workers and their output, Liu observed that the policy of the "iron rice bowl," which prevented firing workers despite poor performance or redundancy, must be abolished because this practice was unique, not existing in the Soviet Union, the Eastern European Communist bloc, or anywhere else (Lee 1978, 131). The policy of the iron rice bowl was considered a special feature of China's socialism but the Weberian-oriented leaders had threatened to modify it based on professional expertise and productivity, which was acceptable neither to the Maoist Marxians in political ideology nor to the unskilled workers whose livelihoods were at stake.

As a group, the workers were largely divided between the skilled and unskilled. The technically skilled workers tended to be older and more established. They were the backbone of production and held permanent or master positions in companies where they enjoyed guaranteed job tenure and promotion based on seniority. They also enjoyed benefits associated with their professional status, including health care, housing, sick leave, and pensions among others (Lee 1978).

By contrast, the unskilled employees were younger and were often apprentices, part-time students, or hired help from rural areas on a temporary, seasonal basis, usually with short-term contracts. Not only were the temporary workers ineligible for any fringe benefits, they were also forced to sign a "contract of adhesion" where the enterprise held absolute power in terms of hours and wages and sometimes made unreasonable demands to maximize profits. In some enterprises, the temporary workers constituted more than 95 percent of the total work force and yet their contracts were renewed on a monthly basis. By the time of the Cultural Revolution, the total number of temporary workers had grown to 10 million; they had little or no job protection and were last hired and first fired (see Lee 1978, 129–39).

The political division among workers took a path mirroring that of the students earlier. The technically skilled were more conservative, as they had been favored by bureaucratic management. They were advantaged by the system, which rewarded them with both financial and social benefits. The radicals were often less-skilled workers who fared poorly under the bureaucratized economic system based on expertise, which prompted their grievances. The original Red Guards and the conservative workers had a personal interest in preserving the current regime, namely the CCP bureaucracy, whereas the radicals had little or none. Similar to the rebel students, it would be more beneficial to the radical workers' self-interest if Maoist Marxians who advocated egalitarian socialism through class struggle toppled the Weberian-oriented pragmatists during the Cultural Revolution.

Under the Chinese Weberians' leadership, Liu had barred workers from participating in the political movement out of concern that China's economy would further destabilize while the Third Five-Year Plan was already on hold. The Maoist Marxians of the Cultural Revolution Small Group manipulated the course of events by inciting the aggrieved workers to revolt against the CCP bureaucracy as the political tide turned in their favor. The workers, they argued, as the proletariat class, should be free to engage in the Cultural Revolution with their full salaries paid. For example, seventy thousand workers in Daqing alone left their posts to participate in the great exchange of revolutionary experience.[7] Party committees had to pay the workers their full salaries and travel expenses in addition to handing out advances, retroactive pay, new bonuses, and even back bonuses (Lee 1978, 139). Soon after the workers' involvement, just as the Weberian-oriented leaders had feared, the society sank into disarray. So many millions of workers left their jobs to participate in the Cultural Revolution that their vacancies left some vital operations such as water, electric, and transportation systems out of normal service.

The CCP bureaucracy was no longer capable of restoring order. It could barely hold on for its own survival. The radicals were rising and homing in on the Weberian-oriented bureaucrats. By December 1966 not only were Liu Shaoqi and Deng Xiaoping destined to be purged, a number of high-level party bureaucrats had already fallen from grace and been removed from duty and publicly humiliated.[8] (See table 3.1.)

Sixty percent of the party and government officials had been removed by 1969, along with 67 percent of the experts in the CCP bureaucracy (Lee, 1991, 80–81). Some ninety central governmental departments were reduced to twenty-six, while the number of administrative personnel was reduced from sixty thousand to about ten thousand (Snow 1973, 14). The massive purging of bureaucrats left little doubt that the Maoist Marxians had gained the upper hand. The seizure of power by the radicals was imminent.

The January Seizure of Power (1967)

The Cultural Revolution fully unleashed its destructive forces when the workers joined the students in the political upheaval. The patterns of factionalism

Table 3.1: Deposed CCP Bureaucrats by 1966

Deposed High-level Cadres and Bureaucrats as of December 1966	Official CCP Title and Position
Deng Xiaoping	Secretary general of the CCP administration
Gu Mu[a]	Deputy director of the State Economic Council Commission, deputy director of the State Planning Commission, director of communications for the political department of the State Council, committee member of Department of Philosophy and Social Sciences, Chinese Academy of Sciences
Jiang Nanxing	CCP appointed president of Tsinghua University, party secretary of Tsinghua University, minister of Higher Education
Li Weihan	First president of the CCP Central Committee Party School, The eighth director of the Office of the State Council, member of the CCP Central Committee[b]
Liang Biye	Deputy director of the PLA General Political Department, head of the Organization Department of the PLA, deputy secretary of Commission for Disciplinary Inspection of the Central Military Commission
Lin Feng	Twelfth president of the CCP Central Committee Party School
Lin Mohan	Vice-minister of the Central Propaganda Department and deputy minister of Culture
Liu Ren	Vice mayor of Beijing, minister of Organization Department of CCP Beijing Municipal Committee, deputy secretary of the Municipal Party Committee
Liu Shaoqi	Second president of the CCP (succeeding Mao Zedong), president of the PRC
Lu Dingyi	Vice premier, minister of Culture, and director of the CCP Central Propaganda Department
Lu Ping	CCP appointed president of Peking University, appointed party secretary of Peking University, member of the CCP Beijing Municipal Committee
Luo Ruiqing	Secretary of Defense, assistant director of State Council, secretary-general of the Central Military Commission, chief of General Staff of Chinese People's Liberation Army, director for the Office of Defense Industry, member of Standing Committee of the Central Military Commission, vice premier, and minister of Public Security Bureau

Table 3.1: Deposed CCP Bureaucrats by 1966 (*cont.*)

Deposed High-level Cadres and Bureaucrats as of December 1966	Official CCP Title and Position
Peng Dehuai	Minister of Defense
Peng Zhen	Mayor of Beijing, member of Central Committee of the CCP, member of the Central Political Bureau and CCP Central Secretariat
Tian Han	Lyricist of the PRC national anthem, head of Bureau of Revolutionary Drama and Opera, director for Bureau of the Arts
Wan Li	Vice mayor of Beijing, secretary of the CCP Beijing Municipal Committee
Wang Zhen	Minister of State Farms and Land Reclamation, member of the Communist Party Central Committee
Wu Han	Vice mayor of Beijing, vice-chairman of Beijing People's Political Consultative Conference, committee member of Institute of History of Chinese Academy of Sciences, committee member of Department of Philosophy and Social Sciences, Chinese Academy of Sciences
Xiao Xiangrong	Deputy secretary-general of the CCP Central Military Commission, director of the Political Department of the PLA, committee member of the General Staff Headquarters of the Party Committee
Yang Hansheng	Deputy secretary-general of Culture and Education Committee of the Government Administration Council, deputy director of the Office of the State Council, prime minister
Yang Shu	Director of Foreign Literature of Chinese Writers Association, deputy secretary-general for China's Defending World Peace, vice-chairman of the Asia-Africa Solidarity Committee, secretary of Afro-Asian People's Council
Yang Xianzhen	Tenth president of the CCP Central Committee Party School, deputy director of the Institute of Philosophy, Department of Philosophy, Social Sciences of Chinese Academy of Sciences
Yu Qiuli	Minister of the Petroleum Industry, deputy chief of the State Planning Commission, member of the Third Five-Year Plan Committee

Table 3.1: (continued)

Deposed High-level Cadres and Bureaucrats as of December 1966	Official CCP Title and Position
Zhang Wentian	Former ambassador to the Soviet Union, vice minister of Foreign Affairs, research fellow of state Department of Philosophy and Social Sciences and Institute of Economics
Zheng Tianxiang	Secretary general of the Standing Committee of CCP Beijing Municipal Committee, deputy secretary of CCP Municipal Party Committee
Zhou Yang	CCP literary theorist, vice-minister of the Propaganda Department of the CCP Central Committee, deputy minister of Culture

[a] Later widely credited as the chief architect of Deng Xiaoping's economic reform and modernization program after Mao's death.
[b] Highest training center for party cadres and bureaucrats.
Source: Yan and Gao 1996, 121–22.

and the crisscrossing subfactionalism that emerged among the workers and the Red Guards were complex. The original Red Guards aligned with conservative workers, and rebel students sided with radical workers. As more actors became mobilized, the internal conflict within each group amplified into violent public confrontations with one another. The culmination of factional strife precipitated the January seizure of power.

In late December 1966 two colossal factions clashed in Shanghai; the conservative Scarlett Red Guard with a membership of eighty thousand mostly skilled, technical workers opposed the radical Workers' Headquarters with at least half a million temporary, less advantaged workers. The Scarlett Red Guard had earlier pressured the Shanghai Party Committee into accommodating its political demands. Later the party committee abruptly retracted its agreements due to the radicals' persistent interference. Infuriated, the Scarlett Red Guard staged a massive demonstration, but it was greeted with physical assault by the radical workers. As the Scarlett Red Guard was en route to Beijing with formal complaints against the Workers' Headquarters, it was intercepted by the radicals and was forced to retreat. On December 30 more than one hundred thousand radicals from the Workers' Headquarters surrounded and attacked the outnumbered Scarlett Red Guard on Shanghai's Kangping Road. After four hours of violent clash, the Scarlett Red Guard relented (see MacFarquhar and Schoenhals 2006, 162–69). By then the city was so immobilized by the prolonged factional conflict that transportation, communication, and production in some operations, including the Shanghai Railway Bureau, harbors, and factories, were at a "standstill," experiencing "slowdowns," or shut down altogether (Yan and Gao 1996, 382).

On January 5, 1967, the radicals seized *Wenhuibao*, the same Shanghai newspaper that precipitated the Cultural Revolution by publishing Yao's Mao-inspired criticism of Wu Han's play. They denounced the conservative faction and ordered the workers to return to their jobs and resume production. A day later radicals gathered at the People's Square and demanded that the Shanghai Party Committee formally recognize the Workers' Headquarters as a legal organization of the proletariat and the replacement of the previous government bureaucracy. The radicals declared that they had ousted Cao Diqiu, the party-appointed mayor of Shanghai, and that the municipal government would be thoroughly reorganized. When the rally ended, the Shanghai Party Committee of the CCP administration was restructured with forty-five of its fifty-six members expelled from the city government. The radical groups essentially assumed all legitimate authority previously reserved for the CCP bureaucracy. On January 9 Mao and his supporters praised Shanghai's seizure of power as an example to be emulated across China and said that "the party, government, armed forces, and people [should] learn from the experience of Shanghai, and take concrete action" (MacFarquhar and Schoenhals 2006, 165). With Mao's approval, the radicals reorganized into what became the Shanghai Commune on January 27, modeled after Marx's Paris Commune, and effectively replaced the party bureaucracy.

As Mao publicly urged the masses to "form a great alliance, and seize power! Seize power! Seize power! All the party power, political power, and financial power," the revolution of Shanghai was replicated across the nation (MacFarquhar and Schoenhals 2006, 168–69). Between March and August 1967 the seizure of power by radicals occurred at every level of government throughout China. While giving no specific instructions on how to conduct the seizure of power, Mao officially endorsed the "triple alliance" policy for the formation of a revolution committee as the new leadership to take over the existing CCP bureaucracy. This revolution committee, now recognized as the new body of government, would include revolutionary masses, radical cadre leaders, and local military personnel. This alliance formally introduced the role of the PLA as a central actor in the Cultural Revolution and initiated its substantial involvement in the political movement.

The radical seizure of power swept the nation in factories, schools, and every level of the party bureaucracy. However, the rebels were unable to fully reproduce the success of Shanghai's revolution at the provincial level.[9] Their failure was partly due to the fierce factional fighting and the chaos that ensued. For example, on January 18, 1967, three radical factions of middle school students marched into the administrative office of Peng Zhen, the fallen mayor of Beijing, and demanded control of his administrative bureaucracy. As they were setting up headquarters on the fifth floor, thirty other rebel federations, mostly of university students and radical workers, cleared a floor below declaring that they had seized power from the party committee. Unknown to the others, a third radical bloc emerged claiming it had been in contact with party members in the same building for negotiation of a takeover. The third radical faction sought to take control of the power structure by subordinating the other two groups (MacFarquhar and Schoenhals 2006). Even after the seizure of power occurred there were constant battles over political power and administrative procedures and processes between the students and workers, the conservatives and radicals, and among the radicals and conservatives themselves (Lee 1978). Contrary to Mao's expectations, the masses could not spontaneously unify themselves for revolution without strong leadership by the cadres; neither could they spontaneously form an administrative apparatus without the expertise of the bureaucrats. At the end of 1967 only eight revolution committees across the country were certified by the central government, and all other attempts at power seizure had failed to replace the existing party structure.

The participation of the PLA brought even more turmoil to the fractious political conflict at the central governmental level. The army was perhaps the most Weberian apparatus of the state. Its organization favored hierarchy, unity, precision, discipline, formalization, rationality, and, above all, order. Although Mao and his supporters ordered the army to assist the radicals in their revolution, the PLA was by its nature incapable of destroying the established order to promote disorganization because this had always been at odds with its fundamental mission. In Weberian terms, it can almost be said that a modern army depends on bureaucratization for its existence: "military discipline and technical training can be normally and fully developed, at least to its modern high level, only in the bureaucratic army" (Weber 1958, 222).

The PLA's Weberian organization and its inclination for stability determined its preference to align with the party bureaucracy. The army generals were reluctant to form a coalition with the radicals on the Cultural Revolution Small Group at the elite level or to provide actual support to the rebels on the ground. For the Maoist Marxians in the Small Group, the forceful takeover was the ultimate outcome of Marxian class struggle, and they advocated indiscriminate seizure of power across the government, including the army. The PLA resisted the order to help the radicals seize power. The army instead supported conservative or more moderate factions by disbanding radical organizations, arresting and killing thousands of rebel activists nationwide. Backfiring, the surge of radical policies contributed to an alliance of the PLA, the party bureaucrats, and the conservative mass factions. This de facto coalition proved to be a powerful force that turned the tide of the Cultural Revolution, later known as the February Countercurrent.

February Countercurrent (1967)

On February 11, 1967, the central government held a conference to assess the progress of the Cultural Revolution. On the one side were the radical Maoist Marxians of the Small Group and on the other were the Weberian-oriented military commanders of the PLA. As soon as the panel discussion opened, Marshal Ye Jianying, a frank military man, went straight to the point and accused the Cultural Revolution Small Group of sabotaging the military. Earlier he had broken a finger while pounding hard on a table in protest to the Small Group's incitement of the radical insurgency against the troops. He charged that the radicals in the Small Group had already made "a mess of the party, a mess of the government, and a mess of the factories and the countryside," but until they could also wreak havoc on the military, they simply would not be satisfied (MacFarquhar and Schoenhals 2006, 192). Another PLA marshal, Xu Xiangqian, accustomed to the Weberian organization of the military, immediately attacked the Small Group for disregarding CCP hierarchy and procedure in the aftermath of Shanghai's seizure of power. He asked why the Small Group never consulted with the Politburo when such a major matter regarding the party-state was at issue (MacFarquhar and Schoenhals 2006, 192).

Party leader Nie Rongzhen asserted that the action of the Small Group was equivalent to dropping stones in a well, and it could never assume leadership with these kinds of tactics.[10] Backing the others, party cadre Li Fuchun, assistant to the premier, even challenged Kang Sheng, leader of the Small Group, to openly investigate him when Kang called him an "anti-Party country-club director" (Yan and Gao 1996, 126). The joint action of the party cadres and the PLA marshals proved too much to handle for the Small Group radicals. As the meeting adjourned, the Small Group took a political pounding from the merciless verbal assaults by the Chinese Weberian alliance.

When the meeting resumed five days later, the discussion turned into another bitter confrontation between the Maoist Marxians and Chinese Weberians. By this time many of the party bureaucrats had been purged and their elite political leaders fallen. However, when the surge of radicalism required the participation of the PLA to maintain order, it opened a strategic opportunity for the Chinese Weberians to regroup, and the PLA adopted the role of the deposed party officials in opposing the Maoist Marxians.

Although the Maoist Marxians' primary goal was to demolish the CCP bureaucracy, they also posed an explicit threat to the military as they sought to dismantle bureaucratic structures, organizations, hierarchies, and stability. Civilian and military bureaucracies are often portrayed as politically neutral in the sense that they more or less faithfully follow the orders of those at the top—even when those in command are enemies or occupiers (Weber 1958, 229). However, bureaucracies also have a strong self-interest in their own survival and, often, expansion. Weber noted that "bureaucracy strives merely to level those powers that stand in its way and in those areas that, in the individual case, it seeks to occupy" (1958, 231). Downs (1967) and other modern theorists of bureaucratic behavior such as Niskanen (1971) repeat this premise, which is supported by some empirical analysis, though not uniformly (Borcherding 1977). In retrospect, it was unrealistic to expect the PLA to revolutionize itself or even substantially to modify its structure. Under Marxians' pressure to debureaucratize, it was almost inevitable that, despite the troubled times, the PLA and the party bureaucracies would align against highly destabilizing forces.

On February 16, led by Premier Zhou, the Maoist Marxians and Chinese Weberians met again. Immediately, conflict reignited as the PLA vice premier, Tan Zhenlin, exploded with anger. When Zhang Chunqiao of the Small Group emphasized the role of the revolutionary masses in the Cultural Revolution, Tan furiously protested that the Small Group had absolutely no regard for the party leadership. He continued with a startling observation: "Your aim is to purge the old cadres. You're knocking them down one by one until there's not a single one left. . . . Forty-year veterans of the revolutions have had their homes burst into and dear ones dispersed. . . . This is the cruelest instance of struggle in Party history, in any history!" (MacFarquhar and Schoenhals 2006, 193; Yan and Gao 1996, 127).

The Maoist Marxians warned Tan that he was protected by the Small Group, in particular by Jiang Qing, Mao's radical wife. Tan countered that he did not need their protection because he worked for the party and not for Madame Mao. Disgusted by the antics of the Small Group, Tan attempted to walk out of the meeting. Knowing what had happened to other party cadres, Tan was composed but disheartened as he asserted that he could no longer follow the party now dominated by the Small Group: "I'll leave you all to do what you like. I quit. I shall follow no more. Even if it means getting beheaded, or imprisoned or expelled from the Party, I must struggle to the end" (quoted in Yan and Gao 1996, 127). "If I had known at the beginning that it would come to this, I would never have joined the revolution or joined the Communist Party. . . . I should never have followed Chairman Mao all those forty-one years" (MacFarquhar and Schoenhals 2006, 193).

The sixty-five-year-old Tan contended that he had never cried in his life until then. Li Xiannan, a battle-scarred soldier of the Long March, also admitted that he wept when he read in the *Red Flag* that all the veteran cadres of the CCP had been expelled. After hours of recrimination from both sides, Tan and others finally charged that the Cultural Revolution was itself depraved and perverse. The next day Tan wrote a surprisingly candid letter to Mao's minister of defense, Lin Biao, stating that he was at the end of his tolerance:

> They [the radicals] are completely ruthless; one word and a life can be snuffed out.... Large numbers of old cadres, high cadres of the provincial level and above, with the exception of those in the military . . . have all been struggled with, made to wear dunce caps, forced to spread like airplanes, their bodies wracked and their families dispersed and broken.... Our Party is ugly beyond repair.... They are only interested in toppling old cadres. They will push you over the edge even for a minor offense.... And yet, can they [radicals] assume authority? Can they take over [seize power]? I doubt it.... How long are we to wait? Wait until all of the old cadres are downed? No, no, ten thousand times no! I will rebel against this one! . . . I will struggle to the end and I will go all the way! (Yan and Gao 1996, 129)

As the political battle exacerbated at the elite level, the situation on the ground was equally tense. The PLA was confronted with a major organizational challenge. Its central mission was to protect the nation and maintain order. Yet it was also instructed to help the radical factions, which were dedicated to destroying the old order and taking control of the government. The future of the Cultural Revolution depended heavily on which direction the PLA would take. However, the army did not move in a unified or uniform fashion. Rather, the PLA itself fractured. In some areas of the country, it crushed the radicals; in others it helped them seize power. Consequently, the only remaining institutional force that could counter Mao's charismatic leadership splintered. The military hierarchy that had remained intact even as its top leaders, Peng Dehuai and Luo Ruiqing, were purged and persecuted now began to crumble. Mao ordered the PLA to respond favorably whenever the radicals asked for military assistance in seizing power. Some military officials, including the commanders of the Nanjing and Fuzhou military regions, had no intention of doing anything of the kind, openly threatening to kill and wage war against any radical who attempted to seize their power. In late January 1967 Mao relented to the military's concern for order and protection of their leadership. He approved a directive forbidding attacks on the military and destruction of military leaders' property and other violence against them (MacFarquhar and Schoenhals 2006, 176).

The PLA waged war against the radicals in various regions. Thousands of radicals were arrested and subjected to barbarous imprisonment while hundreds more were savagely gunned down (MacFarquhar and Schoenhals 2006, 178–79). The PLA's actions spurred riots throughout much of the country, and in response Lin Biao called for military restraint in early April. By then, however, the PLA's actions against the radicals had effectively ended the January phase of the radical surge, and its alignment with the conservatives had stolen the initiative from the Small Group and other Marxian ideologues. The power struggle between the Maoist Marxians and the Chinese Weberians culminated in the summer of 1967 with the bloody battles of the Wuhan Incident.

The Wuhan Incident: The Consummate Clash between Maoists and Weberians (1967)

In January 1967 the Maoist Marxians of the Small Group dominated the central government and endorsed a radical seizure of power of the Weberian CCP bureaucracy. Consequently, radicalism intensified at the ground level. Rebel factions everywhere enthusiastically responded to the calls of their elite political patrons in an attempt to consolidate their own power bases. Political mobilization had similarly developed in the city of Wuhan. Home to 2.5 million residents, Wuhan was the most populous city in central China in 1967. A conglomerate municipality of three boroughs—Wuchang, Hankou, and Hanyang—it was known for its industrial economy and strategic location for railroad transportation between Beijing, China's capital to the north, and Guangdong on the Pearl River in the south, with access to the seaports adjacent to Hong Kong. Additionally, Wuhan was a historical city of revolutionary heritage, famous for the Wuchang Uprising of 1911, the armed coup d'état that was a precursor to the overthrow of the imperial government and the establishment of the Republic of China.

Powered by its historical legacy, Wuhan was already facing a new revolution in early January, fueled by the bitter factional rivalry among conservatives and radicals. As in the case of Beijing, members of the local Red Guard were mostly students from "good" social class backgrounds, and the conservative mass factions drew most of their members from cadres and bureaucrats in the city. Sharing similar interests, the two groups united against their common nemesis, the Wuhan Revolutionary Rebel General Headquarters, whose members included both rebel students and radical workers. Although the rebel headquarters had a large congregation of radical disciples, the massive organization suffered the common fate of a tumultuous union between students and workers; consequently, it broke into three major subfactions.

The rebel students formed their own organization, the Steel-Tempered Second Headquarters, claiming most of the student body in Wuhan. The radical workers split among themselves, separating into the Steel-Tempered Workers' General, with 480,000 members, and the Steel-Tempered September Thirteen, whose associates belonged to either the Wuhan Iron and Steel Corporation or the Ministry of Metallurgy First Construction Corporation. Later the worker factions would realign and reunite as the Wuhan Steel-Tempered Three (MacFarquhar and Schoenhals 2006, 200). The internal and external conflicts among the rebel factions contributed to considerable economic disruption, dislocation, and social unrest—all at the extreme displeasure of the bureaucratically oriented PLA. In contrast to the conservatives, radical groups were generally far more aggressive and hostile toward PLA personnel. Chen Zaidao, the local regional commander of the PLA, believed that the radicals posed a dangerous threat to the military's logistical capacity and should be met with a forceful response.

On January 26 the radical factions sought to seize power in Wuhan but failed to establish control. As soon as the elite radicalism was blunted by the PLA-driven February Countercurrent, the conservative factions on the ground retaliated and denounced the radicals for being counterrevolutionary in their earlier attempt to hijack the government. In March the PLA suppressed an influential radical group, the Workers' General Headquarters of Wuhan, arresting hundreds of its members and dissolving the organization. Meanwhile, the local PLA had formed a partnership with the conservatives and was expanding conservative factions through the army's militia. In April the rebels reciprocated and held a series of protests demanding the rehabilitation of their now defunct organization. Rather than assisting the radicals as Mao had instructed, the PLA in the Wuhan region again sided with the conservatives and mercilessly repressed the radicals under the pretext of establishing order. Summoning their battle battalions in March, the PLA deposed the Steel-Tempered Workers' General, arrested two thousand to three thousand of its activist members, and propelled the demise of the chief radical student organization (MacFarquhar and Schoenhals 2006, 201). Consequently, the conservatives triumphed, regained control of the local government, and reinstated the cadres and bureaucrats in their original positions.

Upon hearing about the situation in Wuhan, the Small Group in Beijing was incensed by Chen's insubordination. In late March Chen and his colleague were summoned to Beijing for a conference. The Maoist Marxians condemned the PLA's earlier actions, but Chen defended the army and insisted that no errors were made. Meanwhile, the situation at the ground level in Wuhan grew even more volatile. To render a public judgment on the Chen-led PLA, the Small Group sent two envoys, radicals Xie Fuzhi and Wang Li, to Wuhan for a comprehensive investigation. After four days, Xie and Wang concluded that the army had committed serious errors in both political orientation and logistical operation. They recommended reversal of the army's earlier positions and vindication of the mass radical factions. However, implementing these findings would constitute a sweeping defeat for the PLA and the conservatives in Wuhan. True to the Wuhan legacy of challenging authority, the conservatives chose to fight (see Lee 1978).

Nourished by the PLA, the local conservatives had now grown into a massive organization under the name of "Million Heroes" with 1.2 million participants, of whom 85 percent were party members. In addition to cadres, bureaucrats, conservative students, and workers, its membership also included soldiers from the Red People's Militia founded by the Wuhan City People's Armed Department. Wang Kewen, president of the Million Heroes, was a member of the CCP Municipal Party Secretariat, and Xin Fu, the deputy chief, was the head of the municipal Department of Organization of the CCP in Wuhan (MacFarquhar and Schoenhals 2006, 203).

On July 20, 1967, with "spontaneous" assistance from PLA officers, the Million Heroes violently confronted the Small Group's delegates at their hotel and kidnapped Wang Li. Agents of the central government demanded Wang's release but were turned back each time. Meanwhile, Wang, now suffering a broken leg, was severely beaten by a mob of CCP cadres and PLA soldiers during the standoff. Worried that Wang might not survive the ordeal, Premier Zhou arranged for Wang's rescue, relying upon loyal military commanders in the Twenty-ninth Army Division and the Air Force of Wuhan. Although escaping in time, Wang Li and Xie Fuzhi were thoroughly humiliated. Adding insult to their injury, the delegates had to make a public appearance in Beijing, which required keeping their plane aloft until the premier landed first so he could honor them by his presence at their reception. On July 25 Wang and Xie were greeted as heroes at a million-strong gathering in Tiananmen Square that included members of the Small Group and Lin Biao, minister of defense, who was now affiliated with the Maoist Marxians instead of continuing his support for the regional PLA leaders (see MacFarquhar and Schoenhals 2006, 210–14).

The Wuhan Incident could be interpreted as a consummate clash between the Maoist Cultural Revolution Small Group and the bureaucratically oriented PLA. Backed by Mao's support, the Small Group dominated the central government and controlled the formulation of national policies. They had imprisoned, persecuted, and purged a massive number of party bureaucrats, but they were unable to fully displace the CCP bureaucracy, which was essential for policy implementation. Later the Marxian Small Group endorsed the radical seizure of power in an attempt to oust the bureaucrats altogether and replace them with Maoist Marxian radicals. From their perspective, a total power transfer would be complete and the "corrupt" bureaucracy would finally be toppled as Mao had envisioned. Unfortunately for Mao and his followers, the policy of seizing power also threatened the PLA's Weberian organization and inclinations. Like the CCP bureaucracy, the army had little or no interest in assisting a revolution against stability, order, and hierarchy. Consequently, the PLA aligned with the party cadres, bureaucrats, and conservative factions to take on the Small Group and their radical followers.

Yet the Small Group was heedless of the political dynamics that had transpired at the ground level, and it continued to attack the PLA, which had openly challenged their authority in the Wuhan mutiny. On July 22, 1967, the radical Madam Mao, Jiang Qing, spoke publicly on behalf of the Small Group in calling on the "revolutionary masses" to arm themselves for self-defense (Lee 1978, 247).

Other members of the Small Group also went to work. The wounded Wang Li reportedly wrote an editorial in the *Red Flag* the very next day, urging mass organizations to continue the Cultural Revolution with more firepower. Zhang Chunqiao lobbied to "arm the left" and sought Mao's approval for distributing weapons to the radicals for a new stage in the Cultural Revolution. The chairman readily agreed and ordered Lin Biao to ensure that the PLA would comply with his desire to provide the "leftist masses" with weapons (MacFarquhar and Schoenhals 2006, 215).[11] The radicals responded in force and again gained the upper hand.

Armed Struggle and Factional War (1967)

Prior to arming the masses the Cultural Revolution had already incurred a heavy human cost. The death toll in Wuhan alone was staggering. Between April and June of 1967, 174 violent struggles resulted in at least 750 deaths and the serious injury of hundreds of thousands (MacFarquhar and Schoenhals 2006, 205, 214).[12] Now that *wudou*, or armed struggle, was promoted as the new official policy, factional conflicts escalated into a new stage of mayhem. Both conservatives and radicals raced to accumulate weaponry and resumed their fighting with heavy firepower everywhere. The central government had essentially formulated public polices to foment a civil war throughout China.

In Beijing there were twenty to thirty armed clashes on an average day, and schools were transformed into battlegrounds (MacFarquhar and Schoenhals 2006, 216; Zhou 154). Fighting strategies were planned, defense projected, and underground tunnels constructed on school campuses (Lee 1978, 261). In Chongqing in one incident alone, ten thousand participants fought with a vast array of weapons, including tanks, mobile artillery, antiaircraft guns, and more than ten thousand artillery shells (MacFarquhar and Schoenhals 2006, 217). In Changchun "radioactive self-defense bombs" and "radioactive self-defense mines" were assembled after factions seized research institutes that stored toxic, chemical, biohazardous, and radioactive materials (MacFarquhar and Schoenhals 2006, 220).

Meanwhile, the last pillar of the Weberian structure started to crumble as the PLA experienced increasing internal factionalism. Some PLA personnel were sympathetic to the radicals and shared their grievances; others continued their support of the conservatives by providing them with more sophisticated weaponry. As Weberian theory predicts, once a polity and society are dependent on bureaucratic organization, its disruption generates chaos and even anarchy (Weber 1958, 229). Cognizant of this, the central leaders of the PLA intentionally neglected to impose order on a disintegrating situation. Communication, transportation, and consumer distribution systems were in disarray and ground to a standstill.

The Small Group's strategy in the summer of 1967 was misconceived. Its attacks on both the PLA and party cadres effectively forced the leadership of these organizations to ally more closely with each other and with the conservative mass groups. By now Mao realized that China was on the verge of total breakdown, which could be reversed only by the sole remaining organization with the capacity to impose order—the faltering but still powerful, bureaucratically structured army. Mao's only functional strategic choice was to promote moderation at the expense of the radicalism he had previously supported. Ultimately, "bureaucracy still ruled" because it was the lone organizational arrangement that could (MacFarquhar and Schoenhals 2006, 218). For example, even in the thick of the factional battles, bureaucrats and bureaucratic classifications determined the level of compensation for individual medical expenses arising from Cultural Revolutionary violence. The compensation available to those injured in "armed struggle" depended on whether they were perpetrators (no compensation) acting to quash violence (work-related compensation) or were simply ignorant of what they were doing (compensated as illness) (MacFarquhar and Schoenhals 2006, 218). One could hardly ignore the irony that the Cultural Revolution was in large part intended to destroy bureaucracy, yet its casualties ultimately had to depend on bureaucracy for compensation.

Deradicalization and Revolution Committees (1967): Mao's Call for Rustication

By the summer of 1967 armed struggle ravaged the entire nation. China was on the verge of descending into mass civil war as the Weberian-oriented conservatives and the Marxian radicals violently confronted each other on the streets. Ever committed to their cause, zealous radicals invited the chairman to lead them in a new round of guerilla warfare. Despite his loyal followers, Mao had other plans in mind. After all, it was not his intention to destroy the entire government structure and let China fall into total anarchy. The central purpose of Cultural Revolution was to initiate a daring reform of the existing government organization so that the Weberian CCP bureaucracy would be reconfigured toward one more suitable for the development of a Marxian egalitarian society. Much to Mao's disappointment, a unified mass revolutionary force that would push for such a sweeping governmental reform never materialized as he had envisioned, be it the student Red Guards, the workers, or the peasants. Instead, from the very beginning the Cultural Revolution was plagued by interminable elite political conflict and irreparable factionalism throughout the society. At last, perhaps even Mao realized that debureaucratizing China's leadership was either a lost cause from the outset or one that would prove far too costly. The immediate problem for Mao was how to deescalate the movement on which he had placed so much hope.

In August 1967 Mao was increasingly critical of student involvement in the Cultural Revolution and called for the separation of the student–worker political alliance. The official propaganda now stressed that students should focus on educational reforms in schools and not interfere with workers' movements in factories. (The schools, closed in 1966, reopened incrementally from 1967 to 1971.) Moreover, they were redirected to disassemble and return to campus or risk being expelled or denied work assignments after graduation. Mao publicly praised the PLA but downplayed the importance of the Cultural Revolution Small Group. Even the Small Group could not evade misfortune. Just a few months earlier Wang Li, the emissary to Wuhan, was a political star among the radicals. Now he was denounced as an "ultra-leftist," along with his colleague Kuan Feng, and both were purged from the Small Group. By National Day (October 1) 1967, Mao stood alongside the PLA generals who had been under attack just months earlier at the Tiananmen Square parade.

In September Mao expedited the implementation of his strategic plan by building a new institution to replace the now tattered CCP bureaucracy. Normally the provincial party bureaucracy included three administrative agencies: the party committee, the provincial government, and the court system. Under Mao's plan, the provincial jurisdiction would be superseded by a revolution committee under which a single administrative bureaucracy would exist, operated by functional groups. Although as of 1967 Mao had succeeded in drastically reducing the number of bureaucrats in government, the new revolution committees still retained a bureaucratic organizational form. For example, in Liaoning, the provincial revolution committee consolidated its bureaucratic staff from 6,694 to just 580 (MacFarquhar and Schoenhals 2006, 239).[13]

In October Mao again called for the "great triple alliance" of the PLA personnel, revolutionary cadres, and revolutionary masses, rekindling his earlier concept for establishing leadership after the abortive January seizure of power. Representatives of this "three-in-one" combination would serve as the functional groups of the revolution committees—the new organ of provincial government. However, problems of the past immediately resurfaced as each functional group sought to pursue its own interests. Bloody factional strife continued even under what was now supposedly a single government organ. With few exceptions, most provinces experienced violent political transitions where each group aimed to annihilate the other by hostile force. In the Guangxi region the interim government had to be installed by force. The PLA's continuing battle against the rebel factions resulted in 60 million yuan in property damage, 50,000 homeless, 10,000 imprisoned, and 2,324 executed (MacFarquhar and Schoenhals 2006, 245). In the end the PLA prevailed and military personnel on the revolution committees dominated the new government organs. Along with the militarization of civilian administration, the army reinstalled Weberian order, discipline, uniformity, and hierarchy to the party and its bureaucracy.

Conclusion: Charismatic Public Administration and Rustication

The Cultural Revolution encompassed an epic struggle between Mao's efforts to assert his charismatic leadership over the CCP's administrative structure and the Chinese Weberians' attempt to ensure that rational public administration, which had taken the form of Weberian bureaucracy, persisted. The need to restore order and the PLA's actions doomed Mao from succeeding in his attempt to infuse China's administrative culture with revolutionary socialist ideals and operational values. Not only did the Chinese bureaucracy perdure, according to my interviewees the bureaucracy was more efficient prior to the Cultural Revolution and corruption was far more limited than after.[14] However, before the PLA reestablished stable, bureaucratic administration in late 1967, Mao was able to use his charisma to control and motivate the bureaucratized administrative system he detested. When he called for rustication in 1967, the administrators involved answered his call with remarkable efficiency and completeness.

Several of my interviewees maintained that the Cultural Revolution stood in stark contrast to Weberian bureaucracy by relying on Mao's charismatic authority to manage administrative operations efficiently throughout the nation. This is surprising in view of much of the literature on and popular image of the Cultural Revolution that envisions China as being in a state of total chaos, if not anarchy. Lan summed up Mao's effort to gain the upper hand against the entrenched bureaucracy by noting, "China had an extremely large bureaucracy in the Weberian sense, the different levels, echelons of hierarchy, rules and regulations including its disciplinary mechanism. That's true. However, Mao was able to cleverly bypass this mammoth organization structure altogether" by relying on "interpersonal relations to get his . . . work done" (I24, 12). Lin, a journalist, contended that Mao used patronage or a spoils system to change the mentality of the bureaucrats and the behavior of the bureaucracy:

> Mao could not use those old cadres, bureaucrats, and administrators because they were all products of the old system. They didn't think like Mao, who is an idealist, a firm believer of Marxian socialism and communism. The bureaucrats and cadres

became practical, pragmatic, and they wanted to rationally develop China's economy. So of course Mao thought they had become revisionists. Mao would not simply let them retire because they had to be toppled. Their thinking, their customs, their rules and regulations, their whole system had to be toppled so that new successors, Mao's own successors, Mao's own "red" bureaucrats and cadres would be bred, produced and mentored under a new system (I28, 3).

Several interviewees agreed that this strategy was effective, at least in the short run. Ding (I6, 2) maintained that "the Cultural Revolution was not a disorderly, chaotic movement; instead it was a highly organized, highly efficient, and highly managed movement. Everything was done exactly as instructed by Chairman Mao." Yu observed that

> Mao's order did not have to go through any normal processes or through different bureaucratic organizations such as the county level government offices, then the local level; it was Mao directly to those who worshipped him. . . . Whatever Mao wanted, it came directly down to the people so the implementation was entirely direct from top to bottom instead of being watered down through the multi–government offices as in the past. The operatives at every level had to implement the policy as they were told. If they didn't then it's over for them. They would be outed as counterrevolutionaries against Chairman Mao, our God, so of course, this approach meant extremely, extraordinarily high efficiency and total coordination among the different organizations. This strategy was a very important factor for the highly effective implementation of the sent-down [rustication] policy. (I50, 12)

The toppling extended to "the children of the political target" (Lin I28, 4) and, indeed, to an entire generation of urban youth whom Mao sought to imbue with revolutionary communist ideals via the "up to the mountains and down to the countryside" policy as an extension of his Cultural Revolutionary objectives. From 1968 to 1978 the rustication program engulfed the offspring of the toppled bureaucrats, cadres, "revisionists," "counterrevolutionaries," and other "undesirables" along with Mao's "little revolutionary generals" and foot soldiers in the Red Guard who were relishing their last days of glory while inflicting disorder upon the cities.[15] All told, some seventeen million urban youth were voluntarily or coercively separated from their families and homes to be sent down for revolutionary socialist reeducation in rural villages, military and state farms, and the Inner Mongolian grasslands.[16] These rusticated youth, mostly aged fifteen to twenty, would on average spend about seven years in rural areas, laboring twelve hours a day, seven days a week under extremely harsh conditions (Pan 2003; Bernstein 1977b; Zhou and Hou 1999). Deprived of a conventional adolescence and a formal education, and in most cases subjected to a tremendously difficult

The Politics of the Cultural Revolution (1965–67) 73

life in rural villages and military farms (as discussed in chapter 5), these rusticated youth became China's "lost generation."

Notes

1. Beida is the shorthand for Beijing Daxue (or Beijing University), combining the first two syllables of the words in Chinese. However, the university continues to refer to itself as Peking University, retaining its original Roman alphabetization prior to the standardization of pinyin that changed the spelling of "Peking" to "Beijing."

2. The Yangtze is also known as Chang Jiang, which literally means "the long river" in Chinese, at about 3,915 miles in total length.

3. The five denoted "bad class" origins include landlord, rich peasant, counterrevolutionary, bad element, and rightist. Capitalist roaders and reactionary academic authorities were later added to the list, making seven bad class elements (Li 1995, 150). At the time, class origin was listed as part of an individual's permanent social records, similar to a social security number in the United States today.

4. In descending order, these were the gentry scholars, the artisans and craftsmen, the peasant farmers, and the merchants and traders. See Fairbank and Goldman 1992, 108.

5. The official five red categories of social origins were revolutionary martyr, revolutionary soldier, revolutionary cadre, worker, and poor and middle peasant. See Lee 1978, 86.

6. In July 1966 the popular couplet regarding revolutionary class was that "If one's father is revolutionary, his son is a hero, and if one's father is reactionary, his son is a bad egg" (Lee 1978, 72).

7. A major oil production field for energy and petrochemicals, Daqing was touted as a best practice productivity model for the whole nation.

8. In July 1966 Liu Shaoqi was displaced by Lin Biao. He was put under house arrest in 1967 until being officially expelled from the CCP in October 1968. He died in November 1969. Deng Xiaoping was purged in 1966 and exiled (*xiafang*) to the countryside in the Jiangxi Province. He was a factory worker until Mao brought him back to oversee day-to-day administration in 1974. Deng was purged again by Mao and the Jiang Qing–led radicals in 1976. After Mao's death, Deng ousted the Mao-selected heir, Hua Guofeng, and reset China's course with his signature pragmatic approach to China's development. Liu Shaoqi was posthumously politically rehabilitated in February 1980. He was subsequently given a state funeral.

9. Even the success of the Shanghai People's Commune was short-lived as it quickly dissolved due to internal factionalism. In less than a month it was replaced by the Shanghai Municipal Revolution Committee.

10. In Chinese, this expression refers to throwing stones on one who has fallen into a well (a metaphor for a trap) instead of trying to save him or her. A rough US equivalent is "adding fuel to the fire."

11. According to China's official reports, Lin and his family died in a plane crash in

Mongolia in 1971 after a botched attempt to assassinate Mao. Considerable speculation remains regarding the circumstances of his death.

12. Although estimates vary according to different accounts, these figures are likely to be on the higher side. See MacFarquhar and Schoenhals 2006, 205, 214.

13. This does not contradict Meisner's finding that the bureaucracy became "bloated" during the Cultural Revolution because his unit of analysis is the nation as a whole and extends beyond the highly chaotic years of 1966 and 1967 (Meisner 1999, 371).

14. See chapter 5.

15. Members of the Red Guard were referred to as "little revolutionary generals" during the Cultural Revolution era, as told by Zheng Yi in his interview. See Leung 1994, 263.

16. See Zhou and Hou, 1999, 12–36.

Chapter 4

Rustication

Policy and Administrative Implementation

> "The young intellectuals and students throughout the country must unite with the broad masses of workers and peasants and become one of them. . . . In the final analysis, the dividing line between revolutionary intellectuals and non-revolutionary or counter-revolutionary intellectuals is whether or not they are willing to integrate themselves with the workers and peasants and actually do so. . . . How should we judge whether a youth is a revolutionary? . . . There can only be one criterion, namely, whether or not he is willing to integrate himself with the broad masses of workers and peasants and does so in practice."
>
> Mao Zedong (1939)

> "The knowledgeable youth must go to the country, and will be educated from living in rural poverty, this is necessary."
>
> Mao Zedong (1968)

In many respects the Cultural Revolution culminated in the unfolding of the rustication program from 1967 to 1978.[1] During that period, rustication represented Mao's last stand in the effort to rid China of the elitist tendencies of bureaucracy and technocracy and return to the revolutionary ideal of building a communist society based on the peasantry. Rustication also offered promise of defusing the civil strife between the radical and conservative factions that resulted in urban disorder and, if not contained or abated, threatened to burgeon into an all-out devastating civil war. As with other facets of the Cultural Revolution, rustication has been analyzed through several lenses. This chapter considers the rustication program from the perspective of the ongoing struggle between the Maoist Marxians and the Weberian-oriented officials in the Chinese Communist Party (CCP) and People's Liberation Army (PLA).

The politics of rustication were a continuation of the contest during the Cultural Revolution between the Maoist Marxians, who wanted to reeducate urban youth to prevent them from being corrupted by exposure to the urbanized, privileged bureaucratic, and technocratic classes, and the Chinese Weberians, who viewed organizational rationalization and technological expertise as central to China's continuing economic and social development. Rustication also reflected disparate views of the appropriate role of rural and urban regions in China's further political development. Mao had an almost utopian view of the peasantry and its role in the ongoing revolution, which was accompanied by antipathy toward the cities, particularly their intelligentsia, and, remarkably, even their proletariat (Meisner 1971a, 21). The Cultural Revolution, as Meisner observed, was a powerful "expression of Maoist anti-urbanism . . . directed primarily against newly-emergent urban elites and the cultural and technological intelligentsia and especially urban-based Party bureaucrats" (ibid., 22).

The Red Guard movement discussed in the previous chapter was Mao's primary weapon against the power and privilege of the urban intelligentsia and bureaucrats. Rustication, by contrast, did not target bureaucrats and bureaucracy per se but rather offered an antidote to urban bureaucratization by reconnecting "corrupted" urban youth with the revolutionary virtues of peasant life, especially hard physical labor and rudimentary living conditions along with a low degree of economic and technical specialization. In this sense rustication and opposition to it reflected marked disparities in policy perspectives regarding the management of human capital. Viewing rustication as part of the larger struggle between Maoist Marxians and Chinese Weberians improves our understanding of the origins and structure of a key component of the Cultural Revolution and tests Weberian propositions regarding the dependency of industrializing economies and urbanizing societies on bureaucratic organization.

This chapter begins with a description of the rustication program. Next it explains how rustication promoted Mao's desire to fulfill the revolutionary ideal of emancipating mankind, including liberating it from bureaucratic and technocratic domination. It then presents traditional explanations for rustication and considers their limitations. The chapter concludes by setting the stage for a fuller exploration in chapter 5 of the roles of public administrative agencies and their personnel in the rustication program as recounted by my interviewees. Chapter 5 also considers how, in turn, my interviewees believe implementation of the rustication program affected China's administrative culture.

The Rustication Program

Sending urbanites down to the countryside for various reasons dates back to 1955. The First Five-Year Plan (1953–57) contemplated vast expansion of China's agricultural capacity, which required that educated workers be transferred from the cities to the rural areas. Urban unemployment enhanced the feasibility

| 1953–57 | Late 1960s | 1962 | 1966 | 1967–68 |

1953–57: During China's First Five-Year Plan and its rapid economic development, educated urbanites went to rural areas and worked with peasants.

Late 1960s: After Chinese society became highly bureaucratized during the First Five-Year Plan, Mao believed that urban bureaucrats were corrupted by city life, and it became a common practice to send down the bureaucrats to the countryside for "reeducation" to reconnect with revolutionary ideals through physical labor.

1962: Rustication became a fundamental part of a broader national program to reeducate the youth in combating urban "bourgeois tendencies" by reaffirming Marxian revolutionary ideals through physical labor.

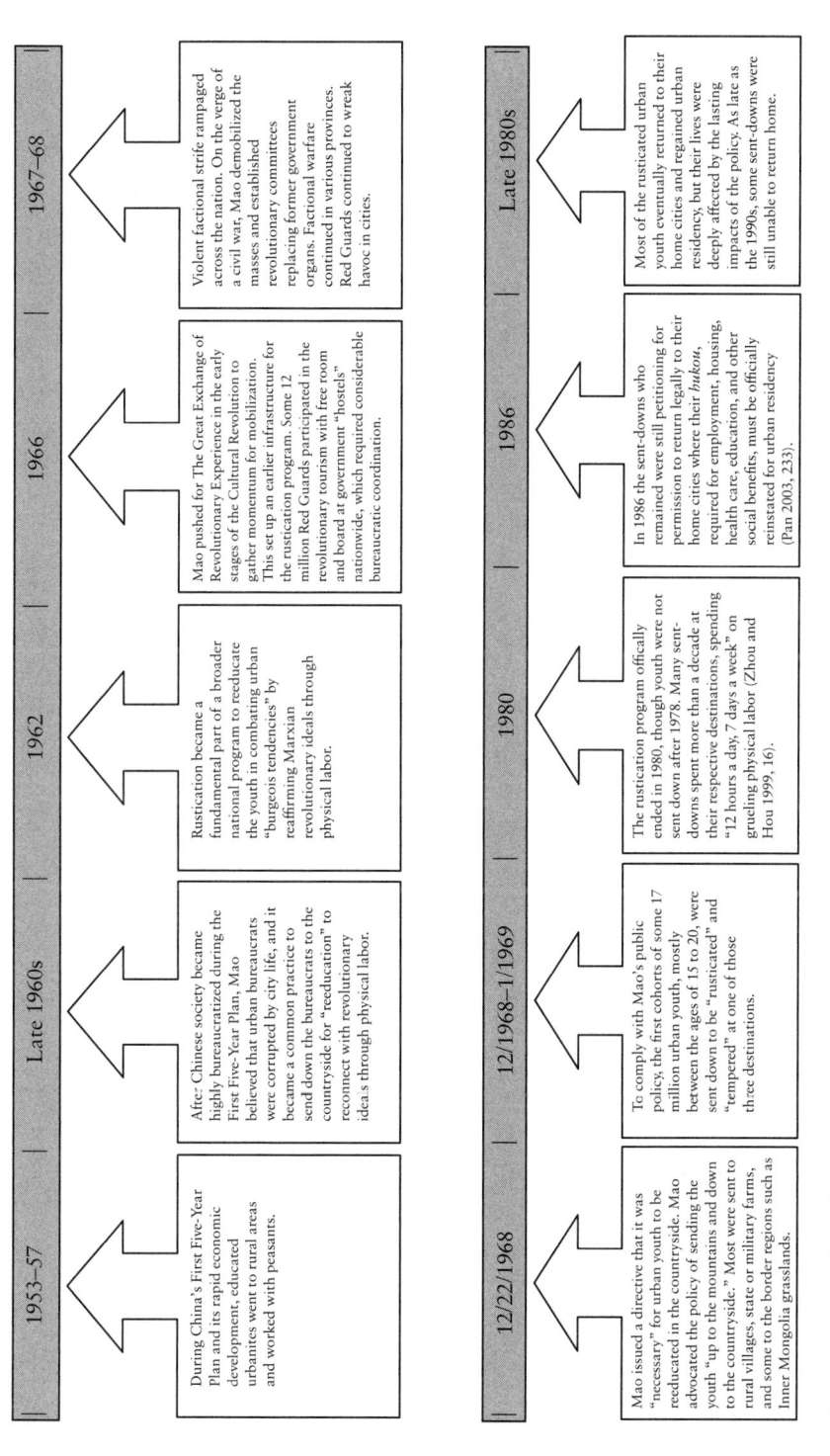

1966: Mao pushed for The Great Exchange of Revolutionary Experience in the early stages of the Cultural Revolution to gather momentum for mobilization. This set up an earlier infrastructure for the rustication program. Some 12 million Red Guards participated in the revolutionary tourism with free room and board at government "hostels" nationwide, which required considerable bureaucratic coordination.

1967–68: Violent factional strife rampaged across the nation. On the verge of a civil war, Mao demobilized the masses and established revolutionary committees replacing former government organs. Factional warfare continued in various provinces. Red Guards continued to wreak havoc in cities.

| 12/22/1968 | 12/1968–1/1969 | 1980 | 1986 | Late 1980s |

12/22/1968: Mao issued a directive that it was "necessary" for urban youth to be reeducated in the countryside. Mao advocated the policy of sending the youth "up to the mountains and down to the countryside." Most were sent to rural villages, state or military farms, and some to the border regions such as Inner Mongolia grasslands.

12/1968–1/1969: To comply with Mao's public policy, the first cohorts of some 17 million urban youth, mostly between the ages of 15 to 20, were sent down to be "rusticated" and "tempered" at one of those three destinations.

1980: The rustication program officially ended in 1980, though youth were not sent down after 1978. Many sent-downs spent more than a decade at their respective destinations, spending "12 hours a day, 7 days a week" on grueling physical labor (Zhou and Hou 1999, 16).

1986: In 1986 the sent-downs who remained were still petitioning for permission to return legally to their home cities where their *hukou*, required for employment, housing, health care, education, and other social benefits, must be officially reinstated for urban residency (Pan 2003, 233).

Late 1980s: Most of the rusticated urban youth eventually returned to their home cities and regained urban residency, but their lives were deeply affected by the lasting impacts of the policy. As late as the 1990s, some sent-downs were still unable to return home.

Figure 4.1: Timeline of Rustication: Policy and Administrative Implementation

of such labor mobility. Moreover, from Mao's perspective, going "down to the villages" to perform agricultural labor side by side with the peasantry was valuable in itself. It offered an avenue for both individual self-actualization and the means to maintain the purity of Chinese communism.[2] By the late 1960s it had become common practice to send bureaucrats down to the countryside for reeducation when they seemed to stray substantially from revolutionary ideals. In addition, some youth and cadres went voluntarily out of a sense of commitment to building the economy and society. Primary school graduates who could not find work in the cities were also sent to rural areas at age sixteen (Bernstein 1977a, 21). Consequently, sending people down to the countryside for various reasons was an ingrained process, not something entirely new when Mao turned to it in 1967 as a potential solution to myriad problems brought on or exacerbated by the Cultural Revolution.

In 1962 sending urban youth down to rural areas became a fundamental part of a broad national reeducation program. The central government began to budget for the resettlement of sent-downs in rural areas, which had previously been the responsibility of local governments. The phrase "up to the mountains and down to the villages [countryside]," used for the fully developed rustication program, was popularized in the early 1960s by Tan Zhenlin, vice premier of the State Council and the head of its Agricultural and Forestry Office (Pan 2003, 41). In 1964 he predicted that six million urban youth would be without employment and would be suitable for being sent down to rural areas (Rosen 1981, 10).

What was new in the rustication program from 1968 to 1978 was its scope and comprehensive administrative organization and implementation. Sending down seventeen million youth required substantial organization and logistics. Some of the infrastructure for rustication had been established during the Great Exchange of Revolutionary Experience program that began early in the Cultural Revolution. Featuring "revolutionary tourism," the program was highly organized to make it possible for students and workers to travel throughout the country. The government set up receiving posts that functioned like hostels in which revolutionary travelers could spend the night and have a meal. Revolutionary tourism was free, and workers not only collected their salaries while participating in it but were also reimbursed for their expenses. Tours included destinations laden with revolutionary importance, such as Mao's birthplace in Hunan and Yan'an, the center of the Communist Revolution from 1936 to 1948. Mao would often greet tours at their conclusion in Beijing's Tiananmen Square. In 1966 some twelve million Red Guard members took part in such trips (Meisner 1999, 323).

From Mao's perspective, revolutionary tourism had the potential benefit of enabling Red Guard units to join up with one another into ever-larger organizations and networks. The PLA was ordered to facilitate the tourism by providing

Photo 4.1: Two young women in Tiananmen Square. The top banner reads: "To fully implement the Great Proletarian Cultural Revolution until the very end."

free railway transportation, lodging, and food. In Beijing, "workers of service trades [were] also . . . mobilized. In many restaurants and dining halls, food [was] served round the clock. Special bus lines connect[ed] universities, colleges, institutions and schools—the suburbs . . . [were] opened, to give the students and teachers from other parts of the country every transportation convenience" (Singer 1971, 22–23). Ironically, even while Mao sought to reduce the influences of bureaucratization, the movement of and provision of transportation, lodging, and food for such vast numbers of travelers required rational organization, which—as Weberian theory predicts—was apt to be bureaucratic.

After rustication became a full-fledged, nationally organized, comprehensive program for sending urban youth to rural areas in 1968, those born between 1949

Photo 4.2: A youth propaganda team promoting Mao's Thought and the Cultural Revolution. The members were later sent down to the countryside.

and 1962 were most affected (Pan 2003, 46).[3] They were primarily junior high and high school students. Most sent-downs went to one of three destinations: rural villages, state and military farms, and Inner Mongolian grasslands.[4] Although the length of stay varied among the sent-down youth, many spent more than a decade or settled permanently in these locations (Zhou and Hou 1999, 13; Pan 2003). According to Pan, about 73 percent went to rural villages, which were organized into people's communes (2003, 62). Sixteen percent were sent to military or state farms. The sent-downs' standards of living and pay varied with their destinations. Those on military and state farms received a regular wage. Military and state farm sent-downs also received a standard food supply, health care, and fixed living conditions (Pan 2003, 62; Bernstein 1977a, 113). The income and food available to those in villages varied with harvests, but they were generally not as secure economically or with regard to food supply as those in the other groups, and many suffered from constant hunger. Generally the sent-downs in villages enjoyed greater personal freedom and ease of visiting home than those on military farms. Among my interviewees, those sent down to the grasslands of Inner Mongolia fared best in terms of food and overall experience (see chapter 5).

Overview of Administrative Organization

The administrative organization for implementing rustication is examined in detail in the next chapter. Here a brief overview based on the extant literature and information provided by my interviewees places the program in a public administrative context. According to my interviewees' accounts, the sent-downs' experiences varied much more than is captured in previous research. This is to be expected because much of the leading work focusing on implementation of the rustication program is based on its early years and, sometimes, is largely drawn on experiences in Guangdong rather than nationwide (e.g., Bernstein 1977a, 1977b; Rosen 1981; Seybolt 1977; Unger 1979), or it adopts a public policy focus that concentrates more on the overall causes and consequences of rustication (e.g., Pan 2003; MacFarquhar and Schoenhals 2008; Meisner 1999; Zhou and Hou 1999). Consequently, the following broad overview is elaborated upon and refined considerably in chapter 5.

The national commitment to rustication was substantial, as were the numbers of administrators, administrative units, levels of government, and individuals involved. At the top, the "number one and two men" in CCP committees and cadres were urged to focus on rustication (Bernstein 1977a, 85). In the middle, the "trade unions, women's federations, and the Young Communist League" were key participants, as were schools, which were instrumental in assigning sent-downs to locations (ibid.). At the bottom "neighborhood or street offices of the government together with the residents' committees" and parents were urged to play a positive role (ibid.). Members of the street offices (neighborhood committees) and *danwei* (work units) were active in persuading eligible youth to sign up for rustication, often by haranguing them at their homes all day and night (Pan 2003, 76–77). Overall, as my interviewees report, the youths' schools, parents' work units, and residential organizations acted in concert to mobilize support for and compliance with the transfer program (see chapter 5).

Final processes for departure were equally "simple" in "bureaucratic procedure" (Pan 2003, 86). The urban youth would visit the local police station (public security office) to cancel his or her *hukou* (residential permit). Each family unit maintained a registration booklet in which the identity of every member was kept on file. The officer would charge a small fee, remove the youth's page from the booklet, stamp it with an official seal, and record the permanent change in residential status. Once without an urban registration, there would be little hope of remaining in the city or returning to it unofficially without incurring considerable difficulties. Under China's tight bureaucratic control, geographic mobility, employment, housing, access to food and other commodities, and additional benefits all depended upon one's household registration status. Even visiting the city for an extended period was prohibited without a permanent *hukou*. The youth would then prepare for departure and wait for mass transportation specially arranged for their designated locations.

The selection of destinations for the urban sent-downs required administrative coordination between the sending and receiving ends. Upon arrival at their destinations, administrators would assign the youth to specific work units. Authorized personnel, who were often local political instructors, would take the youths to their dormitories or reserved housing and help them adjust to their resettlement at the new location. Efforts to socialize the sent-downs to their new locations varied considerably. Some sent-downs went to work almost immediately whereas others were given up to two weeks to become oriented to peasant life before beginning work.[5] The emphasis in rural villages and military and state farms was heavily on physical labor (see Pan 2003, 88; see also chapter 5, this volume). As my interviewees' accounts in the next chapter attest, overall the process for mobilization and implementation of the rustication policy was highly bureaucratized and remarkably efficient. However, there were exceptions, and maladministration on rural communes sometimes led to serious injuries and even death.

Military and State Farms

Many of the military and state farms were located in border areas or territories largely inhabited by minorities, such as the Muslim Uyghur, Dai, Mongolian, and Tibetan populations, who are not ethnically Chinese and have their own languages and customs. For the most part, sent-downs with such destinations had to travel great distances and found themselves in very unfamiliar settings. Life on military farms was highly regimented and collectivized. There was little individual liberty or choice for deviation from mandated routines. Nevertheless, many urban youth preferred to be sent down to the military farms because they would be considered state employees and have a guaranteed monthly wage and access to dining services, medical care, and other benefits. As a division of the PLA, military personnel served as administrators on military farms. In contrast, civilian administrators using a quasi-military organizational structure managed the state-owned farms. In both facilities, the urban youth were organized into hierarchical groupings rising from squads at the lowest level, through the levels of platoons, companies, and battalions to regiments. The youths wore uniforms, male and female alike, and followed a rigid daily routine. There were fixed times for each meal, assigned work, political study, occasional breaks, and sleep.

The jobs required heavy physical labor for long hours under harsh conditions. Work included building dams and irrigation projects, clearing forests, reclaiming land, digging ditches and canals, and planting crops and trees (Pan 2003, 95). There was a Sunday off for every two weeks of work, twelve days of paid

Photo 4.3: Two young men who were sent down to a military farm.

leave for one family visit within the first three years, and an annual leave after the fourth year. Aside from work, there were additional rules and regulations respecting acceptable conduct. For example, romantic relationships were strictly prohibited within the first three years of the youth's arrival, as it would detract from their revolutionary socialist reeducation on the farm. The sent-downs were also forbidden to read classic novels or foreign books, listen to foreign radio stations, or sing traditional folk songs or foreign tunes. Even a trip to the restroom required permission when it was not during one's designated breaks because the youths were instructed to obey the leadership, follow directions, and acquire permission for nondesignated activity at all times (Pan 2003). In addition to strict control, demands were high for individual performance. One had no choice in showing up for work, and the standards for job performance were so stringent that on at least one military farm they simply could not be fulfilled (Bernstein 1977a, 132). Many described life on military or state farms as predictably routine and systematically and bureaucratically organized through hierarchy, discipline, order, and uniformity.

Rural Villages and Inner Mongolian Grasslands

In contrast to military and state farms, communes in rural villages offered more individual freedom but less material security. Although daily life required less discipline in the villages, the prospect of going to the countryside, where many villages were remote, isolated, poverty-stricken, and backward, was also unappealing to many sent-downs. Like other villagers, food and wages for the urban youth depended on myriad factors affecting harvests, including weather, pests, and the efficacy of their own and others' labor. For most urban youth, rural life meant lower standards of living in terms of housing, sanitation, and food and other commodities. My interviewees' assessments of the peasants vary (see chapter 5). However, in general, the sent-downs were unfamiliar with and ill-prepared for rural life. Regional dialects and languages could be completely unintelligible to newcomers (Bernstein 1977a, 134). Spoken Mandarin varied so much that native speakers in one region could not necessarily understand those in another. In some cases, variations in the same dialect made communication difficult if not impossible as one traveled from valley to valley in the same province. Some local dialects maintained distinctive regional sounds whereas others varied linguistically in phonology, grammar, and vocabulary when expressing similar semantic meanings. For example, even youths who spoke Mandarin *and* Cantonese could be sent down to a Hakka village in which the dialect was unintelligible to them (Bernstein 1977a, 134). It could take a sent-down a year to understand the local dialect and as much as three to five years to become fluent in it. Consequently, language alone could be a substantial barrier to sent-downs' integration into rural life.

Upon their arrival in rural villages, local administrators in the work department of the commune would take charge of the urban youths' resettlement.[6] Following the "principle of 'scattered insertion,'" the youths were first separated into groups and then "inserted into [various] production teams," which were organized into brigades (Bernstein 1977a, 124). There was a two-level system of supervision of the urban youth at the brigade and commune levels to provide guidance for their adjustment and integration. Local peasants were often assigned to provide one-on-one attention to the youth settled in their teams to help them gain farming skills and learn production techniques. The peasant political instructors might serve as managers in supervising the youths' daily lives. Once the youth were properly distributed according to the "insertion" system, they lived in collective housing that was either single- or mixed-sexed, with three to ten members per household (Pan 2003, 116). The youth worked in the fields like other peasants and were also assigned to specific projects such as constructing irrigation systems and planting trees, among others. Most of the work entailed hard physical labor, but some worked as cooks for their fellow sent-downs and in other nonagricultural jobs.[7]

Like other peasants, the youth's labor was measured by a work point system, which is described in the following chapter. Individual work points were used to distribute remaining net income and food from production after each member of a work team's basic needs were met. The work points were based on skill and effort (output) rather than production (outcome); consequently, their connection to fulfilling mandatory production targets was imperfect.

Whereas the urban youth received guidance upon their resettlement in the countryside, generally their supervision was not strict. When they first arrived, the rural administrators tended to focus more on the practical side of implementing the rustication policy, such as providing shelter to the resettled youth and assessing the feasibility of absorbing them into the village and commune in one way or another. Once these immediate issues were resolved, the administrators would often turn their attention to matters that they considered more important, such as harvest production. Therefore, the urban youth in rural villages generally enjoyed a higher degree of personal autonomy and a more relaxed schedule in comparison to their counterparts on military or state farms. On the military and state farms, the urban youth's conduct was strictly monitored whereas the countryside youth often spent their off time as they pleased, including reading prohibited books, listening to the Voice of America (a specifically forbidden radio station), and even playing poker in the evenings (Pan 2003, 115; Bernstein 1977a, 128; Duan I8, 40). Although the urban youth toiled in hard labor, they often worked fewer days in the field and took more time off than the local peasants.

Absorption and integration into Inner Mongolian villages was similar. Life on the grasslands could be harsh due to weather and isolation, but the work was generally not as physically hard, and, as reported by my interviewees, the food supply was ample (Lan I24; Sun I41; and Yang I49).

Implementation at the Receiving End

Implementing a program of the magnitude of rustication inevitably presented considerable challenges for administrators on the receiving end. In implementing the transfer program, rural administrators and cadres tended to assess the sent-down policy through cost–benefit analysis regarding settling the urban youth.

In addition to implementing the program and managing the extra personnel, the local administrators also had to consider the potential time and effort needed to address the long-term integration of the urban youth into the larger rural sector. Aside from the financial constraints, the resettlement of the urban youth was an intrusion to the local community, especially when it involved "inserting" large numbers of outsiders who held different cultural customs and social beliefs and perhaps spoke a different dialect into a rural village. Additionally, the urban youth were young teenagers, many between fifteen to eighteen years old. Some were immature, and most had a relatively privileged urban upbringing with little experience in manual or physical labor. From the perspective of the bureaucrats in rural villages or on military and state farms, the urban youth could impose additional commitment of resources, extended supervision, more responsibilities, and longer hours at work, yet their extra labor was unreliable in terms of productivity and other contributions to the local community. The resettlement policy therefore commanded high cost but brought little benefit to the administrators themselves or to their respective communities. According to Thomas Bernstein, whose analysis is confined to Guangdong, rural cadres were typically more concerned with the local harvest than with integrating the sent-downs productively into communal life (Bernstein 1977a). My interviewees, whose experiences went beyond Guangdong, tend to agree with this observation.

The central government allocated funds to rural communities to help offset the costs of absorbing sent-down urban youth into work and village life. In 1973 the central government allocated 480 yuan per sent-down youth, up from the 230 yuan that had been granted earlier (Bernstein 1977a, 134–35). The payment was intended to cover the settlement expenses for a year. However, from the local communities' perspective, the amount was not always adequate, which contributed to continuing friction at the receiving end of the sent-down policy.

Eventually, the so called Chu-Chou model became the "best practices" example for absorbing the sent-downs at the local level. Named after the Chu-Chou region, the model sought to incorporate urban organizations in resettling urban youth in their new locations. For example, an urban work group or factory might help with the construction of housing for youth sent from their area, and urban cadres might coordinate with their rural administrators to facilitate the sent-downs' transfer (Bernstein 1977a, 118). Such cost sharing and coordination enhanced the bureaucratic virtues of standardization and predictability. Overall, however, practices remained flexible with considerable room for slippage in individual cases. The Chu-Chou model may have been limited to Guangdong, to a specific time-period, or not widely used. None of my interviewees mentioned it or described anything like it.

Funds, even when adequate, could only go so far in reducing the local communities' burden of integrating the sent-downs. Additional staff was also desirable. By the mid-1970s large numbers of cadres were sent to the countryside to facilitate implementation of the sent-down policy. The ratio of cadres to sent-downs apparently varied widely from as high as 1:13 to as low as 1:50 (Bernstein 1977a, 146). In addition to general problem solving and liaison activities, the cadres oversaw the sent-downs' political education. More cadres, of course, meant more transportation and logistical support as well as the organizational arrangements to facilitate them.

Bernstein claimed that the rustication program involved too many "uncertainties" regarding destination and length of stay to be "fully institutionalized." He also suggested that flexibilities in the program "provide opportunities for corrupt practices on the part of cadres seeking exemptions" (Bernstein 1977a, 120). As presented in the next chapter, my interviewees' accounts indicate little flexibility on the sending side but much more with respect to when individual sent-downs were able to return to the cities. According to their accounts, the only way an eligible urban youth could avoid being sent down was to join the military, a choice open only to those from good family backgrounds whose parents were able to use *guanxi* (personal networks) to secure their admission into the PLA. Even then, many had to comply with the sent-down policy first.

Jonathan Unger maintains that as time went on the rustication program became more bureaucratic on the sending side, in terms of impersonality and limited administrative discretion. In 1971, he notes, selection became formally impersonal in that it ignored "any of the graduate's own attributes" (Unger 1979, 86). Instead, selection was based on a "sibling policy" requiring a graduate "to rusticate if half or more of his or her brothers and sisters were still at an urban residence" (ibid.). An exception might be made in the case of poor parents who needed the additional income they could obtain if their children were placed in an urban job. Ironically, "in contrast to the 'back door' advantages enjoyed by officials in getting their children *out* of the countryside, here it was those at the bottom of the factory hierarchy who were better able to *prevent* their elder children from being sent-down in the first place" (ibid., 86–87). In 1974 bureaucratic discretion regarding where youth would be sent was curtailed in several major cities, including Guangzhou, Beijing, and Shanghai. Henceforth, sent-downs would be rusticated relatively close to home (ibid., 88).

As both Bernstein and Unger observed, there was a great deal of dissatisfaction with the rustication program. Bernstein emphasizes the substantial social and economic costs in relation to the limited benefits (1977a, 77–78, 295). Villagers at the receiving end had trouble understanding why the sent-downs resented being there, were unable to work hard and adjust well, and were "infected with capitalist ideology" (Bernstein 1977b, 88). Additionally, based on my interviews, they viewed the sent-downs as something of a drain on the food supply. There were exceptions, of course, but overall the sent-downs did not like the physical

Photos 4.4 and 4.5: These two photographs of young women, the first taken shortly before she was sent down and the second of a group of women recently arrived in the countryside, underscore the youth of the people caught up in Mao's social experiment.

labor, the often harsh living conditions, the constant hunger, and rural life in general. Females on the military farms in particular also faced sexual violence and predation. According to Unger, by the early 1970s, thousands of sent-downs were illegally drifting back to their homes in the cities where, without *hukou*, they faced marginal lives (1979, 88–89). Available evidence suggests that complaints from the sent-downs or their parents to higher authorities regarding individual treatment, including subjection to sexual assault, were processed slowly, if at all, and that remedial action was slow and uncertain.[8]

Among the rustication program's many unintended consequences was bureaucratic growth. A program transferring seventeen million urban youth to the countryside, including to military and state farms and Inner Mongolia, could not have been otherwise. As part of the Maoist Marxians' attempt to rid China of the putative countercommunist and counterrevolutionary consequences of bureaucratization and the growth of technocracy, the rustication policy clearly failed. In fact, to the extent that my interviewees' reflections are accurate generally, the rustication program was associated with a dramatic shift in China's administrative culture that gave rise to the widespread use of *guanxi*, including providing hospitality, gifts, sexual favors, and bribes, to obtain favorable administrative decisions (see chapter 5). Yet ridding China of the perceived ills of bureaucratization through socialist reeducation of urban youth in the countryside and connection with the peasantry was surely among rustication's central purposes. As Meisner notes, short of sheer political, economic, and social irrationality, it is the best explanation for the program (1999).

Rustication as Liberation

Rustication had multiple purposes. However, when viewed through the lens of the ongoing struggle between the Maoist Marxians and the Chinese Weberians, it can be seen as Mao's attempt to achieve a final and lasting victory.

The Emancipation of Mankind

The rustication program was a core part of Mao's larger goal of emancipating mankind from exploitation and other constraints brought on by capitalist economic organization, bureaucratic government and political power, contemporary education, and traditional family structures. In 1966 Mao wrote, "Marx said, 'The proletariat must not only liberate itself, but also must liberate all mankind. If it cannot liberate all mankind, the proletariat will not be able to free itself in the end'" (Yan and Gao 1996, 59).

In China, liberation required massive institutional changes. Mao believed in the power of ideas and, as a Marxian, that "the ideological and cultural superstructure could transform the economic base," which was "a reversal of the orthodox explanation for change" (Clark 2008, 26). This partly accounts for the radical nature of the rustication program and its disregard for cost-effectiveness and other economic considerations. By the onset of the Cultural Revolution, in Mao's view China's economic development itself had become a threat to liberation. It promoted the counterrevolutionary—and, therefore, the enchaining—rise of bureaucratization, the undesirable education of urban youth, and technocracy. For Mao, the social and economic costs of rustication, though somewhat predictable, would be offset by the potential gains in reconnecting urban youth with the latent revolutionary ideals that inhered in the peasantry. Mao's *Little Red Book* declares "our enemies are all those in league with imperialism—the warlords, the bureaucrats, the comprador class, the big landlord class and the reactionary section of the intelligentsia attached to them"—excluding the warlords, perhaps, all the potential engine of economic development (Mao 1966, ch. 2).

For the Maoists, the Paris Commune of 1871—at least as interpreted by Marx—presented an archetypal form of liberation. The mythology of the Paris Commune bolstered Mao's effort to prevent bureaucratization of revolutionary socialism because it held the promise of direct mass organization and action that did not depend on bureaucrats and bureaucracy (Meisner 1971b, 485). The rural communes were central to the rustication program because the Maoists thought the future of the revolution—indeed, its very survival—depended on them (ibid., 494). Mao believed that rustication was a key to achieving the ultimate Cultural Revolutionary objective of creating "a one-class generation of many-sided [i.e., nonspecialized], well-educated youths inspired by ideals of service to the people, at home and abroad, contemptuous of personal wealth, and dedicated to a 'world outlook' anticipating the final liberation of man from hunger, greed, ignorance, war, and capitalism" (Snow 1973, 21).

Permanent Revolution and Perpetual Class Struggle

Mao believed that liberation required continuous effort. Rustication was only a step in a much longer-term process, one apparently without end. In 1967 Mao explicitly contended that it would take multiple cultural revolutions for communism in China to succeed (Snow 1973, 65). He asserted that "the class struggle in the ideological [realm] between the proletariat and the bourgeoisie will continue to be long and tortuous and at times will even become very acute" (Mao 1966, ch. 2). "Marxism" he wrote, "must still develop through struggle, and not only is this true of the past and the present, it is necessarily true of the future as well" (Gregor and Chang 1979, 1088). "Disequilibrium," in his view, was "normal and absolute whereas equilibrium is temporary and relative" (Snow 1973, 66). Again, Mao's own words are instructive: "We still have to wage a protracted struggle between the proletariat and the bourgeoisie and petty-bourgeois ideology. It is wrong not to understand this and to give up ideological struggle. All erroneous ideas, all poisonous weeds, all ghosts and monsters, must be subject to criticism; in no circumstance should they be allowed to spread unchecked" (Mao 1966, ch. 2). He specifically indicated that "criticism should be fully reasoned, analytical and convincing, not rough, bureaucratic, metaphysical or dogmatic" (ibid.).

From these perspectives, the massive disruption brought on by both the Cultural Revolution and the rustication program were not abnormal or extraordinary interventions in the polity, economy, and society but part of a continuing, endless "ideological and political struggle" (Snow 1973, 66). Equilibrium was an enemy of liberation because the status quo would inevitably give rise to exploitative power structures, two of which—bureaucracy and technocracy—had long been targets of Mao's rhetoric and political action. Ironically, the Communist Party itself had become a major obstacle to recapturing Mao's revolutionary goals because it had become bureaucratic and more interested in maintaining stability than disorderly endless revolution (see Meisner 1999, 302).

Family Structure

If the rustication program was irrational in normal economic terms and from the perspective of maintaining equilibrium, it certainly made sense in terms of emancipating sent-down youth from traditional "exploitative" family structures. Marxism saw no virtue in maintaining the "bourgeoisie" family structure, which "transformed" "children . . . into simple articles of commerce and instruments of labor" and wives into "mere instrument[s] of production." As "all family ties among the proletarians are torn asunder," "the bourgeois claptrap about the family and education, about the hallowed correlation between parent and child, becomes all the more disgusting" (Marx and Engels 1847). Marx saw the destruction of the family as a prerequisite for successful communist revolution because the family passes on antirevolutionary values from one generation to the next. It forestalls the radical changes required for the communist new world order.

During the early part of the Cultural Revolution, five Chinese operas were produced for mass audiences. None of the central heroes had a family or domestic ties and "ordinary human feelings identified with real families" were downplayed, partly in favor of "dedication to the revolutionary cause" (Clark 2008, 50). Rustication policy was guided by the "needs of the state," apparently with complete disregard of family interests or needs (Bernstein 1977a, 250; see also chapter 5, this volume). Some parents supported the rustication program on ideological grounds and wanted their children to participate. Others, however, viewed their children as "'personal property,' not the 'people's property'" (Bernstein 1977a, 100). Rustication threatened the traditional family structure by potentially depriving parents of the opportunity to promote their children's upward socioeconomic mobility and of the care their children might provide them in old age. For at least some parents, rural labor was downward mobility over which they had no control. Additionally, prolonged rustication caused the disintegration of the nuclear family structure. As the urban youth were sent down, many parents were also separated from their children through *xiafang* (exile) to different locations in downward transfers to the countryside for thought reform through hard labor. As one survivor recounts, "Dad . . . had already been sent to a labor camp in the Great Northern Wilderness [Heilongjiang]. . . . He died of starvation and was buried in his worn-out sleeping mat. . . . My family was completely broken apart. Mom was sent to the countryside, along with my brother and sister. I was left alone in the world" (quoted in Feng 1996, 53, 55). Several of my interviewees also reported that the Cultural Revolution, including rustication, led to the destruction of their family structures (see chapter 5).

The Anti-Confucius Campaign in 1973–74 was partly intended to weaken family relationships (Bernstein 1977a, 102). Confucian thought places great importance on family relationships and roles, which become the basis for harmony throughout society and foundational to the polity. It necessarily supports the status quo in terms of institutions including the family and, in Marxian terms, the superstructure that defines society. Debunking Confucius cannot but include diminishing the centrality of the family to the social and political order. To the extent that Confucian thought remained culturally ingrained, a true cultural revolution could not succeed. During the Anti-Confucius Campaign, Deng Xiaoping was relieved of his official positions in part for his support of Confucian educational principles, including "respect for discipline and severe teachers" and putting "knowledge above all else" (Gregor and Chang 1979, 1074). As early as 1940 Mao referred to Confucius's "old ethical code" as "a slave ideology" (ibid., 1088). The barrier that Confucian ideals posed to revolution was obvious to the Red Guards at Peking University when they proclaimed in 1967 that "to struggle against Confucius, the feudal mummy, and thoroughly eradicate . . . reactionary Confucianism is one of our important tasks in the Great Proletarian Cultural Revolution" (ibid., 1075–76).

Memoirs of the Cultural Revolution recount Red Guard sons and daughters turning viciously against their parents and siblings. Nanchu's personal account captured the depth and intensity: "Ever since the beginning of the Revolution, sons and daughters had stood up to expose their parents, students beat their favorite teachers, best friends betrayed each other, and husbands and wives joined rival organizations and turned into deadly enemies" (Nanchu 2001, 8). In fact, one of my interviewees related that a classmate seemed relieved after her (the classmate's) mother committed suicide because she could now denounce her family and separate herself from her bad family background (Wang I46, 17). The Revolution was about "breaking down the old order and establishing a new world" (Nanchu 2001, 8).

Education for Socialism

Closely related to emancipating youth from traditional family structures often informed by Confucian values was the objective of promoting education for full transformation into a socialist society. The Marxian ideal, it will be recalled, is a society not dominated by a division of labor. The acute division of labor brought on by industrialization alienates people from what they produce and from each other. They lose their humanity as they are separated from their labor when the latter is treated as a commodity. In capitalism, Marx asserts, an individual

> is a hunter, a fisherman, a herdsman, or a critical critic, and must remain so if he does not want to lose his means of livelihood; while in communist society, where nobody has one exclusive sphere of activity but each can become accomplished in any branch he wishes, society regulates the general production and thus makes it possible for me to do one thing today and another tomorrow, to hunt in the morning, fish in the afternoon, rear cattle in the evening, criticise after dinner, just as I have a mind, without ever becoming hunter, fisherman, herdsman or critic (Marx 1845).

Mao's approach to education closely tracks Marx's distaste for specialization. By 1957 Mao had already personally redefined China's education policy as one that "must enable everyone who receives an education to . . . become a worker with both socialist consciousness and culture" (Pan 2003, 20). Combined with their classroom education, primary students as young as nine years old had to fulfill four to six hours of productive labor, junior high students between six to eight hours, and high school students up to ten hours per week. In Mao's eyes, by the end of 1965 even these requirements were creating an elite urban class through "revisionist" education (see ibid., 48). Following Mao's lead, the Marxian undifferentiated ideal was manifested in the "Sixteen-Point Program of the Cultural Revolution," as resolved by the Central Committee of the Party at its Eleventh Plenum in 1966. Point 10 calls for transformation of old educational principles and teaching methods. Education should be geared to "serving proletarian politics" and "combined with productive labor, so as to enable those receiving education to develop morally, intellectually, and physically and to become laborers with socialist consciousness and culture" (reproduced in Snow 1973, 246). It specifically called for students to "learn industrial work, farming, and military affairs" and to integrate themselves with the masses (ibid.).

Point 10 was intended to turn Mao's ideas into action. Mao had been a strong critic of an educational system that "ruins talent and ruins youth" and an advocate of joining classroom education with labor (Meisner 1999, 361). By "ruin" Mao apparently meant that the system fostered elitism. In the mid-1960s he "complained on several occasions that China's education was producing an urban elitist class" (Pan 2003, 48). Urban youth, he charged, were divorced from "social reality" by not observing crops being grown and workers and peasants laboring (ibid., 48). He was critical of just about everything: pedagogy, examinations, and curricula, which in his view were "all exceedingly destructive of people" (ibid.). In late December 1968, after he had reestablished revolution committees to replace local bureaucracies as new government organs, Mao refocused on the national education system. The young, in his view, had to receive reeducation from China's own proletarian class—the landless poor peasants.[9] Mao proclaimed: "It is necessary for educated young people to go to the countryside to be reeducated by the poor and lower-middle peasants. Cadres and other city people should be persuaded to send their sons and daughters who have finished junior or senior middle school, college, or university to the countryside. Let's mobilize. Comrades everywhere in the countryside should welcome them" (ibid., 48).

Within weeks, to comply with Mao's new (re)education policy, tens of thousands of urban youth organized by their schools across the country were rusticated in the countryside as well as sent to military and state farms where they would receive reeducation by PLA officers. Although organized bureaucratically, "the army," Mao thought, "is a big school" for reforming the youths' consciousness by learning "politics, military affairs, and culture and engage in agricultural production" (Snow 1973, 131–32).

Rustication fit this educational ideal well. Moreover, it also served the Maoists well in their struggle to promote revolutionary ideals by eliminating bureaucratic and technocratic advantages. Based on census data and their empirical analysis of the impact of the Cultural Revolution on educational attainment, Deng and Treiman conclude that "the Cultural Revolution was probably the most drastic attempt the world has yet seen to reduce the intergenerational transmission of advantage" (1997, 425). In particular, they found that "there was a marked decline in the advantage of high status origins during the Cultural Revolution.... For nonfarm men from normally advantageous backgrounds, the Cultural Revolution was a disaster. Specifically, the advantage usually associated with coming from an educated professional or managerial family was substantially reduced" (ibid., 424–25). They note that "there is some evidence that the decline was greater and more precipitous for intelligentsia sons than for cadre sons" (ibid., 425). This suggests that even under the great stress of the Cultural Revolution, party functionaries—often bureaucrats and technocrats—retained advantages and that these must have been deeply ingrained in the political and social systems.

It is impossible to know whether Mao's vision of socialist education could have been fully implemented without rustication. Education certainly could have been combined with industrial labor in the cities, and probably with agricultural labor in many suburban areas. However, true socialism required the destruction of class advantage and especially its transmission from parents to child. The rustication policy offered the promise of reducing the importance of education as a substantial component of class advantage. In the short run at least, Deng and Treiman's analysis suggests it was largely successful, a conclusion with which my interviewees largely concur (Deng and Treiman 1997, 425).

In sum, the rustication policy was highly coercive and, given the high social and economic costs—including the sent-downs' opportunity costs—it was not cost-beneficial or even cost-effective in conventional terms. However, from Marxian and Maoist perspectives, it was reasonably well designed as an approach for enabling China to promote the emancipation of mankind from the strict division of labor that robs us of our humanity. Specialization, technical knowledge, and stability—core features of Weberian bureaucracy—were enemies of the Cultural Revolution. They could be defeated by making revolution permanent, weakening the family structure or at least freeing a large number of urban youth from it, reforming education, and reeducating sent-down youth in the countryside. Rustication, therefore, should be understood as a key component of Mao's struggle through the Cultural Revolution to weaken the influence of bureaucrats, bureaucratization, and the growth of technocracy. The importance of rustication in this context appears even greater when the limitations of alternative explanations for the rustication policy are considered.

Alternative Explanations for the Rustication Policy

Rustication is also said to have been a response to the need to reduce urban unemployment and to promote rural development. Although it contributed to these public policy objectives, it was not rationally designed to place them above Mao's desire to instill socialist revolutionary ideals in urban youth as a means of securing China's socialist future and prevailing over the Chinese Weberians.

Urban Unemployment

A leading alternative explanation for the rustication program is that large-scale unemployment in the urban areas caused economic and social problems that could be alleviated by out-migration from the cities to the rural areas. By the onset of the Cultural Revolution, China's urban population had grown much faster than the economy's ability to produce jobs in the industrial sector. Between 1949 and 1957 the cities grew by some thirty-four million people, or by about 60 percent (Bernstein 1977a, 34; Rosen 1981, 9). This growth was fueled by both the birthrate and migration from rural areas. As Stanley Rosen observes, "employment in the modern industrial sector grew by an average of 1.3 million a year, while the labor force was growing by 4 million a year; thus, only about one-third of the annual entrants into the labor force could be absorbed into the modern industrial sector" (1981, 9). A precedent for dealing with urban unemployment had been set during the First Five-Year Plan in 1955, when Mao called for movement from urban areas to the countryside.[10] The failure of the Great Leap Forward contributed to the institutionalization of relying on outward mobility from the cities as a means of dealing with massive urban unemployment. In 1961 "20 million persons were returned to the countryside" (Rosen 1981, 10). Bernstein suggests that the Cultural Revolution was not only associated with an "exodus" of youth to the rural areas but also with a declining urban birthrate (1977a, 37). He notes that during 1961–66 some officials considered rustication to be a means of combating unemployment (Bernstein 1977b, 38).

Unemployment undoubtedly enhanced the appeal of rustication and facilitated its adoption as a national public policy. If labor were in demand in the urban areas, sending employable urban youth to the countryside would make little economic sense. However, treating unemployment as a cause rather than a precondition for rustication faces several serious limitations. If unemployment among youth were the main reason for rustication, why not keep the schools open? Evidence indicates that upon finding their schools closed in 1967, some youth voluntarily departed for rural areas (Yan and Gao 1996, 278). Maintaining the educational system intact and not treating education as undesirable surely would have kept more youth in schools—and, perhaps, subsequently in jobs. Mao's criticism of formal education had a ripple effect on employment as Jiaqi Yan and Gao Gao point out: "The Cultural Revolution despised culture and openly denigrated learning, causing many to look down on education and cultural knowledge. Graduates therefore were not wanted by any office or profession. In addition, revolutionary education excluded science and cultural subjects, depriving the students of the knowledge base needed to qualify them for complex work" (1996, 279).

Another problem with this explanation is that despite the earlier precedents, rustication for the primary purpose of reducing urban unemployment was ideologically unacceptable. According to Bernstein (1977a, 38–39), Liu Shaoqi was criticized for supporting rustication on the basis that it would reduce unemployment (rather than promote socialist reeducation).

Additionally, rustication was an extraordinarily poorly designed program to deal with urban unemployment in a rational manner. There is no convincing evidence that Mao ever viewed rustication in terms of unemployment. As one former sent-down noted, "Maybe Mao never really considered the unemployment problem but thought only of sending the Red Guards away to 'make revolution.' It seems inconceivable, but this is what made Mao what he was" (quoted in Leung 1994, 222).

Even within a rational actor framework, viewing rustication as a partial solution to unemployment faces several problems. First, the historical precedent during which more than a million youth went to rural areas from 1962 to 1966 did not have a major impact on unemployment (Bernstein 1977a, 39). Second, although the countryside was perhaps better able to absorb unemployed youth, as noted earlier, their labor in the rural sector, though hard, was not particularly productive and, as the term "lost generation" suggests, incurred substantial opportunity costs.[11] Third, it seems inconceivable that Chinese policymakers would not realize that the costs of rustication would ultimately far outweigh the benefits derived from the short-term effects of reducing unemployment. Unger notes that the sent-downs contributed "at least *something* to [gross] agricultural production, even if marginally. In the cities they would have been merely an idle, highly concentrated, and perhaps politically volatile body of unemployed" (1979, 89).[12] However, on the other side of the "balance sheet," he observes "the price paid for the program was heavy—more than just discontent among sent-down youth, the peasantry, and urban parents, more than the rising tide of urban crime" because students who knew they would soon be rusticated lost interest in schoolwork and engaged in "juvenile delinquency" (ibid., 89–90). Similarly, Yan and Gao conclude that, whereas rustication "produced some degree of social calm," "its continual onslaught on society and the great injuries inflicted on the spiritual recesses of a generation of educated youth, was not only a shortsighted measure, but a historical mistake" (1996, 281). Even ignoring the massive human and social costs in terms of lost educational opportunity, suffering, dislocation, and stress on families, at a calculable financial cost of over 100 billion yuan from 1968–78, it could not have been otherwise (ibid., 279).

Youthful Unrest as a Cause of Rustication

By 1968 it was clear that the Red Guards posed a danger by fomenting violence and chaos in some cities. With the schools closed or dysfunctional, large numbers of idle teenagers engaged in gang fights and other antisocial behavior. In 1967 in Beijing, many students attended school for only a few hours a day and did not have homework to keep them off the streets afterward. Some played while others, as a State Council document reported, organized gangs, carried weapons, and lurked about seeking to provoke others into fights that occasionally resulted in serious injury or death (MacFarquhar and Schoenhals 2006, 248). Sending youth to the countryside could help solve this problem while contributing to Mao's broader Cultural Revolutionary goal of promoting emancipation by weakening families, freeing youth from them, providing socialist reeducation, and reducing the ability of bureaucrats and technocrats to pass their advantages onto their offspring.

As discussed earlier, rustication was officially presented as a program for reeducation. Several researchers note that restoring order was a major rustication objective even though it was politically risky to say so openly (Pan 2003, 49; see also Bernstein 1977a, 58). This explanation for the rustication policy carries considerable weight—by all accounts, youths' unrest in the cities was a serious problem. However, like viewing rustication as a means of reducing unemployment, it has limitations. If removing youth from the cities were the primary reason for rustication, the policy probably would have been configured differently.

First, the criteria for being sent down did not target troublesome and violent youth. It cast a very wide net in catching the violent ones along with many others who posed no such problems. Several of my interviewees indicated that they had no connection to the Red Guard or the tumult in the streets. Evidence suggests that Shanghai may have consciously sought to send troublemakers to border areas and far-off provinces, which in turn suggests that this strategy could have had more widespread application (MacFarquhar and Schoenhals 2006, 252). However, it was not systematically practiced elsewhere, although Beijing, Tianjin, Hangzhou, Nanjing, Wuhan, Chengdu, and Chongqing did send "large numbers" of youth to such places (ibid., 251). It should also be remembered that the rustication program did not move all seventeen million sent-down youths *at once*, but rather did so over a decade, which left considerable numbers of potentially troublesome teenagers in the cities during the early years of the program.

Second, given the huge economic, human, and social costs of the rustication program, if the main point were to solve the issue of having too many youth with nothing to do, it would have been more rational to focus on reforming the schools rather than closing them. In Mao's view, though, urban schools—however reformed—could not promote the larger objectives of the Cultural Revolution.

Third, in the early years in Guangdong and perhaps elsewhere, inadequate implementation in the countryside made the rustication program porous, which in turn created its own unrest and urban problems. Unger reports that in Guangdong,

> rusticated youths of earlier years—destitute, bored, or disgruntled—already were illegally stealing back by the tens of thousands. . . . The urban Neighborhood Committees and local police offices turned a blind eye to such youths so long as they were not of overly bad background and lived quietly at home. But there were thousands of other youngsters whose parents could not or would not support them. Without work permits, ration coupons, or residence cards, they survived in Canton through petty thievery and prostitution. The city's rate of crime, which prior to the Cultural Revolution had been negligible, began rising rapidly. (1979, 88–89)[13]

This is not to say, of course, that urban unrest was not a factor supporting the rustication policy. Rather, in terms of rational policy design, like solving the unemployment situation, it is at best an incomplete explanation for rustication. Viewing rustication as a key part of the longstanding struggle between the Maoist Marxians and the Weberian-oriented Communist Party officials and technocrats continues to provide a better understanding of the dynamics and overall rationale of the sent-down policy.

Rural Development

A third alternative explanation for the rustication policy holds that it was directed partly at developing rural infrastructure and agricultural production. In 1964 the *China Youth Daily* noted that "cultured youths with socialist consciousness are urgently needed in building a socialist new countryside" (quoted in Bernstein 1977a, 60). Nine years later, in 1973, a *People's Daily* editorial echoed the same theme: "For agriculture to improve, for the villages to change their appearance, it is necessary for large numbers of educated youths to take the political, cultural, and scientific knowledge that they have acquired and unite it with the realities of village class struggle and socialist agricultural production and contribute their strength to build new socialist villages" (quoted in Seybolt 1977, 4). As these editorials indicate, rustication potentially could have contributed strongly to rural development. However, evidence clearly suggests that this was not among the policy's top priorities.

First, rustication was insufficiently funded to promote transformative rural development. From 1949 forward China's development strategy relied overwhelmingly on industrialization in the cities and placed a low priority on the rural sector. As of 1982, "the industrial sectors had received from five to six times as much state investment as had agriculture. Taking the industrial and agricultural output value indexed at 100 in 1952, we see that in 1982 industrial value rose to 2,115, whereas agricultural value only rose to 306" (Pan 2003, 38). Reluctance to fund rustication at the outset undercut the extent to which it could promote development. Youth were sent to places where the state could limit or minimize its investment, not where the need for development was most acute (Bernstein 1977a, 68). Overall, the rustication policy was not accompanied by a dramatic shift in investment and, to the extent that rural development was a key goal, it was seriously underfunded.

Second, rustication was not managed in a fashion that would maximize or even emphasize rural development. Again, the selection criteria made little or no effort to match the youths' skills with the countryside's needs. Development was limited by settling youth in more advanced villages where they could adapt better rather than in poorer places where they might at least theoretically be able to contribute more. Pan observes that by design the program avoided sending youth to the places most in need of development, and all but 1.4 million were rusticated in their "their own home city regions or provinces" (2003, 52). Unger reaches the startling conclusion that "the first lesson" the sent-down youth learned "was that in general they were neither needed nor wanted by the peasantry. . . . In 1968–69, most villages acquired more youths than they could readily accommodate" (1979, 81). In these early years in Guangdong, most youth were "assigned to villages that were labor-rich and land-scarce. This meant that limited harvests would have to be shared among additional hands, lessening each family's income" (ibid.). Many sent-downs, including several of my interviewees as noted in the next chapter, quickly realized that they were more burdensome than helpful to the peasants (Pan 2003, 170). Theoretically, resettling urban youth in relatively advanced villages could have been a development strategy based on the belief that modernization requires a critical mass of skills to take off. However, there is little or no evidence that this was the case (Bernstein 1977a, 65).

Third, rustication was not married to science. Personal accounts indicate that work projects and labor were not systematically based on agronomy, agronomics, botany, and other relevant sciences. Despite the hard labor and massive dislocations, much of the rustication program "produced nothing" of value (Pan 2003, 96), a conclusion with which many of my interviewees concur (see chapter 5). Concrete examples of ill-fated efforts include deforestation, cultivation techniques that depleted the soil, efforts to grow rubber trees in an unsuitable climate, and widespread ecological destruction on the grasslands and elsewhere (Pan 2003, 96, 127, 128). One observer indicated that rustication "committed unpardonable crimes against the land" (ibid., 128). Remarkably, overall productivity even lagged on the military farms (ibid., 138). Eventually, the program included education in agricultural and related rural development, but it appears this was too little, too late.

As in the case of urban unemployment and unrest, it is possible that the rustication program included objectives for which it was poorly or irrationally designed. Still, it is difficult to believe that significantly advancing the rural sector could have been a genuine priority because as a development program rustication was very badly conceived, managed, and implemented for a decade.

Alternative Explanations in Toto

The formulation and administration of any major public policy generally entails multiple goals and objectives. As a large-scale policy that relocated some seventeen million Chinese youth away from their families and cities, rustication was highly complex in terms of mixed objectives. Resolving urban unemployment, becalming the cities, and developing rural sectors are traditionally offered as the main explanations for the Up to the Mountains and Down to the Countryside campaign. However, neither the policy nor its administration was rationally designed to serve any of these goals individually. Conceivably, it could have been a catchall approach to promoting all three objectives simultaneously. However, the program's defects were so substantial that it is questionable whether the whole could have been more than the sum of its parts—or intended to be so. If these were the primary reasons for orchestrating such a massive and elaborate program against widespread opposition by urban families, the sent-downs themselves, and the peasants who received them, the sent-down policy seems remarkably nonstrategic by any measure while incurring tremendous financial, social, and human costs. These explanations cannot fully illuminate why rustication, in such a radical form, was established in lieu of more strategic and less costly alternatives. Officials often touted rural development as a primary reason for sending down youth, but the program continued well after policymakers recognized its high costs, apparent inefficiency, and dubious net results because there were "other reasons as well" (Bernstein 1977a, 238).

Those "other reasons" become clearer by viewing rustication as part of the ongoing struggle between the Maoist Marxians and the Chinese Weberians in the CCP bureaucracy. Rustication could have (re)connected sent-down youth with revolutionary ideals. If families were exploitative, schools were ruining students by turning them into specialists with elitist tendencies, and stability was stifling and an incubator of bureaucratic privilege, then rustication was liberating and could serve the broader goals of the Cultural Revolution. It also could have produced a generation that would succeed Mao in carrying forward his revolutionary goals. Unlike other potential objectives, from the Maoists' perspectives, whether it did so with low benefit–cost ratios was irrelevant. The Cultural Revolution was a struggle against the bureaucratization of the CCP and the rise of technocrats. It favored policy design for China's future based on ideology as opposed to pragmatism. In hindsight, it set China's economic development back by at least a decade or more.

Conclusion: The Irony of Rustication

Rustication was part of the Cultural Revolution's larger struggle against bureaucrats, technocrats, bureaucratization, the intelligentsia, and "degenerative" urban life. Unlike much of the Cultural Revolution, such as the Red Guard movement, which was intended to tear down structures of privilege and elitism, rustication was aimed at building up revolutionary consciousness and virtue in the sent-down youth in addition to mentoring a generation of revolutionary successors imbued with Mao's ideological beliefs. The great irony of rustication is that although it was part of an antibureaucratic movement, it furthered the bureaucratization of China not only by contributing to an increase in the size of bureaucracy, as Meisner pointed out, but also by bringing more of it to the countryside. As noted in chapter 1, precisely how this occurred has not been well researched, documented, or understood (Shirk 1978). Based primarily on my interviews, the next chapter explains the centrality of public administrative design, organization, and implementation to China's experience with the rustication program. By focusing specifically on the roles of public administration, bureaucracy, and bureaucrats, the chapter refines much of the broad overview presented here and provides the most comprehensive analysis of the implementation of the rustication program available to date.

Notes

1. The rustication of urban youth began on a voluntary basis in 1967. The rustication initiative was administratively reorganized and made compulsory in 1968. Urban youth were no longer sent down after 1978, and the program was officially terminated in 1980. However, as late as the 1990s, some rusticated youth were still petitioning for the legal return to their home cities (Tao Fan I9, 51; see also Pan 2003, 1, 233).

2. "Mixed Memories of Zhiqing," *China Daily*, June 15, 2004; www.chinadaily.com.cn/english/doc/2004-06/15/content_339579.htm.

3. See Pan 2003, table 1.

4. As noted in chapter 1, the distinction between state farms and military farms is somewhat blurred because many military farms were previously state farms and employed a mixture of civilian workers as well as military personnel.

5. Chao Duan's village did not know more than a day in advance that a group of nine sent-downs would be arriving, and it made almost no preparation for them (Duan 18, 34). Yu (I50, 14) indicated that one might begin working on the second day after arrival.

6. The rural regions and locations of the sent-downs varied significantly. This section serves to present a general picture of resettlement in the rural villages. The next chapter provides personal accounts of individuals' sent-down experiences.

7. Nonagricultural jobs included barefoot doctors (backpack medics) and school teachers, among others. Such positions were highly coveted, and only a few had the opportunity to obtain them.

8. "Mixed Memories of Zhiqing," *China Daily*, June 15, 2004; www.chinadaily.com.cn/english/doc/2004-06/15/content_339579.htm; and Bernstein 1977b, 98. See also chapter 5.

9. China was not sufficiently industrialized to have developed a large urban proletariat class, and Mao had generally substituted the peasantry for the workers as the "exploited class" of China. Additionally, in "Critique of the Gotha Program," Marx (1875, sect. I) specifically mentioned that "the instruments of labor are the monopoly of the landowners and capitalists." Similarly, Mao had always considered peasants as the landless proletariat class in China's context.

10. "Mixed Memories of Zhiqing," *China Daily*, June 15, 2004; www.chinadaily.com.cn/english/doc/2004-06/15/content_339579.htm.

11. A Chinese doggerel of this generation goes as follows: "When we were growing up, there was the three-year natural disaster [the post–Great Leap Forward famine]; When we were studying in schools, there came the Cultural Revolution; When we were about to work, we were sent to rural areas; When we were about the age to get married, they advocated 'late marriage'; When it was about time to have children, there was the 'one-child policy'; When we returned to the cities, there were no jobs; Now we are about to retire, and we are asked to *xiagang* [step down from the post]." See Hung and Chiu 2003, 204–5.

12. Bernstein suggests that the sent-downs may not have brought a "net benefit" to the countryside (1977a, 238).

13. The extent to which similar problems occurred elsewhere is unknown. Fan (I9, 37) mentioned that the son of a toppled high official stole "all the way to Nanjing [City]" from a Shanxi rural village and was subsequently arrested and brought back to his sent-down location.

Chapter 5

Public Administration and the Sent-Down Experience

"Everything imaginable happened to the sent-downs. Some rose up to the top and prospered but some never even survived their experience and perished."

Ning Lan (I24, 33)

"The moment I got there, I knew I had to get out of this godforsaken place. . . ."

Lina Liu (I29, 11)

"Our generation never experienced youthful dreams, romantic love, or any good days of life in their own time. There was no purpose to our lives. The best twenty years of our lives were completely wasted."

Ying Yuan (I51, 8)

"I had a really good time there for the entirety of my sent-down period, and I was very happy and content every day. Every day was a good day, a good memory, and I was just thinking about it the other day—what a great time I had there."

Hong Sun (I41, 22)

This chapter expands on the broad overview presented in chapter 4 by explaining the role of public administration and administrators in the sent-down experience as recounted by my interviewees. It examines each phase of the sent-down process from the overall administrative organization to how urban youth were selected, induced to comply, sent to locations, transported, settled in the countryside, and assigned work as well as how they experienced daily life and ultimately returned to a city. The chapter also investigates differences in the treatment and experiences of male and female sent-downs. It concludes that public administration was central to rustication and that the rustication program, in turn, had a substantial impact on China's administrative culture. It also strongly suggests that the sent-downs' experiences were more varied than is captured in much of the previous research and memoirs on rustication (e.g., Bernstein 1977a, 1977b; MacFarquhar and Schoenhals 2006; Nanchu 2001; Pan 2003; Rosen 1981; Seybolt 1977; Unger 1979).

Administrative Organization

The Cultural Revolution is generally associated with chaos. However, as noted in chapter 1, some administrative operations continued to run smoothly. Rustication was well organized to efficiently recruit and transport the send-down youth to their destinations but performed poorly in important respects.

Overall Structure and Operation

Formal documents and records related to the structure, operation, and behavior of the administrative units responsible for implementing the rustication policy are not centralized and may not be complete or extensive. Those records that exist are not available to independent researchers, and even the most comprehensive studies of the rustication policy by Chinese scholars contain limited and inexact descriptions of the overall administrative structure and its inner workings (Liu 2009). Jian Zhang, who did professional research on the sent-downs, indicated that the records are scattered and access is restricted and possible only through personal contacts. He also said that official statistics were inaccurate, especially with regard to "bad, embarrassing events" (I52, 5).[1] It may well be that the most thorough available understanding of the administrative organization of the rustication program and the behavior of its units and personnel is conveyed by piecing together the reported experiences of surviving sent-downs. As noted in chapter 1, it cannot be assumed that my interviewees' recollections of such matters are empirically correct. However, the extent to which their descriptions of the sent-down administrative structure and operation correspond with one another strongly suggests that they are accurate. Minor differences in their accounts may be due to changing administrative procedures as the rustication program matured, variations in local organization, the destinations to which they were sent, and their effort to generalize broadly about administrative organization and process as well as incorrect remembrance.

In April 1968 the Beijing Revolution Committee drew on personnel from the political team, planning team, education team, and military exercise team to form a temporary Knowledgeable Youth Up to the Mountains and Down to the Countryside committee to guide and direct the rustication program. Around the same time, the Revolution Committee formally established the Knowledgeable Youth Resettlement Office for this purpose (Liu 2009, 172–73). Subsequently, a

Public Administration and the Sent-Down Experience 105

replica of this office was set up in each province, county, and commune, although not in every village, many of which had informal and flexible administrative arrangements. These subnational offices were largely involved in coordinating the sent-down process in terms of relocation, job assignment, transfers, returning to the cities, and providing direct funding to the sent-downs and the rural villages, communes, state and military farms, and pastoral lands in Inner Mongolia where they settled. Overall policymaking and funding were the responsibility of the national government's State Council and Central Resettlement Office. Funds were distributed through the accounting and finance departments of the provincial, municipal, and autonomous regional governments in accordance with the number of youths received as batches arrived. Primary responsibility for recruiting, selecting, and coercing sent-downs rested with the municipalities from which they were sent. The schools also played a central role in organizing the sent-downs into cohorts for transfer as a group. Brigade leaders or other personnel were largely responsible for dealing with the sent-downs once they arrived at their destinations. Military personnel were generally involved in keeping order in the schools and escorting the sent-downs from the cities to their destinations as well as in some aspects of the logistical requirements.[2] At the lowest level, street offices were active in recruiting, prompting, and coercing urban youth to sign up for rustication.

Although several different administrative levels and governmental jurisdictions were involved, my interviewees agree that the rustication process was tightly managed. Jun Liang, who was sent down to a rural village, explained:

> Knowledgeable Youth Resettlement Offices were established across the country. It was an umbrella system with the central government office at the top (in Beijing), but every province had this office, every county, every commune in every region, they all had the same offices at the lower levels which corresponded to each other. . . . Every commune had a Knowledgeable Youth Resettlement Office, no matter how far or remote the [rural] region was. So when instructions came from the top, that document of order gets passed down through a chain of offices (vertically); the schools at the sending side and the provincial government at the receiving side get in contact with each other (horizontally), and the urban youths' records get forwarded to wherever they were assigned to (be sent down) and then there went the urban youth. In the countryside, the brigade leader [rural street-level cadre] was often in charge of the sent-downs after they were assigned to the villages. The whole organization of the sent-down policy was very tightly controlled because the party system under the Chinese Communist Party is very tightly organized. The whole administration of the process—everything gets passed through the party cadres and select party members who fully followed all directions from the top so the organization and implementation were closely interconnected and passed down through this chain of command under the party structure. Simply put,

there is no way they will miss you and you can't find any loopholes. They will locate you, find you, and send you down. (I26, 19)

Hong Sun, a market researcher who was rusticated on the grasslands in Inner Mongolia, described the administrative structure in similar terms:

> The State Council of the national government had special task forces in charge of the policy, and the corresponding offices were set up to implement the sent-down policy. The State Department has a Knowledgeable Youth Resettlement Office and there were lower-tier Knowledgeable Youth Resettlement Offices at the provincial, county and commune levels with the central Zhiqing [Send-down] Office (in Beijing) giving instructions, orders, and guidance on top. The lower corresponding offices at each echelon followed instructions from above and implemented the policy at the ground level. No matter how far or remote an area, the policy would be able to reach it because even in the most faraway, small, desolate town, at the commune level or at the head office of that township, there were specific people in charge, who were assigned the task of implementing the rustication policy. Therefore, you could say it was tightly organized at every level because the organization was set up in such a way that each office, each agency was closely connected and coordinated with one another, with every section interlinked to the other. For seventeen million youth to be sent down and resettled one batch after another, it took a lot of expenses and the central government allocated a lot of money for this policy. (I41, 26)

Bin Ding, who was sent down to a rural village near his home in Guangdong and later became a municipal official in an urban government, explained the administrative process for sending urban youth to rural communes from the bottom up:

> Because China had a very strict residential *hukou* system, it was quite easy for the local Knowledgeable Youth Resettlement Office to gather all the information at the public security offices in regards to how many families had children who graduated high school or were within the specific age bracket eligible for the sent-down policy. So the office would first send its people to gather this information on whether a family had one, two, or three child(ren) qualified for the sent-down policy. They would know very quickly and have a very accurate picture about each family from the records kept at these public security offices. After that, the Knowledgeable Youth Resettlement Office would send out a notification, a standardized form that states, "Dear comrade so and so, there are X number of children in your family that are eligible for Chairman Mao's proposed policy to send the youth up to the mountains and down to the countryside. Please be advised to educate your child(ren) properly in regards to compliance with the

policy and report to our office on such and such day and time." The county, city, and district Knowledgeable Youth Resettlement Offices coordinated among themselves and worked in conjunction with each other, and therefore, there [were] no loopholes in this process and no matter how small a local district was, not a single family would be overlooked. The office then looks into your [the youth to be sent-down] records such as your family background and a number of relative factors. Even before you report to them, they've already assigned you a specific location, whether it is a post to a factory, a farmland, a fish farm, or to be inserted into a production brigade in the countryside. Once you visit the office and officially report to them, right there and then on the spot, they give you another piece of paper on which your sent-down location is already printed along with a number of things listed for you to do prior to your departure.

At this point, Ding continued, there was no turning back:

After you are handed the location of your destination, you really have no choices; you are leaving whether you want to or not. By the time you receive that form with your sent-down location, your *hukou*, the tickets and stamps for your foodstuff quota have already been transferred to the commune office of the sent-down location. At each commune level, there is also a Knowledgeable Youth Resettlement Office which coordinates with the higher county-level Knowledgeable Youth Resettlement Office and it will receive the sent-down's *hukou*, personal records and files, party dossiers, and the individuals' allocated food stamps from the county office. Everything is done through the organizations and there are corresponding offices at all levels from the sending side to the receiving end.

In the county-level Knowledgeable Youth Resettlement Office, there were about six or seven administrators, and as for the commune-level office, there was usually only one person in charge. For example, let's say a specific commune was assigned to receive 200 sent-downs. Prior to their arrival, its commune-level Knowledgeable Youth Resettlement Office would receive the food stamps for those 200 sent-downs among other important records. However, the Knowledgeable Youth Resettlement Office would not be in charge of food distribution or managing the food stamps, so they would forward all that stuff to the Food Management Office, where every person and his/her various food stamps would be listed in their administrative records. (I6, 18)

Tao Fan, a businessman, emphasized the role of administrative communication in organizing, coordinating, and implementing the rustication program:

At that time, when the central government wanted to issue a new order or announce a new directive, it didn't just go to the specific department concerned, instead, the document was sent to all the governmental offices. For example, any central documents that had to do with the decisions of the sent-down policy, all those documents were issued by the CCP Central Committee, the State Council, the Central Military Commission of the CCP, and the Central Cultural Revolution Committee. These four units jointly issued the documents together, and that's where all those red-letterhead, official documents (directives) came from. The receiving units were the various military regions, various branches of the military, the revolution committees of various provinces and autonomous regions across the country, and the revolution committees of the various departments, agencies, and organizations of the national government. . . . So they didn't just send these documents to the Knowledgeable Youth Resettlement Offices alone, but instead they sent the documents to all the party and governmental administrative organizations, and the directive was passed through the hierarchies of the party structure. From the provincial government, a specific order gets conveyed downward to . . . the county levels. The military conveys the documents to the regional-level government whereas the local government conveys the orders to the county-level government, then maybe through a telephone call, the county-level government conveys the order to the commune-level headquarters, then from there to the brigades. . . . It was through this national administrative machine, the whole system of bureaucracies under the CCP public administrative machine, that the sent-down policy was put in effect, carried out, and implemented from the very top straight down to the very bottom. (I9, 42–43)

Jia Li noted that "the whole process of being sent-down was . . . like recruitment for labor" (I25, 18). Kang Lin viewed rustication from a similar perspective:

From the bottom up, every village can report to a higher body at the top what their conditions were, what they have or what they want. For example, a village may ask for a specific gender, they may want more men or women for this or that reason. They may want expert knowledge in specific subjects because they lack teachers in those subject areas at their local schools. They may only have two empty houses so they can absorb only however many sent-downs, so they tell the top what they have and what they want. (I28, 7)

Lin also noted that, by contrast, rustication at military farms was centralized and top down:

To organize *zhiqing* to be sent down to military farms, that's even smoother and easier for the central government to do because all the military farms were managed under military organization from teams to platoons, battalions, companies, divisions, et cetera. The army administration was highly organized and orderly so when the central government gave them a task of arranging for a number of urban youth to be sent down and resettled, it was done in the military fashion, with order and discipline. And

Public Administration and the Sent-Down Experience 109

so for the military farm sent-downs, the implementation was even smoother because the army structure and process were already in place. (I28, 7)

Street-level administrators were crucial to the overall process, as Liang went on to explain:

> The schools got in contact with the local government and they basically matched the students with different communes, like how many students could be taken in at which commune in a targeted province. On the sending side in the city, the school would give you a form, one of those preprinted official forms where they just fill in our name, stamp it and you are ready to go. This certified that you are "eagerly" responding to the Up to the Mountains and Down to the Countryside policy. . . . With this form, you go to the public security office to cancel your *hukou* and they will record the change in your residential status. After that, they [police officers from the public security office] give you a migration card and with this migration card, you take your *hukou* with you to [your destination commune] and you are no longer a legal resident of Beijing. All your food ration stamps, fabric stamps and whatnot, are all canceled in your name from Beijing. The schools organized the special trains. . . . There were people who chaperoned us on the train and took us to the commune and once we arrived, there were people who came to receive us. At this time, we visited the Knowledgeable Youth Resettlement Office at the commune headquarters where big flatbed trucks came to pick us up and drop us off at our assigned villages. (I26, 16)

Ting Wang, a retired bookkeeper and teacher, explained the role of the schools in conjunction with military farms as opposed to communes.

> First, [the school] notified who was going and where by putting your name and assigned location up on a poster, which they pasted in front of the academic building. If your name was listed, you would already know where you were going and the school administration gave you a piece of paper with a list of things that you had to do before being sent down. The first step required you to go and cancel your *hukou* at the public security office. Also we were given tickets for 25 *chi* [9.1 yards] worth of fabric (for clothes, etc.) and eighteen yuan for our trip, in addition to a set of cotton-padded winter clothes which included a jacket and a pair of pants. . . . The material assistance was probably given to the school by the military farms in the northeast (Heilongjiang) and then the school distributed it to us, the individual students. There were about ten or twelve kids from my class who were sent to the northeast but there were at least several hundreds of other students from our school who were also sent to the same location. So the same procedure applied to all of them, notification on the wall, cancel *hukou*, take materials distributed. After that, the teachers sent you off to the train station along

with the military personnel who came from the farm to escort us back to Heilongjiang. . . . Before we were sent down, the military personnel from the farm already came to the different schools; they probably brought all the material assistance with them to the schools, and their mission was to escort us back to the military farm (I46, 12).

The street offices were also key actors at the street level. These offices assigned individual personnel to each apartment block. The front door of many apartments had transoms or a transparent glass panel through which street office personnel might listen or peer to keep tabs on individuals and families and to intervene in their personal affairs. The personnel were often older women, and the offices were sometimes referred to as the "old hags" committees, "small feet investigation teams" (alluding to their once bound feet), and similar labels. Although street offices were staffed by a mix of paid and volunteer personnel, they all apparently took their jobs very seriously and were considered ubiquitous busybodies. Their role in rustication was basically to recruit youth to be sent down and to make life unbearable for those who were slow to sign up. Ming Zhao, a retired auto worker, explained, "If you were reluctant to go, then the old hags from the street offices . . . would go to your homes and pay you a visit. They would beat drums all day and night to 'welcome' your 'volunteered' departure to leave Beijing" (I53, 7). Wang noted that the pressure to sign up was pervasive: "The old men and women from the street office would visit your family every day to 'teach' you the grand revolutionary theories, and ask you to apply them personally to comply with the sent-down policy and leave the city. Worse yet, some street office personnel visited your parents' *danwei* [work unit] in conjunction to the daily visit to impose pressure on your parents as well." Tactics involved visiting "the homes of those who had not left and (standing) in front of their doors and shouting slogans all day, 'It is glorious and a great honor for the knowledgeable youth to go up to the mountains and down to the countryside!' Or, they would beat drums and bang gongs all day and all night until you just can't take it anymore" (Wang I46, 11, 18). She also emphasized that "there would be the implicit threat of punishment for parents at work. . . . That was the one and only place where they were able to make a living, so of course, everyone was scared by that [administrative] tactic because the parents could lose their jobs if their kids didn't comply with the sent-down policy" (I46, 19).[3]

Ningli Gan also focused on the street office:

People from the street office and the cops from the local public security office constantly visited our family at all hours of the day, sometimes in the middle of the night to "check on our *hukou*." They harassed you constantly but they wouldn't force you to leave physically, like drag you out of your home, because even though my father was a counterrevolutionary, I didn't do anything wrong nor did my mother so they wouldn't do that per se. But let's say I insisted on staying, the cadres at my mother's *danwei* would probably hold a daily meeting with her and talk to her hours on end every day to apply pressure so that I would comply with the sent-down policy. (I12, 12)

Efficiency

Most of the interviewees reported that the administrative system was efficient and thorough. Ding observed that, contrary to "some novels or foreign reports" in which the rustication "process was described as totally chaotic and ineffective," in truth "the whole implementation process from the beginning to the end was orderly, highly efficient, and well organized" (I6, 39).

> For the implementation of this policy, the administrators thought about everything and planned its implementation accordingly—everything they could predict to happen and the things that may happen were all factored into its implementation. The calculation was based on the overall number of urban youth who were eligible for the policy in various age groups.... They considered a number of factors based on that. For example, they matched the gender ratios among the sent-downs so that there would be a balanced number of men and women at the sent-down location. They also thought about the age factor because the sent-downs were matched in age groups. The older and more mature kids were matched with the younger and less capable ones, and the intention was that they would help the younger ones adapt to rural life.... Guys and girls were matched and settled in different villages because men were generally stronger and they would be able to help the girls to draw water from wells, gather and move firewood for winter, and help with various labor intensive tasks that would be hard for women to do physically.... These practical considerations were factored into policy implementation and the sent-downs were matched for a balanced assignment in each village so that they would be supportive to each other. I would say that the whole administration and organization of the Up to the Mountains and Down to the Countryside program were very well organized, and because it was so efficiently organized, the operation of the policy was very smooth. You could say that every base was covered and there were no loopholes in the implementation.... This reflected the centralized power of the CCP which guaranteed strict enforcement according to instruction, fast pace, speedy process, high efficiency, and extreme effectiveness during policy implementation....
>
> Additionally, the implementation was precise. Everything was done in one step perfectly. For instance, how many sent-downs were eligible, how many train cars were needed for transportation, how many administrators were needed to receive the sent-downs were all done in one step—in an orderly fashion with no step that swung back and forth.... They never had to scramble for another car to take people down. There was precision in the implementation. (I6, 34, 35, 39)

Gan also noted gender balance and maintained that "there were no loopholes in the administration and implementation of the sent-down policy" (I12, 17). By contrast, Lin noted that relocation could also be gender specific: "For military and state farm sent-downs, they were supposed to 'put down roots' at these locations so more women were selected specifically as potential wives on these farms" (I28, 7). Zhao also spoke to efficiency: "All the luggage comes with us all the way and nothing was lost" (I53, 3). Yu was even puzzled at the notion that luggage could get lost: "I never heard of anyone who lost his/her luggage. Why would you lose your luggage? We all wrote our names on it so how could it be lost? Actually, to think of it, they didn't have computers back then and everything was done by hand so that was pretty impressive. I heard that when people travel in the US even today, they often lose their luggage. That's just puzzling how people can lose their stuff in the States" (I50, 13).

According to Chao Duan, "The whole implementation of this policy [through the national administrative machine] was absolutely flawless. As the Chinese saying goes, it was very much like a 'heavenly robe that was seamless.' The administration, implementation, and coordination were absolutely seamless. No loopholes" (I8, 34).

Efficiency was enhanced by sending down the urban youth in groups and by providing them with standard-issue wooden trunks (I8, 26). Tan explained, "For us, the same classes in the same grade cohort all went to the same location. We all went to the same rural commune. The villages are organized by communes, then into brigades, and then in smaller teams [under the brigades]. So all the kids from the same class went to the same commune but they might be assigned to different production brigades or different teams. The school was in charge of everything with the whole process" (I42, 10). The number of youth involved varied by school. Bo Tang, vice president of a bank, indicated that his group included six classes of fifty students each (I43, 15). Zhao said, "I estimate, I heard that there were six thousand *zhiqing* who were sent down in my year's graduating cohort [1968] from all over Beijing" (I53, 2).

Efficiency was also promoted by bureaucratic impersonality, disregard of individual preferences and family ties, and the futility of resistance. In Weberian fashion, the rustication administration and administrators worked "without passion or bias" and in "dehumanized" fashion by disregarding basic human values, such as keeping families intact (Weber 1958, 215–16).[4] Wang emphasized that "it was almost like they didn't come to pick up people (the sent-downs); they simply came to pick up a shipment of cargo" (I46, 19). In the case of Duan, "There were five kids in my family, but four were sent down to the countryside and my mother went to a May Seventh Cadre School (for reeducation) and so our whole family was totally torn apart and separated into, let's see, five different places" (I8, 41). Similarly Yanli Wan, a human resources manager, said "there were seven members in our family and we were sent to six different places" (I45, 3). Tingyu Su, a retired administrator who worked in a science institute, also had seven family members sent to six different locations (I40, 7). Li said rustication "separated our family completely" (I25, 17). Liya Song, now head of a travel agency, emphasized the impersonality of the rustication process: "There was no consideration for the family structure in the sent-down policy," and "the whole administrative apparatus was like a game of chess with every piece processed the same way. The whole game was orderly and efficiently organized" (I39, 8, 16). Yun Wu agreed that "there were no considerations for individuals, families, or human factors under this system" (I48, 11). Yan Lu, a retired administrative assistant, said, "The policy completely destroyed our family structure and split us all up" (I30, 6).

Lin touched upon the irony of bureaucratic impersonality being central to the implementation of Mao's ideology:

> A place was chosen based on a specific purpose for having the youth which might be opening up land for reclamation, or perhaps it could be migration as in population redistribution, or resettlement with extra labor to increase food production. But most importantly, all these components were put into consideration to make Mao's theories come true—the whole sent-down policy and the rustication program was an experiment for making his ideas a reality which is to send intellectuals or those with knowledge to the bottom of society in different locations and dissolve them into the proletariat class among the workers, peasants, and soldiers. Mao said that you can tell whether a youth is a revolutionary or not by assessing his/her willingness to integrate with workers, peasants, and soldiers, and whether an intellectual is revolutionary or not by seeing if he or she is willing to [volunteer to] go to the countryside. (I28, 8)

Broad compliance with the rustication program also promoted efficiency. Coupled with the fervor of the Cultural Revolution, many of the interviewees considered it an honor to be sent down and volunteered or welcomed being rusticated.[5] With the exception of those who were able to join the military, those youth who were reluctant to be sent down apparently had no choice, and very few were left behind. The administrative framework for rustication at the local level cast "various nets . . . horizontally and vertically all across the system" specifically to prevent youth from slipping through and evading the rustication program (Fan I9, 27). Fan explained that

> when schools were given the order to organize and mobilize all the students, at the same time, all the public security offices also received the same order to implement the sent-down policy from the top as well. Instead of organizing the students, they are in charge of gathering information and going through all the *hukou* in their respective

districts, and so they will go through the *hukou* booklet and registration for each family in their neighborhood, their district, and they will know exactly which families, how many kids, including their names and age, were eligible and must comply with the mandatory policy. After they examine the *hukou* of each and every single family, they will coordinate with the street offices and send out the old women hags and their various small feet investigation teams to each family one-by-one to implement, to "practically realize" and "to put the policy into effect" for each family unit. In other words, the public security offices and the street offices were coordinated to practically realize the sent-down policy into fruition (I9, 27).

Duan added that even if it were possible, evasion would be disastrous because "if the government revoked your *hukou*, that would be essentially the very end of your life as you know it because it would end your food rations as the cancellation of your *hukou* would mean the government will no longer allocate or distribute any food stamps or other necessities to you and you will basically starve to death without those stamps because you cannot buy any food without them in the city" (I8, 28). Fan concurred that rustication presented a Hobson's choice at best: "If you stayed in the city, you will have no job, no pay, no food, and then your only option is to mooch off your parents" (I9, 24).

In Duan's view, "Nobody wanted to go—everybody wanted to stay in school but there was nothing one could do because everyone had to comply and leave. Everyone had to do it.... Let me put it this way, if you were a human being, you had to go. Simple as that" (I8, 23). In Fan's words, "There was no such thing as having a feeling of supporting [rustication] or not, because you really have no choice but to comply, so regardless of what inclinations you may have, it was of no use" (I9, 23). Lu, a retired administrative assistant, shared the same thought: "There was no way out of it" (I30, 5). Wang observed: "Back then, mobilization and organization really didn't have to take that much effort. Why? Because people were so passive and honest, and whatever the top said, the bottom listened to and this went for both the implementers and sent-downs" (I46, 18). Ding shared the same view: "Who dared to refuse? No one dared to do that" under the political and social climate of the day (I6, 20). Wu concurred with these perspectives: "It was an extremely small amount in number if there were people who refused to go and they would receive some form of unpleasant treatment, which certainly would not lead to any good consequences. But basically there was no one who didn't go as far as I know. I never heard of anyone who simply refused to go" (I48, 6). Kai Wen, a retired administrator at a science institute, put it bluntly: "Not going was shameful" (I47, 12). Yu emphasized the administrative pressures to comply: "The street offices would send their staff to work on you, but not just the street offices alone, their parents' work units would also apply an extraordinary amount of pressure and the parents were subject to

Public Administration and the Sent-Down Experience 115

punishment at work. So a plethora of administrative strategies, tactics, and approaches were used, and all these administrative organizations were coordinated to implement the policy, and therefore, a puny little person like you simply could not fight against it" (I50, 11).

As these interviewees indicate, many youth felt compelled to sign up for rustication. Others, however, recall going voluntarily. One said, "Not only was I supportive of the policy, I was actually pretty excited about it" (I45, 8). Similarly, Liang reflected that "because of our revolutionary passion and youthful romanticism, we were so worried that we were not going to be sent to the farthest places on China's map!" (I26, 3). Gan noted "Ultimately, you can say that I left by my own will, but it was certainly a forced willingness" (I12, 12). Similarly, Li indicated that "it was hard to say whether we were pressured into being sent down but we certainly didn't have any choice" (I25, 17). Yu had no such doubts: "It was more of a sightseeing tour for me because I went with all of my friends, a lot of them, and I was going down to establish my own life with all my buddies, so I mostly felt liberated. I felt it was a process of liberation coming to new freedom. . . . I was excited, joyful, and full of wanderlust" (I50, 11).

Other interviewees explained their decision to comply with the policy as follows:

Song (I39, 6): "It was like a group outing because we were sent down with our friends—all of our good friends and classmates from the same class at the same school so I thought it would be fun. I can't say that I was politically motivated but I was just happy to be with my friends away from home, from my parents' rules which I felt curbed my freedom and cramped my style. Besides, it was just in popular political fashion for you to leave."[6]

Jie Tian (I44, 9), a retired worker at a lock factory: "You may be able to delay the process but in the end everyone still had to go and comply with the policy. It was very hard to resist the zeitgeist of the time, especially one where everyone was sent down, and of course, you didn't want to be the exception."

Wan (I45, 9): "There were no options for you to choose. Not going was a disgrace whereas being sent down was an honor."

Wen (I47, 9, 12): "You had no time to even process and understand what was happening. You were constantly in a total state of shock and confusion and then you were sent down to the countryside. . . . Everyone volunteered to be sent down [in our cohort of 68]."

Ying Yuan (I51, 5–6), a retired personnel administrator in a municipal government: "People . . . back then . . . were so thin-skinned that they couldn't stand losing face. For example, my grandmother was having dinner with me and the old hags from the street office stood outside our door and shouted, 'Well, some people still have a kid who's not sent down' implying that we didn't comply with the policy. But after that, my grandmother could never touch her food again and dinner was totally spoiled for her because she was too upset to eat anything after having heard people mocking our family so publicly. People were easily shamed back then because reputation and family honor meant everything to them."

Although the sent-down policy was reportedly simple and efficient on the sending side, sometimes matters were less so on the receiving end. Zhang, who had systematically studied the rustication process at one time, observed that at the beginning

> there was no system yet in place to arrange for the funding and finance associated with the resettlement. When we were told to go, the Mongolian locals accepted us and initially the local production brigades paid for us and our supplies. The peasants paid for us at first. The pastoral peasants were relatively well off and they paid the cost of our supplies. . . . Later, gradually, the state implemented a system to finance the lower levels. In other places, when the national system for resettlement was not yet implemented, the *zhiqing* faced a lot of difficulties especially in poor countryside villages because if the state didn't provide funding, then the people at these poor regions could not afford to provide better treatment for the sent-downs. Like [this Beijing urban youth], who was sent to Shaanxi when she was 15. The sent-downs [in her cohort] had to live in caves because the state funding had not yet reached the lower levels. Her cave collapsed and everything came crashing down into heaps of rubble. Lucky for her, she was not in it at the time or she would surely not have survived. (I52, 6–7)

Zhao also reported difficulty on the receiving end.

> It was like this—some (military) reps came from the Yunnan farms to our school, and told us that "Oh, you should all come, it's so great there. Everything is so good and the Xishuangbanna is so beautiful and prosperous." They even told us a doggerel that when one is in Yunnan, "one's head touches bananas, toes step on pineapples, and if you trip and fall down, you'll end up grabbing a handful of peanuts." Completely different from reality. When we arrived, we had to first settle in straw houses and we had to use oil lamps for light. In our dorms, there were beds that were made from bamboo sticks but when you sat on it, they completely fell apart because the bamboo was still wet when they rushed to make the beds and now it was already chewed up by termites by the time we got there. . . . In the beginning, we had nothing but our bare hands (I53, 2).

Wu recalled that

> although the process of being sent down was implemented quickly, there were too many urban youth being sent down all at once and the implementation was in such a short span of time that local preparations were hasty and incomplete at the receiving

Public Administration and the Sent-Down Experience

end. For instance, one of my classmates was sent to Shanbei countryside [in Shaanxi]. By the time the cohort arrived in their assigned village, it was already dark and the village cadre sent them to sleep in a storage room for the first night. They lit some candles and were getting ready to go to sleep, but it turned out this was where the village stored gunpowder and somehow, with the candles and all, the whole storage caught on fire. This kid was heavily burned and after the fire was put out, a helicopter had to be sent in to airlift her out of this remote rural location to a proper hospital. I saw her years later and her face was completely disfigured from the burning. But there were a lot of incidents like that—although the local levels received directives for a full implementation, they were still in the process of getting it all together to accommodate the arriving sent-downs, yet they didn't have enough time to get everything ready, and consequently, in the absence of supporting policies and regulations, there were a lot of unexpected dangers in this process for the sent-downs (I48, 11).

Lin (I28, 5) also noted that "the sent-downs first lived in a storage" until funds arrived for settling them in regular housing, and Li (I25, 18) recalled that "when we first arrived, there was no housing or shelter for the sent-downs yet; instead we were sent to live among the Dai ethnic people in their stockade village and in their living quarters which were essentially two-story bungalows." Similarly, Duan recalled that

the village did get a notification earlier that the next day there would be some knowledgeable youth who will come and settle into their village, but they had no idea what that really meant. They thought that we merely came to do some volunteer farm work for the next three days or so and it was going to be a real short stint . . . and consequently they made no preparation whatsoever for our arrival. . . . We were sent to sleep in a classroom in the local elementary school. There was some grass laid over the dirt floor and all of us slept on that in a row, with our padded winter clothes on and that was it. (I8, 34)

He also noted that in a second village to which he was transferred, "Instead of building new houses for us, they settled us in these old vacant houses in the village and they used our settlement money to build a new storage or whatever else. . . . They gave us one of those dilapidated old houses that were unoccupied" (I8, 29).

Number of Personnel

Excluding street office, school, military, and transportation escort personnel, the number of administrators who interacted directly with the sent-downs was reportedly limited. Ding indicated that was because the implementation process was highly effective and efficient; therefore it took a very small number of implementers to get it done. To organize all the *zhiqing* in a county, there were only about three to five administrators in the county-level Knowledgeable Youth Resettlement Office; at the commune- or town-level Knowledgeable Youth Resettlement Office, there was usually just one administrator in charge. At the brigade level, there were no formal administrators, just the brigade leaders. Take us for example, there were five-thousand-plus students to be sent down who came from thirteen different counties, and if you add up all the administrators—there were only like twenty-six or so, at max, it was about thirty administrators altogether who were in charge of the implementation process for over five thousand students which included all the paperwork, village assignments and living arrangements. That's thirty for five thousand, so I would say that's high efficiency. (I6, 34)

Liang concurred that there were "not very many" administrators "in ratio to the sent-downs," as did Gan, who said, "The administrators in charge were very few in numbers," and Wen, who noted that the administrators "were few in number because the implementation was so well done, so efficient and effective that they simply didn't need that many people to run the program" (I26, 19; I12, 17; I47, 17). Apparently this was also true at the street level. Yuan noted that "two of those" street office "women made batches and batches of us leave. Definitely high efficiency. It was their political duty to make sure that the policy was implemented, so there was a lot of political pressure for them to be active" (I51, 8).

If there were three to five administrators at the county level, the total for China's two thousand counties would be in the range of about six thousand to ten thousand. However, those figures undoubtedly understate the total because Ding was referring only to those sent down from small cities to relatively nearby villages. The number of administrators operating in large cities and in sending down youth for longer distances was probably significantly greater. In addition, if there were another administrator in each of the tens of thousands of communes receiving sent-downs, it would push the total much higher. Consequently, though unknown, there is no doubt that rustication was a significant contributor to bureaucratic growth at the subnational party-state levels during the Cultural Revolution (see also Liu 2009, 174–75).

Administrative Culture

Rustication had a lasting impact on Chinese administrative culture. Specifically, it contributed to the growth of administrative privilege, discretion and power, and corruption in the form of bribery, gift giving, trading sexual favors, and using connections to circumvent standard bureaucratic procedures.

Privilege

As discussed in chapter 4, Mao's opposition to the privileges that bureaucrats and technocrats enjoyed was among his reasons for initiating the Cultural Revolution. My interviewees offer a mixed view of the extent to which administrators were privileged. Sun and Tan reported extensive administrative privilege. Sun observed that "at the end of 1966, I participated in the local Cultural Revolution in Jiangxi during the Great Revolutionary Exchange. At the local level, I saw that people were struggling against the local cadres because they were having different kinds of food altogether from the people. They had better dinners from their own separate pots" (I41, 12).

Tan reported that

> for the likes of my family, who were mid-level cadres, there was not much difference between our family and the families of the working class. But my uncle's family, well, my uncle was considered a high cadre, his family definitely had special privileges because when I was young, I often visited my cousins and there were major differences between their family and my own especially in the way we lived. They lived in a different type of housing altogether. . . . My uncle's family lived in a huge two-story house like other [military] cadres at this level, whereas my family, we lived in an apartment in the same complex as my father's colleagues. . . . In theory, my family was relatively well off because my father was a diplomat and had the opportunities to visit abroad. Nevertheless, we lived in a cramped apartment—we lived in a *tongzilou*[7] where the restrooms and kitchen stoves [stationed in the corridors outside the apartment] were shared by multiple families and the stoves were fueled by coal. But my uncle's family lived in a house up on the hill. There were two rows of these houses on the hill, which were all occupied by the high cadres and their families. These were huge houses, kind of like the townhouses in the US today, but they were much, much nicer than those townhouses even by US standards. The cadre families had cooks and maids in their houses and they ate very well, much better than my family did, because their food was supplied by the military. They were very privileged but they were cadres at the very high level. . . . But for mid-level or low-level cadres, their lives were no different than those of the ordinary citizens. (I42, 3–4)

Tang more or less agreed:

> Politically, the cadres were superior but economically they were the same as everyone else. At the time, material resources were so scarce so even using a telephone or having access to a telephone would be considered a privilege. If you count those conveniences (as privileges), then there was a difference between the cadres and ordinary citizens because the cadres would have access to them through their jobs. I guess in some cases,

there were polarized differences because the high cadres had cars with personal chauffeurs which was unimaginable for ordinary citizens. (I43, 3)

Fan, who was the son of a high-level cadre, observed that "in reality, the officials and high cadres of the central government had the very same privileges as they do today. But at that time, privileges were limited to the top and did not permeate or spread out [to the lower levels of government] like today, and so at least on the surface, the cadres—even the high officials—seemed like they were just like ordinary people" (I9, 16–17). He continued to explain that the cadre personnel system provided privileged treatment:

> Prior to the Cultural Revolution in any *danwei*, any institution or organization, let's say a factory, for example, there was a human relations office and a labor capital office. The human relations office only deals with cadres/administrators, whereas the labor office would manage the workers or noncadres. Just think about it—simply by the names of these offices and what they referred to, only cadres were counted in terms of human relations, whereas workers and noncadres were merely thought of as labor and capital. . . .
>
> Under this system, if you were a worker and if you wanted to switch onto the cadre personnel track—you know what? You'd have an easier time flying up in the sky and walking on the moon before that could happen. (I9, 21)

Duan fully concurred and added that Fan had himself been a beneficiary of cadre privilege, including having access to higher-quality food and living in an individual house that was fully staffed with a chauffeur, cook, and other service personnel (I8, 7). For instance, Fan mentioned that "even during those difficult years of the [post–Great Leap Forward] famine before the Cultural Revolution" his father "kept the same habit of having milk, jam, and bread for breakfast when others were starving" (I9, 53).

Zhao observed that "before the Cultural Revolution everyone was so poor but the higher-level bureaucrats still had privileges. They had extra supplies in food tickets and were provided with access to many other materials [that were not readily available to other citizens] from the state" (I53, 8).

Su noted that the cadres' children in her school lived in superior housing and had furniture supplied by the state, whereas "the kids from working class families [workers and peasant families], they all lived in old *pingfang*, these ground-level brick bungalows and their family was not given anything. Their family was not provided with things from the state like we were, such as various household furniture" (I40, 41).

Lijun Yang, who views herself as one of a group of ten students who "jumpstarted the rustication policy" by volunteering to go from Beijing to the West

Public Administration and the Sent-Down Experience 121

Inner Mongolian grasslands in 1967, holds the contrary view that "government administrators and cadres were very much clean and dedicated back then; they were afraid to get special treatment, so society was still very equal—or you could say that class differentiation was minimal" (I49, 5). Zhiyun Meng, a former government bureaucrat, expressed a similar view: "I could not detect any difference between the cadres and ordinary citizens. We could only see that the cadres treated themselves with more discipline and had higher standards for their own behavior" (I33, 3). In general, my interviewees from higher cadre backgrounds were more likely to perceive privilege than other interviewees, who tended to emphasize how the scarcity of material goods in the society promoted equality.

Discretion and Power

The ability to use discretion is a source of power for bureaucrats and bureaucracy as a whole. Some administrators involved in implementation of the rustication program apparently enjoyed discretion and were considered quite powerful by the sent-downs. However, many behaved strictly in accordance with rules and policies, especially in the earlier years of the sent-down program. Several interviewees agreed with Gan, who observed that "the administrators and implementers strictly followed what they were instructed [to do]. Maybe they also had sent-downs in their own families and maybe they felt sympathetic to the predicament of other sent-downs but it didn't matter because they didn't dare not to follow the rules as instructed because Chairman Mao had said so. If you didn't follow what the Chairman said, then you'd be a counterrevolutionary, so of course the administrators had to do as they were told" (I12, 17). Liang expressed very similar thoughts:

> The few administrators at the Knowledgeable Youth Resettlement Office at the county level really had a lot of power because they were in charge of the transfers and recruitment. If they said it or OKed it, then it was done. These administrators were in charge of several thousand sent-downs. Additionally, at every commune, the secretaries are also in charge of the sent-downs. . . . The administrators did whatever they were instructed to do, uncompromised, unquestioned, because no one dared not to. At that time, one's political attitude was above all else. If someone was perceived to have any negative feelings toward Jiang Qing [Madam Mao] or Chairman Mao, then he or she would be labeled as counterrevolutionary so everyone was afraid, did as told, and followed instructions. (I26, 19)

Wu fully concurred: "At that time, the administrators/implementers would be afraid to do something like that [showing favoritism] because implementation of the policy was their political duty and responsibility. Additionally, they were bound by their own ethics (which were quite virtuous back then) and the party discipline" (I48, 10).

Zhao reported what would seem to be an extreme case of going by the book, on the one hand, and a humane bending of the rules, on the other:

> I was 21 years old at the time, and my fingers were mangled flat [by an industrial gum-pressing machine from a work-related accident on the military farm], broken to millions of pieces. After that, I could no longer work properly without the use of my right hand. I wanted to return to Beijing under the sick leave policy. But I was not allowed to return because the Beijing Knowledgeable Youth Resettlement Office said that the work-related injury occurred in Yunnan, so it was their responsibility to take care of it and this was not under the purview of the Beijing office. So my injury, the loss of four fingers, didn't qualify for the sick leave. . . . In other words, the hand injury was not included on the list of conditions that qualified for the sick leave so I couldn't return because of it. . . . I stayed in a Beijing hospital waiting in vain for about three months and finally I had to go back to the farm because they [administrators on the farm] wanted me back at work. (I53, 4)

Eventually, however, the doctor in charge "told me to come up and see him. He said that he knew about my injury, so he was just going to sign my paperwork required for the sick leave" (I53, 4–5). This was after Zhao unsuccessfully tried to fake a heart condition in order to come under the sick leave policy by taking an overdose of aminophylline pills and riding his bicycle under their full effect 20 *li* (6.2 miles) on mountainous roads.

According to Fan, local-level administrators gave "absolute total obedience . . . to the top" but nevertheless gained discretionary power when the rustication policy offered flexibility in assigning sent-downs to different types of work:

> In the first several years, when we were sent down, they [lower-level bureaucrats] had absolutely no power of any kind. The only power they had was to make arrangements for the sent-downs to settle into their new life in the countryside; they never had that kind of power to choose any particular sent-down over another. . . . Later, they were . . . in charge of arranging for and assigning jobs to the sent-downs. In my village, for example, . . . a lot of sent-downs were later transferred to work in the county factory which was a real job with a monthly salary (as opposed to farming with no stable income) . . . and so when all these (transfers) were permitted within the policy, when these policies later came about, the bottom-level bureaucrats ended up having much more power. (I9, 44)

The perception that administrators went by the book did not preclude concern among my interviewees that they might still act arbitrarily. Ding recalled,

There was usually only one administrator at the commune-level Knowledgeable Youth Resettlement Office, but he's in charge of writing up the evaluation reports of the sent-downs and the transfer of a sent-down to elsewhere for a better job assignments, like for example, when a sent-down returned to the city, he or she had to find a receiving work unit to accept his/her records to be considered for a job. The administrator in this office had a lot of discretion on this, and, consequently, received a lot of gifts (from the sent-downs and their families) because if a sent-down wanted to improve his/her standing or chances of returning to the city, you'd want your evaluation report to be written up nicely. (I6, 32)

Guanxi and Corruption

Public administrative discretion can be used in a broad variety of ways. It can be in service of the administrator's conception of the public interest or private interest, a means of fitting general policy requirements to specific cases, a way to pursue equitable treatment, or used to reward or punish individuals (Lipsky 1980; Maynard-Moody and Musheno 2003). When an administrator uses discretion for his or her private gain, it is usually considered corrupt (Gong and Ma 2009). In some administrative contexts, however, using connections or "going through the back door" for favorable treatment is informally institutionalized standard operating procedure (Heidenheimer 1989). For instance, scholars have generally considered *protektzia* (connections) to have been a fundamental feature of the Israeli bureaucracy and administrative culture (e.g., Danet 1989; Nachmias and Rosenbloom 1978). In China, *guanxi* (establishing relationships with administrators) is an institutionalized means of gaining favorable treatment or going through the back door. *Guanxi* can be based on friendship, kinship, kindness, and altruism, but it also includes using third-party or direct connections as well as bribery, gift giving, and providing hospitality or sexual favors.[8] Today, *guanxi* is considered a central feature of China's administrative culture. However, based on my interviews, it is reasonable to conclude that it was insignificant at the beginning of the rustication program and became fairly common only toward the end, especially in regard to the sent-downs' return to the cities. This is what my interviewees had to say with respect to *guanxi*:

> Ding (I6, 26): "As time went on, the sent-downs would find every possible reason, every excuse there is, to wheedle their way back home. The sent-down would beg their parents, ask their parents to use every kind of *guanxi* or connection possible to get them back to the city. This is when the parents who were able to help their children started buying gifts, taking friends of influence to dinner, establishing relationships with those who were in charge or had discretion over the sent-downs and basically the beginning of using *guanxi* and going through the back door because these push factors became a

breeding ground for the wide use of *guanxi* and personal connections. For example, at where I was [sent down], some parents were able to get their children recruited to the local factory; some were able to get their children into the PLA; and some were able to get their children jobs in the nearby mining area. It didn't matter what the job was—they took any reassignment as long as it took their children out of the countryside. That's when the trend of giving gifts and taking people to lavish dinners in exchange for favors proliferated and swept across the nation. Prior to the Cultural Revolution, these incidents were very rare."

Duan (I8, 9): *Guanxi* became prevalent "around 1975 during the returning stage of the rustication policy . . . when it came to the time that the sent-downs were allowed back to the city under various policies and as more possibilities opened up, such as being recommended for a university placement in the city. Mao then said something like, 'Among those who used the back door, there are also some good (qualified) people.'. . . From that point on, the use of *guanxi* and going through the back door became prevalent and people no longer even bothered to hide it. They were brazen if not proud about their *guanxi* which became rampant and standard operating procedure."

Fan (I9, 41), whose parents worked for the national government, personally benefited from "a certain access to the back door through *guanxi* and that's why [he] came back so quickly in only two and a-half years . . . [whereas] in general the other sent-downs stayed for five or six years."

Gan (I12, 8): "The old cadres were so upstanding. They never treated themselves or their own family members differently than others. In fact, you know when *guanxi* and the practice of going through the back door started? It was during the Cultural Revolution when the old soldiers and military officers wanted to help their own children. If they didn't go through the back door, then how could their children be recruited into the PLA? . . .

"*Guanxi* and the use of connections became rampant only during the Cultural Revolution. Think about it, everything was chaotic, even killing people was OK and not legally prosecutable, and so *guanxi* became no big deal. In fact, it became OK and natural to give gifts and use *guanxi*. Like when all the paperwork was ready for my husband's transfer, the school district director in the Inner Mongolia countryside would not release him (as a teacher) and said that they needed more time to reconsider and process his transfer. That was obviously a euphemism asking for gifts. That's when I said, I came here prepared and I got out my liquor and cartons of cigarettes and said that he could have them all. After he took the gifts, the director immediately approved my husband's transfer and stamped the paperwork right away."

Lin (I28, 10, 13): "*Guanxi* and back door connections became super important and widespread and it all started when the bureaucrats used their connections to send their kids to the military to become soldiers (instead of being sent down) and it got worse when it came to the end when it was time for returning to the cities. Previously, however, . . . cadres and administrative officials were generally good, clean, and especially the street-level bureaucrats were. . . . Materialistically, everything was so scarce, even if the cadres wanted to be corrupt, there were simply not enough material goods to go around [to be offered as bribes of any value]. To give you a crude example, even if a cadre wanted to seduce and have sex with a woman in exchange for favorable treatment then, he probably didn't have the space or place to sleep with her because all housing was public and he certainly won't have a place of his own for the assignation to occur. Similarly, if there are no material resources to begin with, then you can't be corrupt even if you wanted to. The society couldn't have been that unequal because . . . everyone was equally poor. Politically, there was much less tolerance. If you were perceived to have special privilege or treatment, people would probably put out big-character posters to expose your behavior, so no one dared to do anything too much outside of the parameters (of the normal rules and regulations).

". . . When *guanxi* and corruption really became sweeping and rampant and came down like a tsunami—it really started when the sent-downs were returning to cities—when men had to present material goods such as cigarettes and liquor to administrators both locally and in the city to secure their placement [back home] and women had to sleep with local administrators in exchange for favorable treatment."[9]

Su (I40, 15): "The practice of going through the back door or using *guanxi* only happens under certain conditions. When there is no competition or when everyone's opportunity is equal, there is no need for relying on connections—however, the sent-down policy really activated these certain conditions. For example, people were sent down to the military farm in Inner Mongolia where everyone wanted to leave and when there is the desire, there is the demand and fierce competition for limited opportunities (to return)—and especially because the specifications for eligibility under the returning policy were subject to administrative discretion, and consequently, the conditions for the use of *guanxi* became ripe and were set in motion."

Sun (I41, 11, 29): "Going through the back door or using *guanxi* was not prominent at the beginning of the sent-down policy, and in later stages, technically, people were not using connections because the criteria for returning to the city were already possible under the policy. They just had to find a way to become eligible under those specifications." However, he noted that "the returning era really activated the beginning of using any means [sexual favors] or strategies possible such as relying on *guanxi* or connections of any kind."

Tan (I42, 6, 12): Before the Cultural Revolution, *guanxi* was "extremely rare because even if you used *guanxi*, you still couldn't get too far. Material was so scarce, so you just couldn't get that much out of it, even if you relied on personal connections and used *guanxi*. But let's say you did, it still had to be within the possibilities; it had to stay within the parameters of what was regularly allowed under the policies. [However,] definitely, people did start using *guanxi* when all the *zhiqing* were set to return to the cities."

Tang (I43, 18): "That's how the old cadres were in those days [prior to the Cultural Revolution]. They were extremely clean and upstanding in their behavior, especially at their jobs. No cadre used *guanxi*, and if one did, it was extremely rare. Back then, the administrative culture was so clean as was the political atmosphere."

Wan (I45, 14): "During the Cultural Revolution and the subsequent rustication era, all the regular, normal procedures and processes were disrupted. Once there were loopholes in the policies, every parent tried to fish out their own kid from wherever they were sent down through their own personal connections. However, there must be general policies which allowed the transfers or returns; otherwise no matter what connections you got, you still couldn't get back. Unlike today, [when] the individual cadre or official can actually create a new set of rules or add on a new set of categories for their own benefit, back then, they must stay within the general policy. When the rustication policy loosened up and when there were possibilities to come back, only then could you use connections or *guanxi* to help your own cause (kid)."

Yu (I50, 7, 22): "It [*guanxi*] started around the middle stages of the Cultural Revolution, after the sent-down policy was being implemented and before returning to the city happened. . . .

"When new possibilities opened up as they were permitted under the policy [for returning] and having realized that we had permanently lost our right to return to the cities, that's when the demand for favors and *guanxi* came about. This was the beginning of it all—when the widespread use of *guanxi* started in the Chinese society."

Yuan (I51, 3): "I feel that China was an equal, egalitarian society before the Cultural Revolution. The cadres—most were clean and uncorrupt. Maybe some of the cadres were corrupt and bad but that's like 1 percent of 1,000. Today it's 1,000 out of 1,000 percent! Heck, it's 1,200 out of 1,000 percent."

Zhang (I52, 7): "A lot of this taking officials to dinners, giving gifts and bribes came during the rustication era, which was especially connected to the returning period of the sent-down program. . . . It was in 1973, '74 when I first heard about these incidents. . . . So taking officials to dinner and bribery or gifts came from the returning period at the end of rustication. But this was not absolute, of course, [offering] bribery and gifts has been a historical tradition when dealing with the Chinese bureaucracy. . . . But the old cadres back then were so naive in their ways of thinking. The society was so poor. They were poor themselves and they didn't desire much [materialistically], and so there was no rampant corruption problem back then."

Zhao (I53, 6, 7): "Bureaucrats and officials, especially the street-level bureaucrats were clean and upstanding prior to the Cultural Revolution and the sent-down era; it was unheard of having to take officials to dinner. . . . From what I know all this inviting people to dinner, bribery, and trading for favors definitely happened during the later stages of the Cultural Revolution and the rustication era."[10]

To the extent that *guanxi* was relevant to the sending side of the rustication process, it was probably with respect to the military. Lin claimed that "anyone who didn't go up to the mountains or down to the countryside and instead was

Public Administration and the Sent-Down Experience 127

admitted into the military used their family connections" (I28, 10). Lu said, "Back then [before the Cultural Revolution], the cadres were so clean and upstanding.... However, to place the stamp of bureaucratic corruption in the Cultural Revolution era, I would say that using *guanxi* or going through the back door began during the time when the sent-downs competed in getting into the PLA as a way to evade being sent down" (I30, 4). Tian fully concurred: "For those who went to serve in the army instead of being sent down, if you had no connections, there was no way in hell you could get in. It would be an utter impossibility" (I44, 13). So did Wen: "Anyone who went to the military in lieu of being sent down had some sort of personal or family connections or *guanxi* to the PLA. If you didn't have any *guanxi* in the PLA, there was absolutely no way you could be recruited" (I47, 17). Tan and Tang agreed that "those who were admitted to the army instead of being sent down all had connections. This was absolutely true. Maybe not every one of them but definitely the majority of them. The major portion got in through *guanxi*. Like in my high school, when the army admitted people, most of them had *guanxi*. Take my uncle's family, all his kids were admitted into the PLA—not a single one was sent down—and he had six children" (I42, 6 speaking; I43, 6 agreeing). Yu said flatly, "Anyone who could get into the PLA, 100 percent had *guanxi* or connections" (I50, 8).

Guanxi, including sexual favors, was also widely reported to be used after 1973 when sent-downs' admission to universities as worker-peasant-soldier apprenticed students (*gongnongbing xueyuan*) depended on approval and recommendation by rustication administrators (Ding, Fan, Gan, Haoram Han, Li, Lu, Wenbin Mo, Peng, Tan, Tang, Tian, Wen, Zhang). As Zhang pointed out, "Some say that the majority of those girls who were recommended or allowed to go to universities were those who traded sexual favors during this time" (I52, 5). Officially, sent-downs were supposed to be selected on the basis that they had excelled in their reeducation, reformed their bourgeois thinking, and integrated themselves fully with the masses. *Guanxi* continued to be used even after 1977, when university admission depended on one's performance on national examinations. Tan reflected that in her experience,

> no one was in charge. The whole admissions process was so disorganized.... At the time, no one knew how to manage admissions because the universities had been closed for so long. So the whole system and the organization of it were a total mess. Everything had to be done through the back door because the administration was so unorganized and there were no regular procedures or guidelines yet in place, and so every step of the admission process was plagued by going through *guanxi* because no one knew what to expect.... So at that time, even if you passed (the admission requirements), you still had to use *guanxi* to get into a university because the admission process was just too messy. (I42, 11)

Based on my interviewees' responses with regard to China's administrative culture immediately prior to and during the Cultural Revolution, it is reasonable to conclude that (1) high-ranking cadres and military personnel were afforded substantial material benefits, including food, housing, and personal services, that were unavailable to the general public; (2) other cadres may have enjoyed limited conveniences such as access to telephones that were not generally available to ordinary citizens; (3) during the first several years of the rustication policy, administrators' discretion was limited by strict adherence to procedural regularity, used within the framework of extant policies, and only very rarely swayed by *guanxi*, including bribery and hospitality; (4) administrators' discretion was more flexibly exercised during the later stages of the sent-down program and especially as increasing numbers of urban youth sought to return to the cities; and (5) such discretion enhanced the power of individual administrators over the lives of the sent-downs and fostered the use of *guanxi*. It does not appear that my interviewees were romanticizing the honesty of bureaucrats prior to the widespread use of *guanxi* because all of them who expressed a view on the subject agreed that administrators were upstanding and public administration was clean.

Transporting the Sent-Downs to Their Destinations

The overall efficiency of the rustication program should not belie the logistical complexity of transporting seventeen million urban youth to a variety of rural destinations, some of which were very remote from the major cities. Transportation was primarily by train, truck, and, for some, horse-drawn cart and foot. Train transportation involved amassing sent-downs at train stations and transporting them in cars specially designated or added for them. Some trains were devoted to sent-downs only; others carried regular passengers in separate cars. Military personnel escorted the sent-downs to military farms and, sometimes, to other destinations as well. Teachers also served as escorts on some trains. Overall, my interviewees indicated that getting to their destinations was well organized and smooth, if sometimes arduous.

The schools played a major role in organizing transportation from the point of departure. As one interviewee explained, "It was all organized by the school. They sent along all our files, arranged for our 'special trains,' had people send us there and pick us up" (Wen I47, 12). Another remarked, "I remember that day so distinctly. In the morning, we just brought our luggage to school and there were already cars waiting for us to send us down. It was all organized by the school" (Tan I42, 15). Ding recalled debarking from the local Knowledgeable Youth Up to the Mountains and Down to the Countryside Resettlement Office:

Public Administration and the Sent-Down Experience

Photo 5.1: Transportation of sent-down men on a flatbed truck to rustication destinations.

On the day we reported to the office, all the sent-downs were led to the downtown plaza together as a group, where the town residents gathered for a "warm send-off" ceremony in our honor. Every sent-down was given a big red-flower boutonniere and we pinned it on our jackets over the heart. Everyone was singing the revolutionary song, "going to the borders, going to the countryside, going to where the country needs me. . . ." By the time you reported to the office, everything has been prearranged by the Knowledgeable Youth Up to the Mountains and Down to the Countryside Resettlement Office. Once you reported to the office, you are given a form, which told you where you were going to be sent, along with information on what kind of transportation, which train car, which seat was assigned to you. That would be the normal process for urban youth from Beijing or Shanghai sent to Shanxi or the northeast for example. But for us [in Guangdong], because our sent-down villages were within our county and our destinations were only about 140 kilometers [87 miles] from our county town, so it was relatively close and we didn't need to get on a train for transportation. Instead, we got onto these big flatbed trucks that belonged to the specific communes in the countryside. For us, once we finished the ceremony, the trucks were lined up for each commune.... The whole administration was streamlined and extremely well organized. It was like military organization and administration. The student sent-downs were all organized like soldiers in the military—each grade was a company, each class was a platoon, and then into smaller teams and subunits. (I6, 19)

Beginning in 1967, after official policy shifted to resuming classes and making revolution in the schools, the military assumed supervision of different agencies, institutions, and organizations across the nation, including schools, and played an extensive role in transferring sent-downs to their destinations. Zhang explained that

the military management played a major role in getting the kids to the countryside. I remember that when we were sent to the countryside, the military personnel were on the whole trip until we arrived in our assigned villages. They were making sure that we would be taken to our intended destinations, whether it was forceful escort or a "friendly, cheerful send-off" as they put it, it was hard to say—but they only left after we got to our assigned destinations. Once you got to the villages, then they just disappeared and that was it. (I52, 10)

Several interviewees had long journeys to the countryside. For example, Zhao explained that

our destination was so far away and at that time there were no direct trains to take us from Beijing to our sent-down location in Yunnan. We had to take trains from Beijing to Chengdu and then another train from Chengdu to Kunming [the capital of Yunnan Province]. After that, we got on these big flatbed trucks for another four days—so that's four days and four nights of train, two days of rest, and then four days of trucks, and finally it would just reach the general area of our sent-down location. Then it takes another two hours by horse carriage to reach the destination of our assigned teams. The trip took exactly ten days from Beijing to where we were sent down. (I53, 2–3)

Gan also had an arduous trip to the countryside:

I was sent to Tuzuoqi (Inner Mongolia), about ninety *li* [twenty-eight miles] from Hohhot. First, we took the train from Beijing to the Tuzuoqi county where we stayed on for a day. The office there distributed winter coats to us and provided food and

Public Administration and the Sent-Down Experience

temporary housing for us overnight. They even arranged for a movie to entertain us, and we were given these buns made out of white flour, which was actually considered really good food because the local peasants were too poor to afford eating something made of flour. After one night there, the next morning, they took all our luggage and put it on these horse carriages, so our luggage left first and we left on these flatbed trucks later in the day. It took about sixty *li* [nineteen miles] to reach the commune. The trucks dropped people [sent-downs] off one group at a time along the way at different stops. . . . About ten of us were assigned to Heihe brigade and by the time we got to the general area, the brigade already sent a horse carriage to pick us up and take us to our ultimate destination. . . .

A military representative from our school served as a chaperone on our entire trip to our sent-down location. When we got there, there were people who came to receive us. Once the military rep handed us to them, he was gone—mission accomplished. (I12, 11)

Those traveling such long distances involving trucks and horse-drawn carriages faced particular difficulties in returning to their homes for visits. By contrast, Tan and Tang were sent down to the rural outskirts of Beijing and could return home for brief visits by an hour's bicycle ride (I42, 10; I43, 10).

Settling into the Countryside

The schools largely established the sent downs' destinations, although some of the interviewees were able to choose their place of rustication from among a few alternatives and others volunteered for locations to which they were virtually certain to be sent. Based on my interviewees' responses, destination made a huge difference in the overall rustication experience.

Rural Villages

Rural villages were organized into work teams, production brigades, and then into communes, which housed the headquarters for overall administration. Urban youth sent down to rural villages were managed like peasants and essentially became peasants. For the vast majority of peasants, grinding poverty and almost constant hard work were the rule. In large part, this was due to the taxation system, which a former local government official, Ding, who was rusticated in a rural village, explained:

China was under a planned economy and it was completely controlled and planned accordingly. Material was scarce so the production of everything was limited by a quota system under a preset quantity and then distributed by tickets or stamps. Food, fabric (for clothing), sugar, salt, oil, coal, you name it. In the countryside, the women from our village even needed stamps to get sanitary napkins for their period. . . . Anything you can think of—it required stamps for you to get it. There was a set amount [quota] for each person for any given material, and each person had a little booklet to keep track of his/her quota such as how much soy sauce he or she had already been given. (I6, 5–6)

This rationing system was particularly harsh on the peasantry, Ding explained, because

the peasants must turn over to the government a preset number of things per average farm—how many eggs, how many ducks, how much pork, must be turned over—and after all that was turned over to the government [as farm taxes], only then would the peasants be given the food stamps and material tickets needed to sustain their basic living. . . . The Bureau of Commerce was probably in charge of the administration and management of the food stamps, material tickets and the records of the quotas allocated for each individual and their families in the cities, whereas the Supply and Sales Cooperatives [at each commune] were in charge of the peasants in the countryside. . . . The peasants were the backbone of China's economy but they had to turn in all their profit whether it was grain, beans, oil, sugar, or cotton, all must be rendered to the state unconditionally. . . . In fact, peasants must turn over everything to the state without getting paid because that's the farm tax, a quota that must be met. After the grain tax, peasants must sell the "surplus" to the state at a fixed price [as additional surplus tax]. . . . After that, the peasants end up getting the food back at a much higher price [with food stamps] from the government. . . .[11]

Let's say you could only pay 80 percent (of the taxes) even with everything you've got because your harvest production was low this year due to some unforeseeable events. In this case, you will have to find a way to pay for what you didn't turn in, the remaining 20 percent that you owe to the state, otherwise you will not be allowed to farm next year [because the state owns the land] which means you will have no food and will essentially starve to death. This is why the peasants were always on the brink of starvation and lived in perpetual destitution. . . . Because if a peasant produced more, he may have enough to eat after all the taxes. But if not, then there would be nothing left for him after the taxes to even feed himself. . . . You must come up with the fixed amount of taxes you owe to the state and if you couldn't do it—and let's say if you were lucky enough and somehow you were given a break when you couldn't pay up—then you would certainly have to pay everything back plus more the next year to the state, but for this current year, you will have nothing to eat for the entire year because you would not be given any tickets or stamps to purchase the essential materials needed to sustain your basic existence. (I6, 5–6)

Public Administration and the Sent-Down Experience

For the sent-downs, the most obvious result of this system was the need to work hard to enhance production either directly or indirectly by freeing up someone else's labor. Ding said that at his destination "housing and shelter were already arranged for us before we got there, and as for food, the first week of our food rations were also arranged by the brigade, and by the second week, they expected you to work and contribute to the production of your own food. Whether it was gathering firewood for cooking or drawing water from the well, or some other sort of farm work, either way, by the second week, you are expected to work [in any way that you could]" (I6, 20). Tan recounted that the sent-downs were managed "just like all the other peasants because you've become a peasant yourself. Every morning the team leader would ring a bell when the sun rises, then you take your tools and walk with all the other peasants to the field and they assign you a specific task [whether it's planting, seeding, or getting rid of weeds in the field], then you do as you were told and work along with all the other peasants" (I42, 14). Tang concurred that "the *zhiqing* were managed like other peasants" and added that "the commune had built a row of houses for the sent-downs to live in. Women and men were separated into two different dormitories and each room was shared by two *zhiqing* residents. There was a kitchen specifically reserved for *zhiqing* and some *zhiqing* stayed in and cooked for the rest of us while we worked in the field" (I43, 14).

What did it mean to be managed like a peasant? Liang explained that he was

> exhausted because in the northeast, the sun rises very early. During the summer harvest, the sun rises at 3 AM and so that's when you had to get up and go shovel the dirt in the field. You take a pancake with you for food and off you go with your shovel and hoe. The seedlings are all below your waist level and they were always wet and so you get wet while crouching down and it was always in the freezing cold. The climate in the northeast was really cold even during the summer season, so you were always in the freezing wetness on those morning days. I probably worked ten hours or more every day but somehow you just get used to it. (I26, 18)

He added, "You can't imagine how backwards everything was. Everything made, used, produced, and consumed depended on human labor" (I26, 18).

Ding had a similar experience:

> Every day was like that from 6:30 AM to 6:30 PM with two added hours of overtime so we would finish and call it a day about 9 PM or so. At that time there was no "machinization" or mechanization for any farm work and so everything was done by human physical labor. We were the oxen. Literally, because each production brigade only had four oxen and so there were simply not enough oxen to go around for plowing. Consequently, all the plowing was done by human labor and we were the oxen that plowed

the land. We dragged plows like oxen. We replaced the animals with our labor. In the countryside, everything, every task, every related errand was done by human labor and we were the labor to do it. (I6, 25)

Tian and Wan explained their experiences in similar terms:

In the morning, if you don't show up for work, then the peasants would drop by and wake you up. Everyone in our team [all sent-downs] always overslept and couldn't wake up on time because we had to get up and work as soon as the sun rises. Even if the peasants came to wake us up, we would drag our feet and stretch it out and it would take us a long while to get going but then we would carry our hoes or whatever tools to the field with the rest of the peasants. The team leader would assign different tasks to everyone and we would start working. We worked until noon and then took a break for lunch. . . . We often skipped meals because there was not enough to eat. Those days on the farm, we prayed for rain because only on rainy days we could stay in and didn't have to work in the field. Peasants don't have holidays. They don't have Saturdays or Sundays off; every day is a workday, and so we had to go into the field every day unless it rained. . . .

The worst job was "deep plowing" the land—which was supposed to be done by tractors but we were the tractors who did the plowing when the field was completely frozen solid. And when you did try to plow, all the shrapnel of ice and frozen dirt would fly in your face and get in your eyes. (I44, 11–12; I45, 11–12)

Wan added, "The 'deep plowing' was the worst, which was totally useless in reality. It was just absurd. It was pointless to hoe a frozen field. If all this labor produced something then that would be one thing, but the fact is all this extensive labor we put in only destroyed our health and didn't produce anything" (I45, 12). Tian added "life was so difficult even the basic necessities of life were hard to come by"—including adequate and safe drinking water (I44, 16).

Food was a constant concern. Within the overall framework of the national food taxation system described earlier, allocation was strongly related to work performance. Ding explained the system, which was used throughout the rural villages:

Work points directly affected your food ration, or one portion of your allocated food amount, which was called the labor grain ration. For example, the factual points of a day were calculated by multiplying the base numeric value of your daily work points earned and that would be your factual points for that day. Let's say you earned 10 points for the day [the maximum], after it gets converted to numeric values in factual points, it would usually come out to be one *jin* [1.1 pounds] of grain, which would be

Public Administration and the Sent-Down Experience

what I earned for my labor grain ration for that day. So the factual points would produce one *jin* of grain as my labor ration, and if you add that to your assigned basic food ration [of one *jin*], then you have two *jin* of grain altogether. However, in reality, two *jin* of grain would only produce one *jin* and seven *liang* [0.11 pound] of rice after you grind it down, and for me, that would be just enough for one meal. So if you slacked off for even one day and didn't show up for work in the field, then you would not have your labor grain ration and you will have to get by on that one *jin* of basic ration of food assigned to you. But for guys like me, we need at least two *jin* of food to survive, so if I didn't work it would mean that I will have to starve because I won't have enough to eat [without the extra portion earned from the labor ration].

Therefore, the ration system for peasants [individually] is comprised of two parts: the first is one's basic ration, and the second is the labor ration. What is the basic ration? The basic ration has to do with how many people there are and it is calculated by the total amount of food getting averaged out among the total number of people. The labor ration is the ration of food that you earn through your labor at work. The basic rations were given to us, but for children and the elderly, their values were counted much higher and so their basic rations would come out to be much more than ours in actual quantity of food. In other words, the values of their basic rations were higher than the values of our [capable workers'] basic rations because these people do not have the adequate capabilities or the manpower [required for heavy farm work]. To ensure the capable [male peasants] will work in the field every day, there is also the system of labor ration added on, because for us, the numerical value of our basic ration was much lower, and the resulting food from that itself would be absolutely not enough for guys like me. Only when we work every day and get the second portion of the labor ration added in, do we have enough to eat. . . . (I6, 29)

Ding went on to explain how the work points—so necessary for survival—were assigned:

The assessment process of assigning work points for your contribution of the day was done publicly in front of everyone, and in that sense, it was really democratic. This process was generally fair, just, and open. . . .

At the end of the day, the team leader would call out someone's name, like, for so and so, how many points should he get today? Then one of your peers may shout out a number, so he may say, "Let's give him an 8.8." Another would shout that down and say, "No, that's too high because he goofed off and took a break at such and such time, and so he should only get an 8.5." So there is a little discussion or debate among your peers in assessing your work performance and how many work points you deserved to earn for the day. There is a person assigned to take charge of recording and keeping track of everyone's work points and you may also keep a record on your own. (I6, 30)

This system presented significant problems for many sent-downs. Ding noted that the "peasants were . . . honest in that . . . if you worked hard, then they would give you the points you earned" (I6, 30). However, he went on to say, "Some sent-downs were given lower work point values because some of them were really lazy and inept, and even though they did show up for work, they didn't put in the labor or adequate effort required which was easily observable. Another reason that the sent-downs were given lower work points was that they didn't know how to do anything. They were urban kids and grew up in the city; they simply had no experience with any kind of farm work" (I6, 30). "After all that exhaustion" in the field, Yu recalled, "the money that we earned from work points couldn't cover us for anything. The majority of us had to rely on our families in the cities to send us money" (I50, 15). Even worse, the basic ration varied with uncontrollable factors and events. It depended on what remained after taxes, which, with poor harvests due to droughts, floods, pests, and weather, could be little or nothing.

Difficulty might also come in the form of local cadres who inflated the harvest reports upon which the grain and surplus taxes were imposed because they

> wanted to show off their leadership skills and . . . boast about their leadership prowess. So if the village leader next door reported 120 *jin* [of harvest production], then this guy here would report 220 because it looked bad for him in comparison to the next guy and if an administrator could not measure up or stack up on his performance as a leader, then he might lose his job. For them, it was more important to keep their own jobs than to care about the plight of their constituents, so certainly there was bureaucraticism [bureaucrats putting their self-interest above that of the public good] at the lower levels. (Sun I41, 10)

The taxes, of course, had to be paid on the reported harvest, not the actual one, thereby potentially leaving little or nothing for the peasants (I41, 9).

According to Ding, in Guangdong, the peasants' food supply for the entire year was delivered in December. When the basic ration was insufficient or nonexistent, the peasants had to do whatever they could to secure food. For the most part, once the sent-downs reached rural villages, the rustication bureaucracy paid little attention to them. Nevertheless, the overarching Chinese bureaucratic system could contribute to hunger and starvation because one needed certification from his or her commune to beg or travel (I6, 31; Yu I50, 15). In summing up the relationship of the peasants to the government, Ding said, "You know what their [the peasants'] biggest hopes and dreams are? They only hoped that the local officials or current officeholders are not too corrupt and won't take too much from them so that there would be a little food left over to keep themselves fed [and] they would be able to go on living" (I6, 41).

Public Administration and the Sent-Down Experience

Although agricultural conditions varied throughout the country, for many sent-downs in rural villages, rustication meant not only very hard physical labor and exhaustion but also constant hunger. Tian recalled that when she got to her destination, "there was a severe drought that probably happened once in a hundred years. The previous year they had a really good harvest and a lot of grain and other foodstuff, but the moment we got there the food supply shrunk, and there was no more wheat so we had to eat buns made out of yam powder, which gave you constant symptoms of indigestion." She noted that "we often skipped meals because there was never enough food. There were many days when we starved—it was a frequent occurrence" (I44, 11). Wan added, "Anyway, we very often gathered for 'mental feasts' [when we had no food]—we would get together and discuss what it would be like to eat our favorite dishes and describe them down to the tee in every detail about the local favorites that we enjoyed in Beijing" (I45, 11).

The Peasants' Response to the Sent-Downs

Rational implementation of the rustication policy would require administrative effort to make the peasants on the receiving end accepting of the sent-downs and interested in benefiting from the knowledge these urban youth brought to the countryside. As noted earlier, there was limited administrative contact with or attention to the sent-downs once they settled into their village destinations. This suggests that the rustication administrators may not have adequately prepared the peasantry to gain the greatest potential benefit from the sent-downs in their villages. What did the interviewees say about the peasants' response to their presence?

Their experiences differed, but on balance the majority of those interviewees who provided an assessment of their treatment by the peasants felt that they were unwanted and discriminated against, albeit for rational reasons. Duan, Fan, and Lu made the most positive statements about the peasants. Duan said, "They were much nicer to us than the people in the city. The peasants were really good kind-hearted people" (I8, 37). Fan added that "the peasants were much nicer than the folks in the city who were bent on struggling against us and making our lives a living hell. They were much better and nicer people . . . [who] never thought about all that political BS" (I9, 37). Lu agreed: "The peasants were really pretty nice to us. I mean, they even sent someone to cook for us until the very end when all the sent-downs in our village returned to the city so they were really pretty good to us. Additionally, they let us live in the new cave housing, which was far better than the homes of the local peasants" (I30, 9).

A few interviewees suggested that the peasants were grateful to the sent-downs for what they could do for their villages. Lin (a control) was well integrated into peasant life as a returning youth rusticated with his grandfather in a rural village on the outskirts of Beijing. He provided the most detailed appraisal of the overall relationships between the peasants and the sent-downs:

> *Zhiqing* brought a lot to the peasants. For example, in many places, electricity came only after the *zhiqing* went there. They also brought peasants knowledge, culture, and technical expertise such as scientific farming methods or financial acumen like bookkeeping. Also, *zhiqing* were neutral, unlike the peasants who were defined by family ties. Many families had long-term feuds and they wouldn't trust each other to be the bookkeeper. They didn't think members of the other families could be fair. But *zhiqing* were removed from these kinship relationships so they were neutral and the peasants wanted *zhiqing* to do the accounting and other finance-related tasks. In my village, the peasants didn't care one way or the other about the *zhiqing* because the policy by then had been relaxed and the sent-downs were on a two-year rotation from Beijing. So a set of *zhiqing* would come into the village for two years, get reeducated, and they would all return back to the city. Then a new set of *zhiqing* would come and repeat the same process. However, the local bureaucrats and the village cadres really liked *zhiqing* because they were idealistic and enthusiastic. When the village cadres asked the local peasants to work, none of them would really work hard. In the morning, the team leader always had to ring the bell multiple times and the peasants would act like they didn't even hear it and delay showing up, but the *zhiqing* were motivated and eager. They would always show up for work on time and work really hard. So the village administrators welcomed the *zhiqing* because they were easy to organize as a labor force and listened to directions well. In the poor and remote areas, *zhiqing* had a harder time because the locals thought that the sent-downs competed with their food supply, but in other realms, they brought a lot to the peasants, like knowledge and culture, and many sent-downs taught in the local schools. In these remote villages, it was often the case that they didn't have a middle school or even an elementary school. The villagers couldn't afford hiring teachers from outside and they didn't know much themselves so they couldn't educate their children. But when the sent-downs arrived, all they had to do was to provide food and they finally had a force of educated personnel to teach their children. (I28, 5)

Fan also made the point that the arrival of electrification and the sent-downs coincided:

> Any village where the *zhiqing* were sent down had their electricity turned on. . . . Is it because they [local government] didn't have the capabilities earlier although they certainly didn't seem to care all that much about those poor ole peasants in the dark, or is it because the arrival of the sent-downs promoted local development? Who could say? But the fact is that after one year, any village that hosted the sent-downs had their electricity connected and turned on. After another year had passed, just about every

village in that region had their electricity turned on because the neighboring villages that had no electricity now started protesting, clamoring and making trouble, and so soon thereafter, all the villages were powered with electricity. (I9, 36)

Several other interviewees were far less sanguine. Ding and Tian specifically mentioned the sent-downs' impact on the food supply as an overarching cause of peasant discontent with the rustication program. Tian said, "Of course they [the peasants] didn't welcome us. Each village was given about ten sent-downs and that meant there were ten extra mouths to feed, and we took another chunk of the pie, so of course they didn't really want us" (I44, 11). Ding concurred that "when we entered the picture, we made the pie even smaller for each villager" (I6, 24). He also said that as time went on, "for the sent-downs who wanted to leave but could not, they were in a permanent state of restlessness. . . . They were just waiting aimlessly for any opportunity to get back home" and were burdened with feelings of "hopelessness, sadness, despair, and indifference" (I6, 27). "Plagued by hunger," Ding continued, some "started engaging in petty theft such as stealing the peasants' chickens, dogs, anything for food. Their work performance suffered as well and they would malinger at work, putting in only a perfunctory effort at best or the bare minimum to get by" (I6, 27). As a result, "the local peasants disliked the sent-downs even more and their relationship became even more strained and things got really tense where I was [Guangdong]" (I6, 27).

In contrast to Lin, Wan suggested that the peasants eventually gave up on trying to gain anything positive from the sent-downs: "At first, they may intervene and try to manage us, but after a few years, even they stopped trying, because we really could never do what they did, to live like them, to blend in with them among the local peasants and so what else could they do? We were all underweight and small so even if we exerted ourselves and maxed out our physical labor, it still wasn't much in the field so the peasants simply stopped bothering to try to acculturate us into that lifestyle" (I45, 13). Liang, who came from a bad family class, said, "the peasants either avoided us or discriminated against us. When you were working . . . they assigned you the worst, the dirtiest, the most exhausting work whereas the other guys (local peasants) would be given good cushy jobs. However, the peasants were still pretty fair about the work points" (I26, 17). Although experiences clearly differed widely, overall, it is reasonable to conclude that the rustication administrators at the local level might have done more to forge positive, productive relationships between the peasants and the sent-downs.

Military Farms

The sent-down experience on military farms differed substantially from that in rural villages because adequate food, shelter, and reasonable health care were guaranteed. Wu described his military farm as "like a microcosmic society. There were clinics for medical care, schools for the children, little shops and other facilities" (I48, 11; Wang [I46, 13] made the same point). With one exception among my interviewees, those sent down to military farms also received a fixed monthly wage. The work may also have been more varied, with some overhead and service positions available to sent-downs. Some of my interviewees were aware of these differences prior to being sent down. Wang noted that she wanted to go to a military farm in Heilongjiang because there was "a fixed monthly wage, so at least I could survive, whereas for Inner Mongolia and Shanxi, the students would be inserted into production brigades in the countryside and [without a steady income] their basic survival would be in question" (I46, 10).

Military farms were organized bureaucratically and followed strict military discipline. The sent-downs were organized into platoons, companies, battalions, regiments, divisions, and corps. Meng termed the management "very formal and strict. Nothing strayed a little left or right outside the box from the prevailing rules and regulations" (I33, 7). Su thought her newly established military farm in Inner Mongolia was probably managed more strictly than others: "Our military farm was managed exactly like the military because it was an extension of the PLA. . . . All the administrators, even those at the company level were PLA officers or soldiers on active military duty. . . . We were treated exactly like soldiers in the PLA because it was exactly the same management system" (I40, 7).[12]

However, the competence of military farm staff varied, as did their levels of kindness and venality. Wen observed:

> We found out after the establishment of the military farms that those who were dispatched for administrative positions on our military farm were mostly from two kinds of people. Those who were either ineffectual or incompetent and those who had "committed errors and mistakes" in the military and were essentially no longer wanted by the army but they had no place for them elsewhere in the military and so they were sent to our farm. . . .
>
> These military administrators [who committed errors and mistakes] were all of questionable character and we looked down on them because of the way they did things. (I47, 3, 13)

His military farm was probably typical in this regard. According to Zhang, "All the lower-level personnel on the military farms were undesirable rejects from the Red Army, people who had been up to no good, made mistakes, too old in age, from bad family background and including those who were politically persecuted among them" (I 52, 10).

Wang noted that "some administrators were very nice and some were absolutely horrible. This was true in every company" (I46, 13). Coming from a "bad

Public Administration and the Sent-Down Experience 141

class"—a counterrevolutionary son of a bitch—Wen said, "Those who tortured me were the military personnel, particularly . . . those on active duty" (I47, 3).

Among my interviewees, the sent-downs' rustication on military farms varied greatly. Wen had the most difficult experience. He described his experience as "just pure hell and endless suffering" (I47, 4). He considered "the superior officer in charge of us (sent-downs) . . . was completely sadistic and . . . my prime torturer. He took pleasure in seeing me suffer and he was the man behind everything. He was the superior officer of my company and that's why everything had happened to me, the humiliating public struggles against me, the surprise physical attacks from the other guys [his peers and fellow sent-downs]" (I47, 4). He continued,

> I definitely thought about killing myself. Actually, I came back from death because I really put in a good effort to commit suicide. I went into the woods intending to kill myself on this freezing winter day. It was so weird because the snow powder was up to one's knees and somehow there was an old shepherd out there—why would you be grazing sheep when there was nothing but snow? I was wandering about in the woods for a long time, and being alone and all, I really let it out. I bawled my eyes out because I felt so wronged and life was so unfair. After that, I put my neck through the loop on the noose that I hung over a tree branch [but was saved by the old shepherd]. I just felt so hopeless and was in such despair and misery. I never knew what was going to happen to me next. Life was so unpredictably disorienting and I never knew what was coming to me next. Not even the next minute, hour, let alone the next day. I had absolutely no control of my life because other people were completely in charge of me and I never knew when I was going be dragged onto a stage again being publicly humiliated, struggled against in front of the others, or beaten again by my peers. I had to face so much discrimination and hostility and I was treated like a subhuman. The cafeteria would only serve me when everyone else was finished with his/her meals. I slept on a ragged broken mat, which always froze during the night. Kids like us, the "counterrevolutionary sons of bitches" were segregated from the other sent-down youth and we faced extreme discrimination because of our political background and we were given the worst of all worst treatment . . . .
>
> Well, maybe a small incident can serve as an illustration. On the day that the administrators on the farm found out that my father was a "traitor who belonged to the Liu Shaoqi clique," in the middle of that night [at 4 AM] and right in the coldest weeks of winter, I was dragged out of bed. The company instructor told me there was an emergency letter that I had to deliver to the regiment headquarters. My company was twenty-five kilometers [15.5 miles] from the headquarters. Of course, there were horses and other means of transportation in my company but I was not allowed access to any of that. They told me to rush the delivery on foot and that I had to return and report back to the company within 24 hours. The snow was so deep. It was up to one's

chest. You simply could not walk. You had to open up a path with your body and push the snow out as you went. Each time I moved, I had to use my body to push forward through the snow, and remember this had to be fast, because I only had about a day's worth of time for both the delivery and getting back. Somehow I got to the headquarters at 2 PM in the afternoon. I still don't know how I did it. I just pushed through it all so desperately with the last ounce of life in me and somehow I got there. I almost gave in. Think about it—I had to do this without any preparation, yanked out of bed in the middle of the night—and they simply did it for fun. You thought they assigned you an important task, but all it was, all it was—was a blank piece of paper. That was the emergency letter. When I delivered it to the administrators at the headquarters, they opened it up in front of me and I saw it. It was just a blank piece of paper.

. . . . People like me, who were from the five bad categories were quarantined from the other sent-downs. Kids like us lived in a segregated dorm with the worst facilities and we would be led in a row like prisoners and marched to the cafeteria only when the others were done with their meals. . . . We were second-class citizens and we were deprived of any human dignity. . . . It was such inhuman treatment and all your human rights were taken away from you but we were housed and fed. In reality, we were treated like prisoners. (I47, 15)

Meng provided the following overview of his stay on a Heilongjiang military farm in the northeast:

In the mornings, the bugle woke us up, then it was PT [physical training] and we practiced with guns, real guns, during our PT. At night, we take turns to stand guard. The first two to three years, it was strict military management. We were strictly managed under the military system. Later, after Lin Biao's death [in 1971], they took our guns away and the management style gradually relaxed. It was reverting back to the state farm system before and so it became less formalistic and militaristic. However, in the first few years, it was extremely ridged, strict, and disciplined management. Totally like how it was in the military. . . . There was one day off for rest, Sunday, but not during the hectic seasons. During the busy seasons, there was no rest because we had to work every day to pick up harvest, which could not be delayed and we worked fifteen-, sixteen-hour shifts during those seasons if not more. (I33, 7)

Although not treated as prisoners, the sent-downs at Meng's military farm were used as human subjects.

Also, we *zhiqing* just went through so much. At some point in time, we [China] were helping the Vietnamese to fight against the Americans, and so we were used as guinea pigs for military products. Vietnam's got a tropical climate and they got a lot of mosquitoes there so they came up with something like a netted scarf for the soldiers. But

Public Administration and the Sent-Down Experience

they had to do some product testing first to see if it would work and we were the subjects who tested it. We had to put on these scarves over our heads and we were told to go into the forest when the mosquitoes were most active which was usually at dusk. We were told to go in and stay there for thirty minutes and thirty minutes it was, not a single minute less. We were bitten so badly that our whole body was swollen. So this military experiment failed. Then we were given a new cream and had to repeat the same experiment again in the woods, this time to treat the bug bites which also failed. But we were eaten up alive and left with so many mosquito bites everywhere that our whole body ballooned up. (Meng I33, 7).

Su described her experience in Inner Mongolia:

In the morning, we awake to the bugle, and at night, we must take turns to stand guard. It was just like the lifestyle in the military. We got up at 6 AM and then PT, then each class had one person who stayed for domestic logistics such as getting the water bottles filled, et cetera. Then we come back to wash up, brush our teeth and after that we have breakfast. We also studied Mao's *Selected Works* every morning. Then we go to work. Mostly we had to do agricultural work in the field. At noon, we return to have lunch in the cafeteria and then go back to work until late afternoon. We ate dinner at the cafeteria, then studied Mao's *Selected Works* again, and lights off at 10 PM. We had a daily assigned quota of work each day and you had to finish it. Also the agricultural work was seasonal, and so during seeding and harvest season, we had an extended workload and very grueling long hours. We were the oxen, the animals in the field. During the winter season, we were sent out to find firewood in the desert and had to process animal manure. However, the most difficult job was irrigation because we really couldn't control the flow of water which was so rapid and would wash out all the seeding. On those days, no matter how cold it was, whether or not a girl was on her period, you had to jump into the icy water and use your body to block the water source and slow down the irrigation. That's why the women sent-downs had so much gynecological problems. Because even if the girls were on their menstruation, they had to work in the freezing cold water for a very long time just like the men. We were allowed a home visit after two years, but it was very strict. You must return on time, not a day later. (I40, 9)

Song said her schedule on the Heilongjiang military farm was similar, although the "physical work was much more demanding and grueling. During the harvest or hectic seasons, it seemed that we never rested. We worked fifteen hours a day or more" (I39, 10). Li reported a similar but more relaxed and less regimented daily schedule, with construction work requiring an "exorbitant amount of physical labor" ending around 5 PM (I25, 19).

Wang noted that conditions varied substantially from company to company at the military farms in Heilongjiang. She emphasized the work differentiation:

"The princes did machinery work, the princesses did domestic logistics, the prisoners did agricultural and construction work" (I46, 2). She became a "'princess' who worked in the domestic logistics unit" and noted

> that was a really good job because you just had to put in few hours of the day to cook several meals in the cafeteria, but you can goof off the rest of the time in between. Additionally, you can pick the best food for yourself when it comes down to mealtimes. But how much better could the food be? Well, it just means that you could pick out the less burned buns for yourself and give others the more burned ones, but that's about it, really. The best thing about the job is that your workload is not that heavy and you don't have to be toasted and sunburned to death in the field every day starting in the early morning. (I46, 5)

Zhao also complained about the food: "The food was horrible. We always ate what we produced for that season so we would eat squashes every meal, every day for three months" (I53, 6).

Wang was later downgraded to a "prisoner" and transferred to an agricultural job as punishment for overstaying a home visit. She described a typical workday in the fields:

> In the northeast, the sun rises much earlier so often we had to get up at 3 AM in the morning. When you hear them banging the gong, you know it's time to get up. The workload was extremely heavy on the military farm. . . . Unlike the countryside, all the farms' got was land—endless, endless land. In the summer time, we have to get up at 3 AM when it's still dark outside and go to the field for hoeing. Why did we have to get up so early? Because it took us over an hour on foot to walk over to our own company's plot of land that we had to hoe—it was that far. Every company had several thousand meters of land. . . . The only thing that did not fully depend on human labor was when harvesting wheat because there were machines for that. Everything else—hoeing, seeding, growing, picking up and drying food—all depended on human labor. In the northeast, everything had to be done in one season. By winter, there was not much to do [because the ground gets frozen solid] but you couldn't just sit around. They will certainly find something else for you to do. Usually we would have to strip the outer layer of hemp that's been decomposing in the pond so that later it could be made into strings of rope. However, the most tiresome work is hoeing in the field. Every night, you had to sharpen your tools, otherwise you would be too slow during the day and fall behind the others. . . . Usually someone would deliver breakfast to us in the field—there were people who delivered food and water—and we would eat our lunch in the field as well. There was a short break after lunch and then you resume work in the field until it got dark. . . . The happiest times of our lives were when we could stay in our

dorm and strip the outer skin of the hemp which stunk to high heaven but it was not too bad physically, and we could just sit around and chat while we worked. (I46, 15)

What can be concluded about rustication on the military farms? Experiences varied substantially with the character of the administrators and the nature of the work to which one was assigned. The food may have been unappetizing and insufficient, but unlike the sent-downs in the rural villages, those on military farms did not suffer from constant or severe hunger. As workers, they also earned a fixed wage. In most cases, they also had better access to clinics and health care. However, life was regimented along military lines and sent-downs to rural villages generally had more freedom. Zhang, who had a chance to review some of the historical records regarding incidents that occurred on military farms, concluded that "the military farms' control of people including its utter disrespect to human rights was much worse than the countryside. It was like concentration camps. It was human-subject prison. It was hell on earth" (I52, 9). As discussed later in this chapter, that conclusion may require qualification based on gender and social class.

Inner Mongolian Grasslands

Only four of my interviewees were rusticated on the pastoral lands of Inner Mongolia. Overall, this group had an easier and more enjoyable time than those who went to rural villages and military farms. A main difference was that they were warmly welcomed by the ethnic Mongolians, they were subject to generous hospitality, they ate well, and they had sufficient supplies of clothing and other necessities. Additionally, for some, the work was herding and generally enjoyable.

Rustication on the Inner Mongolian grasslands began with the voluntary departure of Yang and nine others from Beijing. Yang recounts:

October 9 [1967] was one of the most memorable days of my life. The twists and turns of life began on its winding road, and for me, it started in Tiananmen Square before the Golden Water Bridge. That morning, the ten of us went to Tiananmen Square where we were greeted by thousands of well-wishers, classmates, parents, and friends all gathered for a warm send-off ceremony in our honor organized by the Beijing Municipal Labor Bureau. We stood before the Golden Water Bridge in front of the portrait of Chairman Mao at the gate of the Tiananmen Square, and swore our oaths and gave our pledges. As I made my pledge, I was filled with a sense of mission and I realized that though our mission was glorious, we had to live up to the heavy responsibilities and duties of our oath and we took it so seriously that we felt like the soldiers before going onto a battlefield. Two days later, news stories about our departure were splashed across the front page of the *People's Daily*; they even devoted a whole editorial about us. Soon, various other media also picked up the story and reported on us, such as the *Beijing Daily* and China National Radio. Later, some reporters came all the way to Inner Mongolia and visited us in our yurts for more interviews.

No one would have thought that what these ten high school students did on October 9, 1967—the regular urban kids like us who volunteered to leave Beijing and settle in the West Inner Mongolia grasslands—would jumpstart the policy that would eventually send tens of thousands of urban youth from various cities to the countryside villages and the pastoral grasslands. The number of sent-downs later exceeded over seventeen million, which was equivalent to the total population of a mid-sized European nation. When the ten of us made this life-changing decision for ourselves, it was not possible for us to think about all the impact and social consequences that might come from our action. At the time, we never had any idea that our mission would inspire Chairman Mao to formulate and implement the Up to the Mountains and Down to the Countryside policy nationwide. (I49, 4)

Not surprisingly, this interviewee thrived during rustication. In 1970 she was transferred to a county Revolution Committee office and, after four months, became a cadre on the Inner Mongolia Autonomous Region's Party Committee. She described her decision to leave the grasslands for an administrative position: "I already became a model *zhiqing* who had made a significant contribution in both my work and political performance. But I really didn't want to leave because I came to reform myself through labor and by placing myself in the countryside. I thought about all those other sent-downs who volunteered to come because of me (whom I persuaded) and I didn't want to leave them there and go elsewhere myself. However, I was pressured by the administrators at the top" (I49, 6–7).

Whether due to or despite her celebrity status, Yang shared a typical sent-down's experience on the grasslands during her first three years in Inner Mongolia.

If you have not been to the pastoral lands in Inner Mongolia, you cannot even imagine the lifestyle.... It was very hard both in everyday life and with your physical work, but not because we didn't have enough to eat or had nothing to wear against the cold, or even that it was so physically exhausting and we couldn't handle it. It wasn't that at all. We ate very well. We drank milk and ate a lot of meat so that was not it. Actually, we ate better than we did in the city [Beijing], but then again we only ate those things. There were no vegetables. No stir-fried dishes like in the city that we were used to. It was completely a different kind of culture and lifestyle. When we worked as shepherds and herded sheep, it was really hard not physically but the climate was so harsh and it was very cold and I felt very lonely because the job only needed one person. Also I didn't speak or understand the local dialect so I couldn't communicate with the locals.... So it was really a different kind of hardship mentally and physically. (I49, 7)

Public Administration and the Sent-Down Experience 147

Sun was in the same group of sent-downs as Yang. As captured by his statement quoted in an epigraph to this chapter, he thoroughly enjoyed his rustication. He recalled that

> the local pastoralists were very warm to us and completely welcomed us as their guests and they really took very good care of us all. They gave us milk tea and meat, and food was never a problem because we always had plenty of everything. We joined the brigade to share their physical work and it was just herding animals. In less than ten days, the work was done because by the time we arrived we had already missed the harvest season. The brigade cadres told us that there was not much else for us to do and why don't we just hang out for the winter. . . . They also brought in the meat supply and other foodstuff and told us that we were all set for the entire winter season and we should just sit it out and kind of hang out and stay in for the winter. They didn't give us any more work because they were worried that we couldn't take it working outside under the harsh climate. The cadres said to us, the weather is too harsh right now and the snowfall is too great, it would just be too hard for you kids to work under this kind of weather but I went to see the leadership and persuaded them and said that anything the local pastoralists could do, we could do it as well. Finally, they relented and agreed that the male sent-downs could participate in lower-level production activities and work at the breeding stations [which required less physical endurance], but the local cadres would not let the women [sent-downs] breed animals, and it was actually very interesting work. (I41, 20)

He also worked as a shepherd and was struck by the vastness and low population density of the commune, which was about eight hundred square miles. It was organized into five production brigades of about two hundred people each. The headquarters had roughly five hundred people who provided a variety of services (I41, 24–25). Sun enjoyed his rustication partly because he was housed with locals who "took me in as family and treated me like family" (I41, 22).

Lan concurred that "the local Mongolian people were so hospitable that they really tried to take care of the sent-downs. In fact, at night they wouldn't leave until they saw us in our beds and kind of tucked us in before leaving [our yurts]" (I24, 19). He also enjoyed the work. "Every day you just enjoyed your own time out there and soaked up the sun under the sky. It was not the heavy physical work that was so typical of the sent-downs elsewhere, like those who were sent to agricultural sectors or military construction corps where the workload took a heavy toll on them. In contrast, our jobs were really pretty chill and kind of easy" (I24, 24).

Gan was rusticated in a village in the Inner Mongolian countryside rather than on the grasslands. Her commune "was organized into progressively larger units: production teams, production brigades, and the commune itself." The production brigades were divided into two production teams with three leaders each, one of whom was for political education (I12, 13). Like my other interviewees who went to Inner Mongolia, she had a good experience because after one year of farm work she became a "barefoot doctor" (backpack medic), which she said "gave me so much satisfaction because I was able to help people and I was good at it" (I12, 4). She noted that, aside from her militia battalion commander who thought she was unfit to be a medic due to her bad family background, the other administrators and the peasants treated her well. Additionally, the sent-downs in her location were guaranteed 550 *jin* [618 pounds] of food per person. The first year it was paid for by the government, and afterward by the sent-downs themselves. Hunger was not a problem, and it turned out that they could not consume that much so they "sold what we couldn't eat at a much higher price than what we paid for it. We also got smart the second year because, by selling the coarse grain, we were able to buy finer food like flour and rice. We [the sent-down girls] would pool our remaining food together and sell it off. We also raised pigs and we took one pig to the market at the commune headquarters and sold it for 130 yuan!" (I12, 13). Lan said "my life actually improved," in part because the local administrators "treated us very well; very personal and humanized treatment for the sent-downs" (I24, 21).

Location, Location, Location

It is evident that among my interviewees location made a great deal of difference.[13] As Lan summed it up, "Throughout the Up to the Mountains and Down to the Countryside movement, of course, each region and locality was different. For example, in Yunnan, a lot of things happened [alluding to sexual assaults on female sent-downs]; in Shanxi and Shaanxi, the sent-downs were starving and didn't have much to eat. But for those who were sent down to the pastoral grasslands, we were extremely fortunate" (I24, 20). There was also considerable variation in the experiences both among and between those who were rusticated in rural villages and military farms. Overall, those in the countryside had more freedom but less food security than those on the military farms. One major difference mentioned by my interviewees is that at least some of those in rural villages, such as Fan, Wan, and Yu, could "return to the city to visit our family every winter" when the planting, growing, and harvesting seasons were over (Yu I50, 15). As a whole, those on military farms probably had better living conditions overall but less freedom. My interviewees who rusticated in Inner Mongolia report the best experiences.

It is impossible to know how representative these experiences were. Of those interviewees who were rusticated in the countryside, Ding, Duan, Gan, Mei Fang (now an editor for a television station), Gan, Han, Yishan Huang (a director

Public Administration and the Sent-Down Experience 149

in a steel technology company), Liang, Liu, Mo, Yuxin Peng (a director of a real estate company), Tan, Tang, Tian, Wan, and Zhang said their experiences were representative of sent-downs generally.[14] Wen and Yu asserted that their experiences were representative of those from bad and good class backgrounds, respectively. Several interviewees believed that they were highly representative of sent-downs generally (Ding, Gan, Wanxin Jin [a former bureaucrat], Lu, and Yuan). Interestingly, these interviewees remained at their sent-down destinations for eight or more years, which is longer than most of my other interviewees. Of those who were sent down to military farms, Xiaolin Gao, a highly talented writer; Chengfei Gu, a mid-level CCP bureaucrat; Haoyu Guan, a deputy director of a research institute; Yong Hao, a general director of an investment banking firm; Hui Hu, a retired high school teacher; Jianhua Jiang, a television program producer; Jin; Zhi Kong, head of a financial investment firm; Li; Liangyu Liao, a radio news host; Cheng Luo, a retired vocational school teacher; Linfen Ma, a retired bus ticket seller; Meng; Ling Ren, a retired bookkeeper; Lei Shen, a newspaper proofreader; Chaowei Shi, an actor; Song; Wang; Wu; and Zhao stated that their experiences were representative. Among those sent down to Inner Mongolia, Lan, Sun, and Zhang considered their experience to be representative, whereas Yang thought her experience was representative of "that one-third of the total number of sent-downs" who had high revolutionary consciousness and "thought just like I did" (in wanting to dedicate their service to the nation by going to the countryside) (I49, 6). Su claimed that she was representative of those sent down to pure military farms who were given a very small monthly allowance (5 yuan) rather than a fixed monthly wage (35 yuan) (I40, 7). Several interviewees who said they were representative also thought that they might have fared better than others. These include Li, Meng, Wang, Wen, Wu, Yu, and Zhao. Li declared, "I think that among all the sent-downs, I was very lucky" (I25, 25). Tan and Tang said they were

> especially representative of the last cohort of sent-downs who were inserted into production brigades for a little while, so we had some experience of it but didn't experience too much hardship. By the time we were sent down, the policy had relaxed so much. We were just sent to the rural areas on the outskirt of the city [an hour outside Beijing by bicycle] and there were already signs that the times were changing. A year after we were sent down, universities reopened and the national exam resumed. We were allowed to take it and were able to pass it because the Cultural Revolution was less disruptive to our education. . . . For the sent-down generation, our cohort was extremely fortunate! (Tan I42, 16)

Tang added, "The most determinant factor in improving one's life chances [and increasing one's upward social mobility after the Cultural Revolution] was getting a university education. The earlier sent-downs who couldn't get higher education were never able to change the course of their destiny later in life," which is why he agreed that his cohort was fortunate (I43, 18; Fang [I10, 15] agreed with Tan and Tang). Based on these responses, it is fair to conclude that the experiences of my interviewees with respect to location were representative of at least a substantial proportion of those sent-downs who returned to the cities.

To the extent that the interviewees' experiences are representative, it can be concluded that bureaucracy and public administrators played different roles depending on the location of the receiving end. Rustication bureaucrats were not prominent in the rural villages, apparently considering their job complete once the sent-downs reached their destinations and settled in. However, the bureaucracy associated with China's agricultural taxation systems was highly salient to the nutritional and economic welfare of the sent-downs in rural villages. The military and state farms were clearly organized bureaucratically, staffed by either military personnel or a mix of military and civilian administrators. Here, though, the agricultural tax system was irrelevant. Despite what may have been a substantial number of commune headquarters personnel and administrative units, assignment to the grasslands or rural villages in Inner Mongolia probably provided sent-downs with the most day-to-day freedom and the fewest bureaucratic constraints. It may also have been the case that the local culture, which was very welcoming, affected the administrative culture in Inner Mongolia, making it more responsive to the sent-downs' concerns than was typical elsewhere.

Returning to the Cities

As noted earlier, several of my interviewees believe that the current use of *guanxi* started or escalated substantially in association with the sent-downs' return to the cities. This strongly suggests that the rustication bureaucracy and its personnel were central to the return process. According to my interviewees, this was indeed the case. However, bureaucratic discretion was exercised within the broad parameters of the return policy, and the policy itself underwent significant changes over time. Of my interviewees, Ding offered the most general and comprehensive description of the administrative organization of the return process.

> The procedures for returning were very simple. Once the Knowledgeable Youth Resettlement Office approved your return, then the office takes care of all your required paperwork.... Let's say you were set to return to the city—this office already approved your eligibility for returning—you will be given a notification form certifying your returning status. You then take this form with you to change your *hukou*. When one came to the countryside as a sent-down and was inserted to a production brigade, the brigade office holds your *hukou* because you had become a rural resident of their

village. Now that you are eligible for returning to the city, you take that notice of eligibility from the Knowledgeable Youth Resettlement Office earlier and go to the brigade office and ask to be approved for the certification of release and they will have all the information, your files and records, your *hukou*, et cetera. You then take that approved certification of release to the public security office of the town where you are returning and reinstate your *hukou* as a legal urban resident of that town or city. . . .

As for foodstuff, you will have to visit the Grain and Foodstuff Management Bureau. In the countryside the peasants get all their food ration supply in December of each year [in Guangdong] and now that you are returning to the city, you must return your left-over food supply back to the Grain and Foodstuff Management Bureau, essentially you are returning your food supply back to the state. . . .[15] All these agencies were well coordinated and the administrative process was meticulous, detailed, and very much regulated according to the established regulations and procedures. You can't skip a single step. . . . When it comes to the management of people, don't you worry, the Chinese bureaucracy's really got it down pat and it's an expert in handling and processing multiple cases just like you. Of course, this returning process all depended on the official approval of your return. (I6, 37–38)

It was at the approval stage that bureaucratic discretion became most pronounced. Some criteria were clear, such as sickness and a prohibition against married sent-downs leaving the countryside, but eligibility for returning to the cities involved an administrator's assessment of a sent-down's performance, years of rustication, and political background. It also depended on other factors, such as the quota of available placements in a workplace or university. Ding emphasized the amount of administrative discretion involved. Based on reported demand for workers from work units, the Department of Labor notified the county-level Knowledgeable Youth Resettlement Office of available slots for sent-downs. That office then scheduled interviews with eligible sent-downs and "basically would say something like, 'So and so, you've been here for a while now and you've received enough reeducation. You are now pretty well reformed so why don't you go to such and such place and do this or that job there'" (Ding I6, 38). Song confirmed that this was the administrative process.

A different process was used when the sent-down's return to a city was based on illness. First the street offices would have to determine whether the illness matched fixed criteria for returning. This potentially involved considerable discretion, as Li explained:

When a sent-down comes to the street office with a documented form of ailment from a doctor, the first step is to identify and differentiate which illness is in fact listed under the returning criteria because some sicknesses were simply not included as it was not possible to specify every form of illness. Or perhaps the wording of the illness description is not an exact match under the classified categories [such as Zhao's lost use of four fingers, mentioned earlier]. There was definitely some flexibility, which required administrative or bureaucratic discretion. Consequently, many people visited the street offices first trying to establish connections or looking for *guanxi* to "get things flowing" so that the bureaucratic discretion would later fall in their favor, should ambiguity arise in their case. Only when the street office gives a green light and gave it a go can you step up the organizational chain and progressively petition your case for returning. The street office was the determinant first step for the return process, because only when the street office [in the specific urban neighborhood where you will reside] grants its approval and stamps your application will the administrative organization at your sent-down location even consider giving you permission to leave. Only after you get through that first tier in the city are you eligible to move up incrementally in the administrative bureaucracy and its chain of offices and begin the process on the other end at your sent-down location. (I25, 11)

Similarly, if the reason for returning to the city were "family difficulties," such as aging parents in need of care, which Chinese culture traditionally considered a child's filial duty, the parents' workplace was a crucial gatekeeper. It would have to send a certified document to the sent-down's local administrative organization, which had discretion whether to approve the sent-down's return. If the approval were granted, the paperwork would go to the street office in charge of the sent-down's original neighborhood residence. Here, too, the street office had considerable discretion in whether to support the sent-down's return (Li I25, 12). Additional criteria for eligibility for return included being a widow or widower, divorced, or unmarried and reaching an age at which it would be difficult socially to find a spouse (as in the case of Wu [I48, 12]). In order to qualify, some sent-downs divorced, with or without the intention of remarrying their spouse after returning to a city (e.g., Gan, Lu, Wang).

Bureaucratic discretion invites a variety of patterns of street-level administrative behavior (Lipsky 1980; Maynard-Moody and Musheno 2003). Favorable treatment based on *guanxi*, *protekzia*, and bribery and other forms of corruption is only one such potential outcome of broad street-level discretion. "Creaming," discrimination, triage, and too strict or too lax enforcement are additional patterns that are found in street-level administration. In the context of China during the Cultural Revolution, at least two additional patterns of differential treatment were noteworthy—those based on gender and family class.

Street-Level Administrative Behavior, Gender, and Family Class

It is well known that female sent-downs faced particular difficulties and hardships. Sexual abuse of females by the authorities responsible for their welfare

Public Administration and the Sent-Down Experience 153

was common. Comprehensive statistics do not exist. In the chaos of the Cultural Revolution, this historical record was "bruised" (as it is said in Chinese), and individuals were, and remain, reluctant to report what happened to them and their families. However, partial statistics show that in Liaoning Province alone, 3,400 rapes of sent-down females were recorded between 1968 and 1973. In Sichuan Province the number was put at 3,296 (Nanchu 2001, 113). These statistics are far from complete. Moreover, data on the number of rapists involved are also incomplete because many were not charged, prosecuted, or punished (Liu 2009, 192–94). Overall, my interviewees confirmed the maltreatment of female sent-downs, including sexual violence. For instance, Zhang said "there were . . . a lot of girls who had to trade sexual favors to return to the city but it was all because of the historical and social conditions at the time. . . . It was the only way out when there were no other ways out. . . . For female *zhiqing*, their circumstances always made them vulnerable and submissive. Cases like that were simply too many to count" (I52, 5). Collectively, the interviewees offered a more complete and subtle description of the special circumstances faced by sent-down women.[16] Again, the sent-down's location made a substantial difference. Sexual predation and violence were most pronounced on military farms whereas in the countryside women faced a variety of pressures to provide sexual favors and to marry locally.

Military Farms

Officially, the treatment of male and female sent-downs on military farms was equal. Meng (a male) stated flatly that the difference between young men and women was "negligible on the military farms" (I33, 8). As noted earlier, Su (a female) indicated that equal treatment was not ideal for women as many developed gynecological problems due to having to do certain kinds of work while menstruating. Li (a female) concurred that "basically they [males and females] were treated the same. They did exactly the same work, same amount, and were paid the same wages" and consequently "countless female sent-downs reported that they had major gynecological problems because they had to engage in extreme physical labor [often in severe whether] when they were physiologically unfit to do that kind of work," often involving immersion in freezing water (I25, 23). Wu indicated that in his division on the Heilongjiang military farm, women "were not given any special treatment" except that "if the tasks required a very high degree of physical strength then these tasks would not be assigned to women," presumably because they were less effective than males in performing them or simply could not do the work (I48, 10).

Equality at work did not protect female sent-downs from sexual violence and predation. Wen (a male) said, "Personally, I knew at least over ten cases where the sent-down girls were assaulted by the military personnel on active duty. Some girls did it willingly. But to be honest, it was probably their only way out and the only way they could have survived under the circumstances. However, in some cases, the girls were forced to give in" (I47, 13). Min Deng, a woman who was sent to a factory and is now a bookkeeper, explained how traumatic sexual violence could be, not only for the physical violation but also for the social stigma:

> My cousin, my aunt's daughter, was a sent-down from Shanghai to a Xinjiang military farm. She was a very beautiful and delicate girl. After being on the farm for a while, she really missed home and went to see her military supervisor hoping to receive a home visit. During this meeting, she was raped by the military administrator on the farm. She was so distraught and traumatized by the sexual assault that she went mad. She could not let go of what happened to her and later committed suicide by drowning herself in a lake. Because of the political climate at the time, there were no places [for her and her family] to appeal for justice against a military personnel. Her family had to endure all that pain and mourn her passing in silence. In fact, we didn't even know what happened to her until years and years later, long after the Cultural Revolution had ended and many years after that. My aunt never mentioned a word to us because at that time (and even now in many places), a woman being raped is considered extremely shameful both for herself and her family. If it were known, it would be very hard, if not impossible for the girl to ever get married because no man wanted "damaged goods" as a woman's chastity was extremely important and especially valued traditionally in the Chinese culture. Therefore, being the victim of a sexual assault would bring extreme embarrassment to the family and would permanently stain her reputation. By seeking justice and having her grievance addressed, everything would be aired out, all the dirty laundry, every detail of the event would be recorded in her personal files and party dossier which would follow her for the rest of her life—when she applies for a new job, when she applies for a promotion, when she applies for admission to school—no matter where she goes, her records would follow her, and her past would always catch up with her as a topic of gossip. Under that kind of political and social climate, the victim and her family would rather suffer in silence than be humiliated again publicly by identifying the rapist and petition for justice. Unfortunately, it led to her death in this case, and that was it [no repercussion for the perpetrator]. The end for a sweet beautiful young girl who never survived such a brutal world. (I5, 16).[17]

Recourse for the victims of sexual predation, including rape, was generally limited. Wang (a female) and Wu noted that military personnel at Heilongjiang were executed for raping female sent-downs (I46, 15; I48, 10). However, despite some well-publicized executions, many perpetrators—probably the overwhelming number—escaped punishment or sanctions. In the case mentioned earlier by Wang, "It wasn't until after this regiment commander raped the niece of a high official in the State Council" that he faced punishment and was executed even though "he had raped a number of girls before [who] . . . were too afraid to do

Public Administration and the Sent-Down Experience 155

anything and no one said a word" (I46, 15). Wu agreed that "It was just impossible for women to seek legal recourse" against rapists (I48, 10).

Short of actual sexual violence, predation was a serious problem for female sent-downs. Speaking of the same regiment commander who was executed, Wang explained, "Even in our battalion, there were girls who, well, in today's terms, perhaps you may not call it rape but consented fornication" (I46, 15). She attributed this to "their fragile psychological state where they felt a total sense of hopelessness":

> Once these hopes [of returning to their home cities] were dashed, they were completely defeated mentally and they no longer had the strength to carry on. When all your hopes had died and all possibilities were over with, what difference does anything else make? A woman's chastity was extremely important—if that's taken away from her, it's like taking half of her life away. Therefore, if a woman knew she would eventually be able to go back home someday, she would be able to get married, start a family and have a new life back in the city, she'd rather die or get killed instead being raped. That's what I mean by the hope factor—if those girls had any hope of returning, any sense of the future, they would fight back and they would never submit themselves to those local administrators. They would rather work in the field every day year after year; they would take the political persecution, public struggles or what have you even if the regiment commander took revenge on her and made her life a living hell, but even then if she knew there were any chances in her future [to return home], she would never consent to their sexual advances. (I46, 16)

Lan reported that "the military rep of the county level Song and Dance Ensemble was a real lech . . . I was really repulsed by the guy. Anyway, this guy did a lot of that kind of stuff [trading favorable treatment for sex] with the female sent-downs. In these cases, sometimes, the women were beneficiaries of the situation and other times, victims. For the former, the women benefited in getting promotion to a higher personnel grade level, getting into a university, but sometimes it was purely forced upon the women" (I24, 25–26).

Pressure to trade sexual favors for favorable treatment with regard to returning to the cities was mentioned by Li, who said, "Yes, those kinds of incidents definitely happened where women used various other means (sexual favors) to gain favorable treatment and consequently returned to the city. Because at that time, one's destiny was singularly dependent upon a specific administrator in charge [at the sent-down location] and his bureaucratic discretion." Consequently, "Your whole life rested in his administrative palm" (I25, 13).

Fan (a male) indicated the same was true with regard to gaining placement in a university: "On military farms, the military political commissars seduced young girls into trading sexual favors because they took advantage of how these girls desired more than anything to go to school, to get into a university. Things like that happened so frequently, specifically because these street-level administrators had all the power in their administrative palm, and they had the sole discretion on the actual implementation of who will be sent to a university for higher education" (I9, 14).

Zhao (a male) added that sexual predation was also common in the context of approval for a visit home: "The military guys [administrators] on the farm were truly vile. When girls [sent-downs] asked for home visits, these men would not grant it unless the girls slept with them. Those things [sexual predation or assault] definitely happened, and it was very hard for a woman to petition her grievance against her superior because it [a woman losing her chastity] was such a social taboo and the process will bring shame and extreme embarrassment both for the women themselves and their families" (I53, 5–6; Gan [I12, 8] concurred). Zhao indicated that this kind of predation pressured the female sent-downs to "immediately find themselves a boyfriend. If a girl doesn't have a boyfriend, if others knew that she didn't have a man, it was much more likely that she would be harassed and assaulted [sexually]. The presence of a boyfriend would protect her. If a girl doesn't have a man then she is definitely in danger. She'll never know where or when a pervert will strike out and take her by force" (I53, 6).

That was the reported situation in Yunnan, which became "notorious for their high incidents of sexual persecution of women" (Wang I46, 20). In Heilongjiang, by contrast, Song observed that romance was "the biggest taboo" because the "social mores were so leftist, everyone thought they had to dedicate themselves fully to the revolutionary cause and romantic relationships interfered with this total devotion of the self" (I39, 10). However, she drew a distinction between sex and romance in indicating that "it was a common occurrence that women would sleep their way back to Beijing. . . . Some women definitely volunteered; others were perhaps pressured or forced into it. There were many reasons and various circumstances as to why or how this happened" (I39, 14). Apparently "sleeping one's way" back to a city was not as common in Yunnan, where sent-downs were returned to the cities in large batches and administratively processed as groups, which "probably prevented an individual sent-down being singled out and isolated by administrators (for harassment), and therefore having to resort to other means to get back to the city" (Li I25, 29).

Rural Villages

The experiences of my interviewees who were sent down to the countryside diverge with regard to differential treatment based on gender and subjection to sexual violence and predation. This is probably due to being in different locations, communes, or brigades. There is general agreement that the peasants posed no

Public Administration and the Sent-Down Experience 157

sexual threat to female sent-downs. For instance, Ding (a male) observed that "no female sent-down was ever bullied or harassed (sexually) in our region [Guangdong]. The peasants were generally simple-natured and they wouldn't dare to impose themselves so brazenly. Incidents like that usually happened on military farms" (I6, 36). He continued to explain that the peasants' attitudes had a spillover effect that probably limited predation by administrators as well: "The traditional rural customs made that a total impossibility" (I6, 39–40). Duan (a male) noted that "as far as I know, there were no male peasants who dared to touch the female sent-downs" (I8, 45). Tan (a female) agreed with this characterization of the local peasants (I42, 16). Tian and Wan (both female) agreed that "no girl was ever bullied (sexually) in any way in our sent-down location [Shanxi]," as did Yu (a male), who was sent down to Shaanxi (I44, 12; I45, 12, concurring; I50, 15). Gan indicated that she "didn't know any girl who tried to trade sexual favors" for favorable treatment (I12, 18). However, Liang (a male) claimed that "there were many female sent-downs who were raped by the brigade-level party secretary" in rural Heilongjiang even though "rape of a sent-down was treated as a heinous crime, so the government really made an example of those offenders" (I26, 21). He also said he "heard of many such cases" of women trading sexual favors for the opportunity to return to the cities (I26, 21).

Apparently the main differences between male and female sent-downs in the countryside were that (1) women earned fewer work points because they were less adept at hard physical labor or might be given easier jobs that were worth fewer work points (Duan I8, 35; Liang I26, 18; Lin I28, 6; Tang I43, 16); and (2) they faced greater pressure to marry local peasants. Regarding marriage, Yu explained:

> For girls who married the locals, it was mostly because of practicality based on economic survival because they simply could not handle the physical work. Also, these girls were often older in age than the other sent-downs. In the countryside, the custom was that once a girl got married, she would no longer work in the field. Instead, the husband would do all the farm work year round and support the woman who stays at home. That's the rural custom. Under those circumstances, some girls, after one or two years, would look into local men for potential husbands because there was just no way out for these girls. Like this [sickly] girl that I knew, she was physically unable to do any of the farm work that required to even sustain her basic survival. Similarly, those girls were probably not thinking about their future. They could not even resolve the immediate threats to their existence, and under those circumstances, marriage to local men became an attractive option because it was probably their only way out. (I50, 17)

There were additional incentives to marry for female sent-downs from bad family classes, as Ding explained:

In our sent-down village, it was easy for girls from bad family backgrounds to get married, and they usually married those poor peasants who were rather unpleasant looking. But if a guy from a bad family background wanted a wife, it would be harder than walking atop the sky, because no woman, however poor, uneducated, or hideous, would even consider marrying someone from a bad family background. Everyone was afraid of being associated with that kind of political liability or falling into the treatment of those in that category. As for the girls, they could not be picky. You see, women from bad family backgrounds simply had no option to be selective. They merely wanted to marry someone who was politically reliable as a way of securing their immediate survival. There was no romantic love—just a practical way to survive. For example, a gorgeous sent-down girl may marry a poor peasant, no matter how ancient or repulsive-looking he was, and perhaps he was even disabled with a limp or blinded in one eye, but even so a sent-down girl from a bad family would marry this guy. Because once she married him, she would be counted as family of the poor peasant, and she is now a reformed person who embraced the total "integration with the workers, peasants, and soldiers" and she would no longer be struggled or discriminated against by others. Once she gets married, she now has good "political composition" and so would her children on their birth certificates. Consequently, just for her offspring, there would be plenty of motivation for her to marry this old, ugly, poor peasant with a limp, let alone the fact she won't have to work in the field again. However, for the sent-down guys from bad family backgrounds, no matter how educated, how good-looking or sophisticated he might be, no girl would dare to marry him because of the association that she would bring to herself, her family, and her future offspring. (I6, 10–11)[18]

Zhang (a male) made a similar point:

The biggest difference between male and female *zhiqing* is that women married the locals where they were sent down much more often than the men because they could not adjust to the intense physical labor required on the farmlands. . . . Usually girls who married the locals came from bad family backgrounds because they didn't have many options otherwise, but for men it was different. If a guy came from a bad family, he would always remain a bachelor because no girl would want to marry him. It was actually pretty brutal stuff. Like where I was sent down, those boys from bad family backgrounds were actually quite impressive; every one of them was polite and good-looking, but no girl would even look their way. If a son of a bitch married a local farm girl, then it will show that he had reformed his bourgeois thoughts through physical labor and integration. But for female *zhiqing*, it was different. When they marry local men, their (political) chastity returns like shuffling a deck of cards. They start from a brand new hand, and they are now washed clean. Consequently, all these factors contributed to the higher incidents of female *zhiqing* marrying locally at their sent-down location. (I52, 4–5)

Public Administration and the Sent-Down Experience 159

Ding was an exception to this generalization because the woman he married had lost her virginity and, consequently, had very few, if any, other prospects:

> If I were not a "son of a bitch," there is no way in hell I would have married my ex-wife. My ex-wife is from a poor peasant family background, and, consequently, I in fact "hypergamied" her. I felt absolutely no romantic love for her whatsoever. However, I was so exhausted by everything I had to face. I was assigned the dirtiest, most disgusting jobs—jobs with the heaviest load and other unthinkable tasks such as burying the dead. I was young and I just wanted a home. However, the moment I married her, the social treatment for me changed drastically overnight because it was proof that I succeeded in my thought reform! Almost immediately, I was reassigned as a teacher at the local schools. Because teachers would not work in the field . . . [but] these jobs would only be open to those from good/red family backgrounds. (I6, 11)

Fan (a male) indicated that "those girls who married local men almost all came from a KMT family background[19] . . . [and] probably felt that they would never have a chance (to return to the city) and had no future in life" (I9, 39). For instance, Lu married out of desperation: "All my hopes and dreams were crushed, and I felt that the only possibility for me was to settle in this village for the rest of my life and so I found someone in the village. . . . I found comfort in the company of a local man and we got married." However, "after about two years, [Lu and her husband] separated and got divorced" because her family was adamantly opposed to the marriage and refused to accept her peasant husband (I30, 11). It is impossible to say how prevalent such marriages were, but female sent-downs clearly had greater incentives to marry locals than did the males.

Conclusion: The Rustication Administration and the Cultural Revolution

As explained in chapter 1, this study was prompted in part by Susan Shirk's probing question regarding how the rustication policy could have been implemented on such a broad scale with so few supportive constituencies. Based on my interviewees' responses and stories, I am now able to provide an answer. The rustication administration, coupled with several components of the larger Chinese bureaucracy, simply left urban youth in the appropriate age category no viable alternative. The sent-downs were caught in a bureaucratic pincer. Vertically, the pressure to participate in the rustication movement reached from the national Knowledgeable Youth Resettlement Office down through equivalent offices to the county and commune levels for rural villages and through the PLA for military farms. Horizontally, the street offices, schools, and local public security offices (police stations) augmented this rustication bureaucracy. Through their neighborhood units, the street offices were able to eavesdrop on apartments, keep a watchful eye on individuals, and intrude upon their lives. Moreover, rustication bureaucrats and street office personnel were highly motivated and efficient in their efforts to reach all eligible youth and move them quickly to their rustication destinations. The transportation bureaus also participated by arranging special trains and train cars, as did school and military personnel by escorting the sent-downs along their journeys.

Bureaucratic control was aided by widespread willingness by the urban youth to comply with the policy. Compliance was generated by the revolutionary fervor and adulation of Mao at the time, as well as by the administrative process of sending down the urban youth in groups composed of school classes and other cohorts so that the sent-downs went with their classmates, friends, and acquaintances. In retrospect, sending urban youth together in this fashion was propitious because it tapped into the desires of some teenagers to get away from their parents and to be with their friends on an anticipated great adventure. The low level of information urban youth and their families had about the actual conditions in the rural villages and on the military farms also fostered compliance. Parents who outwardly voiced their opposition the Up to the Mountains and Down to the Countryside campaign could be labeled "counterrevolutionaries" by the street office personnel and face untold hardship. Throughout much of the rustication period, many families were already in disarray due to actions by the Red Guards, the toppling of parents from their administrative posts, the reeducation of cadres, and struggle sessions against parents, which at least for some urban youths enhanced the attractiveness of going to the countryside and military farms.[20] Potential opposition to the send-down policy from military personnel may have been defused by their ability to use *guanxi* to get their children into the PLA directly or after a short period of rustication.

In sum, as my interviewees reported, some urban youth were eager to go, others ambivalent or reluctant, and some opposed. However, for the overwhelming majority of sent-downs and their parents, there was no way out. Except for those who joined the military, those who were permitted to remain in the cities because their rustication would cause severe hardship for their parents, or those who were sent to factories to receive reeducation from workers, very few eligible youth avoided rustication.

The public administrative performance of the rustication bureaucracies and administrators presents many ironies. First, as this chapter explains in detail, rustication, which can be viewed as the capstone of the Cultural Revolution, depended very heavily on the form of organization—bureaucracy—that Mao partially launched the Cultural Revolution to reform and reduce. Second, the quality of the administration deteriorated in conjunction with the processes involved in returning sent-downs to the cities. There is a strong consensus among my interviewees that China's administrative culture was corrupted by the use of *guanxi*, including bribes, gifts, hospitality, sexual favors, and the use of personal connections, as increasing numbers of sent-downs sought to return to the cities. Some women "slept their way" back to their home cities, as my interviewees pointed out, and many of those on military farms were expected or extorted to do so for favorable treatment. Third, beyond the return process, lawlessness in the forms of sexual predation and violence by administrators was a significant feature of rustication, especially on the military farms. Fourth, insofar as the Cultural Revolution was intended to eliminate bureaucrats' privileges, the return processes provided crucial decision makers with opportunities for private gain. Finally, rustication contributed to the overall growth of bureaucracy in size, power, and discretion. These are hardly the outcomes Mao sought in launching the Cultural Revolution and the rustication program.

Notes

1. For instance, Zhang said, "You better believe that the recorded stats of these incidents [of sexual assault and predation] were significantly lower than what really happened by leaps and bounds, just like the official stats today" (I52, 5).

2. It is interesting to note that disorder in the schools was so acute in 1967 that assignment to them was considered "frontline training" for military personnel. Keeping order and escorting were the responsibilities of separate military units (Zhou I54, 3, 14).

3. Jobs were assigned by the government, and there was very little if any independent job mobility.

4. "Sine ira ac studio" is variously translated as without "anger or bias," "anger and fondness," "scorn or bias," and "hate and zealousness" (Weber 1958, 215).

5. Overall, my interviewees' accounts show a more nuanced mix of willingness, social pressure, and coerciveness in the sent-downs' decisions to participate than Zhou and Hou (1999, 16). Several reported that their decisions were a mix of push and pull factors, rather than push alone.

6. The same point was made in very similar words by Du (I8, 23).

7. A *tongzilou* was an apartment building in which each family usually occupied a one-room apartment. Common restrooms were shared by multiple families on the same floor. The building had no individual kitchens, instead a number of coal-fired cooking stoves were stationed in the corridors for shared use. *Tongzilou* buildings had no showers; one had to visit a bathhouse to bathe.

8. Altruism may be based on the perception that an individual or his or her family has suffered an injustice, as in cases reported by Wan (I45) and Wen (I47).

9. The situation of women in the rustication and return processes is discussed later in this chapter.

10. Li and Liang agreed that *guanxi* became pronounced during the sent-downs' return process (I25, 11; I26, 22).

11. The stamps and tickets enabled one to buy items. Money was used for the actual purchases. In practice, the peasants did a lot of bartering among themselves.

12. This is the interviewee who did not receive a regular wage but rather an allowance or stipend of 5 yuan per month.

13. My interviewees' accounts with respect to daily work in rural villages and military farms are basically in accord with Zhou and Hou (1999, 16) and Pan (2003, 92, 118–19) but show more variation in work assignments. The accounts of the interviewees who were rusticated in Inner Mongolia are not in keeping with most of the literature on rustication, including Zhou and Hou (1999) and Pan (2003).

14. Duan (I8) and Fan (I9) thought their experiences were representative except that they both spent less time in the countryside than most sent-downs and left under atypical circumstances involving *guanxi* (Fan I9) and a policy allowing one of two or more sent-down children in a family to return home under some conditions (Duan I8, 41; Fan 9, 41).

15. Ding returned the food by physically carrying it in two buckets hanging from a shoulder pole.

16. The terminology, "men and women" should not obscure the fact that many sent-downs were under the age of eighteen. The interviewees frequently referred to themselves and other sent-downs as boys and girls.

17. Deng is one of my controls, noted in chapter 1, who were sent down by programs not under the rustication bureaucracy's jurisdiction.

18. Ironically, despite being a "son of a bitch," Ding was able to marry a woman from a poor peasant family background.

19. That is, they came from Kuomintang (Chinese Nationalist, anticommunist, antirevolutionary) backgrounds.

20. Although most cadres were sent to May Seventh Cadre Schools for reeducation, others were sent to political prisons (Fan I9, 42) or prison-like hard labor camps. Gan's father died in such a camp (I12, 2–3).

Chapter 6

Conclusion

Rustication as Public Administration

> "I learned nothing useful from being sent down. You can learn nothing from the ignorant, and except for a few new cursing words, I learned nothing. Now looking back, there was no purpose to my life and it was a life completely wasted."
>
> Ying Yuan (I51, 8)

> "The direct legacy of the Cultural Revolution and the rustication era brought a total crisis of faith, convictions, and ideals that did not exist before."
>
> Bin Ding (I6, 42)

> "You know, when you are a photographer, you are trying to capture the world through your lens and sometimes you catch a glimpse, a fraction, a moment in the fragile beauty of life. You can only catch that moment when you understand life and when you can read the world better. That perspective of beauty, hope, love, and serenity is a reflection of you—your inner world, your heart and soul. Prior to being sent down, I never had such a perception or even knew how to read this world because I never had such an awareness about life. That's what I learned the most (from my sent-down experience)."
>
> Kai Wen (I47, 18)

The Cultural Revolution failed to achieve its goal of reducing the influence of bureaucratization and bureaucrats in China. By the close of the Cultural Revolution in 1976 and the rise of Deng Xiaoping to leadership of the CCP, the Chinese Weberians had clearly prevailed over the Maoist Marxians. Rustication contributed to an expansion in the size and scope of bureaucracy during the Cultural Revolution. The rustication administration reached from the national government to individual urban apartments and remote rural villages. Very few youth eligible for rustication who did not join the military or work in factories eluded the street offices, local public security offices, and schools in an effort to avoid being sent down. Moreover, based on my interviewees' accounts discussed in the previous chapter, the rustication program was associated with a change in China's administrative culture that made bureaucrats' self-serving behavior and the use of *guanxi* more common. In my interviewees' eyes, the ills of Chinese public administration are much greater today than at the start of the Cultural Revolution (e.g., Duan I8, 8–9; Fan I9, 8–10; Gan I12, 9; Lan I24, 28; Liang I26, 13, 23; Meng I33, 3, 9; Sun I41, 10, 31; Tan I42, 18; Wang I46, 6, 22; Yuan I51, 9; Zhao I53, 9). However, even as the rustication program detracted from Mao's goals regarding bureaucracy, it may have contributed to another central objective, that of reeducating the sent-downs with respect to socialism.[1]

Socialist Reeducation

As discussed in chapter 4, socialist reeducation was a major objective of the Cultural Revolution. Mao had long been a vigorous critic of the way youth were educated in China. As early as 1919 he condemned "a bastion of bureaucrats who exercised a fierce monopoly over" formal education (Zhou 1994, 1). After the People's Republic of China was founded in 1949, Mao called for a variety of educational reforms, including combining "education and productive labour" (ibid., 8). However, prior to the Cultural Revolution, Mao contended that the Chinese educational system retained a "bourgeois ethos," a condition that was addressed by closing the Ministry of Education from 1966 to 1975 (Milner, n.d.). During this period, reeducation of the sent-downs would be through integration into rural peasant life and military farms; for "bourgeois intellectuals," it would be "through physical labour" (ibid.). Mao consistently advocated subordinating expertise to socialist consciousness and favored the red over the expert (Poon, n.d.). Integration of the sent-downs with the peasantry would provide socialist reeducation because, in Mao's view, the peasants "possessed a high degree of proletarian class consciousness, and a firm class standpoint in this socialist society where there was still constant life-and-death class struggle" (Pan 2003, 165). The socialist reeducation of sent-downs had at least three components to which the rustication bureaucracy was relevant: the study of Mao's Thought; connecting the sent-downs to the masses, particularly the peasantry and peasant life; and tempering them through physical labor.

Socialist reeducation was a substantially developed CCP objective and process well before the start of the rustication program. For example, cadres were sent to May Seventh Cadre Schools for reeducation, personal reform, and training through labor and the study of Mao Zedong's Thought. Such study was supposed to be a major feature of the rustication program as well. Ultimately its quality would depend on the rustication administration, particularly military and civilian personnel on the military and state farms as well as cadres in the rural villages and on the grasslands of Inner Mongolia. How central and effective were the study of Mao's Thought to the sent-downs' experience?

Mao's Thought

Based on my interviewees' responses, a great deal of time and attention was devoted to Mao's Thought, but a substantial amount of it may have been perfunctory. In Meng's case, Mao's Thought was taken very seriously:

> In the morning we had to reflect on Mao's Thought, and at night report about our own thoughts and consciousness. For example, let's say I had a wheat bun for lunch, but because the bun was half spoiled, I only ate parts of it and threw away the rest. Although I did this privately and no one else knew about it, at night I must report myself and my wrong consciousness, and tell the others what I did by reporting the account of my behavior that day. Then everyone would help you analyze the behavior according to Mao's Thought. They would critique it and collectively deconstruct your behavior and your motivation behind it for a while, make suggestions to you how you can improve yourself to achieve higher consciousness, and then move on to the next person. That was the method of studying Mao's Thought, and we did it every day. (I33, 7)

Ding and Wang also reported strict attention to Mao's Thought:

> When we returned at night around 8:30 or 9 PM, we still had to study Mao's Thought. We studied for half an hour every night. At every meal, we must also do our pledges and bless the chairman. We would say, "Long live Chairman Mao! Long live!" Then we'd read some pages from Mao's quotes, from Mao's *Little Red Book* and whatnot, then we would chant in unison to complete the ceremony: "Chairman Mao, may you live ten thousand years of a glorious life! Ten thousand years of glorious life! Ten thousand years!" After all that, we would eat. This was done at every meal, every day (like how some religious folk would pray at every meal in the West). (I6, 25)

> There is always time for Chairman Mao's *Selected Works*. Of course, you have to find time to study it no matter what else happened. Our cafeteria also served as an auditorium for meetings and there was a stage in the center. Every day before we had our meals, we took out our *Little Red Book* in one hand and greeted the portrait of Chairman Mao, and pledged our dear love for the chairman with the other hand. We did this several times a day. . . . That's every meal, every time you enter the cafeteria, you go in front of Chairman Mao, whether you mean it or not, you stand in front of him, bow down, then pledge or bless or whatnot and then you go eat. . . . Because everyone was there in the cafeteria, there always was someone ready to expose you (for

Photo 6.1: Three sent-down women happily studying Mao's Thought for the camera.

your bourgeois tendencies). Let's say you went to eat but forgot to do your pledges or bless the chairman, you would certainly be struggled against at a later time, if not that very evening. We met several times a week after dinner to study Chairman Mao's teachings. When it rained so hard that we really could not work in the field, we had to stay in and study Chairman Mao's Thought. . . . You had to participate whether you wanted to or not. (I46, 15)

Su also indicated that Mao's Thought was central to her daily routine, with both morning and evening sessions (I40, 9). For Li, however, studying Mao's Thought was thankfully only a morning activity: "No, [not in the evening] thank goodness. It's only for the morning. It's a daily scheduled must for the morning only" (I25, 19). Sun took "Chairman Mao's *Selected Works* and . . . a notebook to study in the snow. [He] would write self-reflections and poems in the falling snow, studying the chairman's books on [his] own." He did this because he was enamored with Mao's ideology, and there were no organized study sessions on the grasslands of Inner Mongolia due to the isolated nature of herding animals (I41, 22–23). Fan suggested that the "organized study sessions" at his village were not so much the result of administrative plan as

> because we had a sent-down leader among ourselves, [a] knowledgeable youth whose father . . . was the secretary-general of the then North China Bureau. He was also

the brother of . . . the Party secretary of the Health Ministry. This guy assumed the leadership position among the sent-downs at our village and had become a political instructor. This kid was born to become that typical, classic depiction of the CCP cadre as portrayed in those old revolutionary movies, and he was born for this kind of thing [political reeducation] and had been ready for it since birth. (I9, 38)

By contrast, Tian and Yu devoted no time at all to Mao's Thought. Both indicated that they had no time for Mao's Thought and suggested lack of attention to it may have been common among sent-downs in rural villages. Tian said she did not study Mao's Thought because "we were not on military farms. We were peasants and after all that physical labor, who had time?" (I44, 12). Yu's response was similar: "No, we had to make dinner! That's what we felt was the most unfair! All those other local guys, they worked in the field all day but when they went back home, their wives already had dinner waiting for them. For us, we busted our chops all day in the field and were dead on our feet and still we had to make our own dinner!" (I50, 14).

Two interviewees provided an example that suggests some of the study may have been perfunctory or even irreverent. Liang reported:

> Every day you had to read the paper and study Mao's *Selected Works*. When it rained, we would get together for meetings or do struggle sessions. Once, on one of those rainy days, everyone was called to come out for a struggle session against Liu Shaoqi. Everyone from the village, about seventy or eighty people sat all over the place in the production brigade house and even spilled into the courtyard. The brigade leader told us, "Today we are not going to work because it's raining, but we are still going to record the work points." He said that everyone had to speak, and give a speech of a few words to criticize Liu Shaoqi. If one did not, then he or she would not get the points and so everyone talks a bit. But there were two brothers who were very uncultured. Worse yet, they both had some sort of speech defect, especially the younger one who could barely squeeze out a few sentences a year to his wife, and then maybe only during, you know, intimate moments. It took the older brother a very long time and a lot of effort to express himself but he managed to roughly repeat what the guy before him had said, so he got off. Then it was the younger brother's turn, the last one to speak. He tried pretty hard but just couldn't come up with anything to say. Finally, the party secretary got impatient because the younger brother was holding up the meeting. The secretary said fine, he couldn't get the ten work points then because obviously he had nothing to say. Upon hearing this, the younger brother got so infuriated he jumped up and cursed out loud, "Liu Shaoqi, I fuck your mother!" People went nuts. Everyone split a gut laughing and cheered him on in an uproar because in the end this one fuck earned him ten points. And that's what struggle sessions in the countryside were like. (I26, 18)

Liang also indicated that studying Mao's Thought was not part of the village routine because "the peasants were illiterate and uncultured. They could not possibly understand Mao's writings. That's like graduate-level work in Chinese literature" (I26, 18).

Lan said that study sessions on Mao's Thought often turned into gossip sessions at his Inner Mongolian location:

> During these meetings, it was like a social get-together and if they thought that I wasn't there, they would start gossiping in Mongolian (because the other sent-downs didn't understand it) especially about the local romances. There might not be a lot of people in the pastoral lands, but they got a lot of those things going on. . . . There might not be a lot of people around but there were a ton of interpersonal relationships between men and women. . . . Anyway, whenever we had these sessions to "struggle against capitalism and criticize revisionism," that would be all they talked about among themselves. They would say, "I spotted so and so together with so and so and they were doing such and such." They would be gossiping up a storm. (I24, 25)

For at least one interviewee, the sent-down experience actually detracted from studying Mao's Thought. Tang explained, "Yes, we were all so passionate about it [studying Mao's Thought] before we were sent down. But once I was sent down, we became much more practical and realistic. We still studied Mao's writings almost every night though" (I43, 16). Tian noted that after Mao died, interest in his thought waned: "But it was already 1976. The chairman had already died by then, so had Lin Biao and Premier Zhou Enlai and so we were not as fanatic as we used to be, like when we were back then in the city" (I44, 16).

Based on these accounts, it is reasonable to conclude that the rustication bureaucracy did not uniformly promote or coerce the study of Mao's Thought. Sent-downs in some villages apparently had very little or no exposure to Mao's writings as part of the rustication program. In others, attention to them may have been pro forma. Study was probably more rigorous on military farms, with twice-daily sessions as part of their inflexible schedules. On the Inner Mongolian grasslands, Mao's Thought was clearly optional.

Connecting with the Peasantry and Peasant Life

Mao believed that the sent-down youth would benefit physically, morally, and ideologically from developing a strong connection to the peasantry and peasant life. Through their sent-down experiences, my interviewees clearly became more connected to the peasantry and the hardships they faced. However, for some, the impact of exposure to the peasants was contrary to Mao's objectives, and for others the price of gaining a better understanding of peasant life was too high. From an administrative perspective, these responses raise the question of whether the rustication program should have better prepared the sent-downs intellectually and physically for immersion in the countryside as a means of advancing the reeducation objectives of the Cultural Revolution. The absence of attention to integrating the sent-downs into their new settings was noted by Ding:

> The administrators only cared and organized things for the initial settlement of the sent-downs such as making arrangements for their food and shelter. However, once they were settled in, the administrators' jobs and responsibilities were done.... They were not there to help us integrate with the local people or continuously monitor us or anything like that because they were not assigned with the task of acculturating the sent-downs and helping them to be absorbed among the people. To them, you were now a peasant like everyone else, so the less you bothered them, the better. (I6, 28)

As discussed in the previous chapter, many of the sent-downs were transferred to the countryside in a matter of days and without any formal briefing or other preparatory sessions. Some went to work almost upon arrival whereas others had as much as two weeks in which to be socialized into peasant life. The settling in process was generally—though with many exceptions—effective in terms of paperwork, housing, and housekeeping matters. Nevertheless, it sometimes fell short with respect to educating the sent-downs about rural life and socially integrating them into their villages. In some cases, as noted earlier, language was a substantial barrier to communication and connection with the peasants. Based on my interviewees' accounts, it seems clear that reeducation through exposure to the peasantry and peasant life would have been more effective if the rustication program had provided the sent-downs with guidance or training about rural society, its administrative and social organization, and agricultural production.

Several of my interviewees indicated that they learned a great deal more about China through life in the countryside. Some used almost the same words. Liang said, "I saw for the first time how some people lived in China. I couldn't fathom that some people lived like that in China. The countryside was so backwards, so impoverished" (I26, 22). Tan noted that she learned "what China was really like and I understood China more because it was a life we never knew before.... It was being in the countryside, experiencing firsthand how the peasants really lived that made us understand China so much more" (I42, 19).

Fan described the peasants' living conditions most graphically:

> Once I saw my surroundings, my heart sank into a bottomless pit. I couldn't believe that I was sent to such a godforsaken place! ... In this peasant household, there was an open outhouse within the courtyard which was reserved only for the women in this

family but because we were guests from the city, they also allowed us, the sent-downs, to use this restroom. You have to understand, this was first-class privilege because they gave us access to something that they thought was their best facility and they all treated us so much better than the local (male) peasants. But what really tops it all—and this really tells how backwards this place was, only the details of everyday living can explain to you how completely backwards this place was—this so-called bathroom was simply a hole in the ground about three meters deep and that was the extent of their best facility! And this was the bathroom reserved for their fair maidens only, mind you, and it was considered super deluxe. When you entered the restroom, there was a basket full of hardened mud balls and that's what they used for toilet paper! At that time, this was how the peasants lived and this was the actual living condition of China's countryside. In this sense, one could certainly understand why some at the time said that it was absolutely necessary for the knowledgeable youth in the city to go down to the countryside because it would at least open their eyes. It would help these city folks understand what China's rural areas were like, and how those other people lived. Well, so far, just this one incident alone, mission accomplished. Being sent down to live in the countryside really did make the urbanites such as ourselves understand the abject poverty in China's countryside, which was previously unimaginable to us, and this includes the people who became China's high officials today. (I9, 31)[2]

Fan continued to relate his dismay at peasant life:

Seriously, you cannot believe what else, how backwards everything was. Each family had only one *kang* [mud bed with a built-in stove for heating]. On one side there are the grandparents, on the other, the parents, and in the middle are the kids. All their conjugals are done on this very same *kang*. That's really how it was. In the summer, maybe you can get some privacy elsewhere, but in those long winter months, there is no other source of heating in the household other than what's in the *kang*. So what else can they do? Also in the countryside, the family generations are very close in age—each generation was within twenty years of one another. They have children at fifteen or sixteen, latest by seventeen or eighteen. By the time the adult son has a child of his own, the grandparents are not even forty years old. That was the age difference between the generations and yet they all slept on the same bed because the peasants were so poor (that they couldn't afford any better living arrangement). Honest to God, unless you were there and saw it for yourself, the total backwardness of China's countryside was unfathomable. You simply could not imagine how poor the people were and how backwards everything was. (I9, 32)

Yet the impact for some was precisely the opposite of the Cultural Revolution's objective. Yu came away believing the communist system was completely faulty as applied to the rural sector:

> This system killed all motivation on the behalf of the peasants. When the system doesn't distinguish good or bad, efficient or inefficient, performance individually, then the enthusiasm for anything was all but killed because any rational actor would question why he or she should contribute more when not compensated for the effort. This was the result of the communist system in rural villages. When we first arrived in the countryside, we were so upset to see that the peasants were barely working. Instead we exhausted ourselves every day but later at the end of the year, we realized why they were not working hard because the system was so screwed up. No matter how much time or effort you put in, you would never get a fair share. You just could not beat the system. However, once in a while, we would get an assignment where individual performance mattered, like if you finished your job early, then you'd get to go home early. On those occasions, it was shocking to see how much more competent, how much faster and better these peasants worked compared with us, the sent-downs. The sudden transformation of these guys was astonishing. This was when they got so enthusiastic because their individual performances mattered. (I50, 25–26)

Furthermore, Yu concluded that one of the core tenets of Mao's Thought was woefully misguided:

> It was not like how Mao had indoctrinated us that the landowners were the root of all evil, and the wealthy peasants were nothing but full of greed whereas the poor peasants were the best and most glorious of all. In reality, it was exactly the opposite. That's what I learned from my sent-down experience. The real poor peasants were the layabouts, the loafers who were too damn lazy to do anything productive, and consequently they were poor. . . . Poor peasants were either lazy or inept. The really competent and hardworking ones were the wealthier peasants. Not only that, those wealthier peasants who were supposed to be such evildoers, not only did they work longer hours and harder workloads, so did their offspring. Even their kids were resourceful and hard workers. These people got wealthier simply because they worked hard, but according to Mao's theories, they were the greedy bad guys who exploited everyone else and should be struggled against. . . . I learned firsthand that Mao's political prattling and his understanding of class differentiation among the peasantry were completely wrong. (I50, 25–26)

Gan had a very similar analysis:

> I learned how difficult life was in China, and I learned how painfully hard the peasants' lives were. However, what I learned most was that ole Mao's analysis on social classes was total BS. Once I got to the countryside and lived there, I found that the class differentiation in reality was nothing like Mao had described in his grand theories. The poor peasants were impoverished because they would not contribute their productive

labor. They would not work and they would not lead a regular life like everyone else did. Most of them would smoke opium, they would grow opium instead of food on their plot of land, and so of course they were poor. There was no class exploitation at all. Because I was a barefoot doctor [backpack medic] and I made house calls, I went to just about every family from all different class backgrounds in the village. Sometimes I would visit a mid-level wealthier peasant and ask, "Do you think life is better now or before the Communist Liberation?" They would always say, "Life was better then, because we were able to feed ourselves and had enough food back then [under the old system] instead of now." I then asked, "Did the landlord exploit you back then?" They said, "Why would the landowner exploit us? If we had a bad harvest and didn't have enough to eat, we could go to the landlord's family and take some food for free.". . . The peasants were very respectful of the old landowner families. But, alas, it was during the Cultural Revolution and the peasants were asked to hold struggle sessions against the former landowner families. During those meetings members of these families would go on the stage and the peasants would joke around and banter with them for a while and that was the end of it. I thought it was pretty funny how everyone goofed off in what was supposed to be a struggle session. (I12, 19)

Duan also found a disconnect between "what you thought China was like" based on "CCP propaganda and how they told you it was" and the reality "when you experience some hardship—that's when you learn by yourself, your own sense of how China really is" (I8, 55). Li noted that "if the rustication program was meant as a reeducation program, its objectives were never clear," and she wondered "what exactly were our learning objectives? What exactly were we supposed to learn from these ignorant peasants? Because they really had quite a bit of character defects and so I'm not sure exactly what we should learn from them" (I25, 33).

Tang and Tian were among those who thought the price paid for reeducation was too high and that they "should never have been put through it" because "the price in exchange for this reeducation was the best years of our lives and prime of our youth" (I43, 19; I44, 17). Fan concurred that "for the impact on one's life chances and opportunities, this [rustication] was simply a farce. It made an absolute farce out of our lives" (I9, 53). However, he went on to say that "if dear ole Mao didn't do this, I guess that we at best would have only a superficial understanding of the countryside and think it was all good and merry" (I9, 53). Zhang passionately summed up this line of thought:

> Our sent-down experience transformed our understanding about life, and we were awoken by our experience because for the first time we understood what China was really like, when we saw with our own eyes how people lived at the lower levels, and it was such a harsh, naked exposure. In this process, most of the sent-downs were

awoken to reality, which was completely at odds with the propaganda that had indoctrinated us. After that, we found everything so extremely distasteful and offensive, which ultimately led to a total negation of the policy itself but the price we paid was too heavy. We cannot justify the Up to the Mountains and Down to the Countryside policy just because we had a better understanding of things as a result of those long years being sent down to the countryside and living in abject poverty. That was too much of a price. Mao wanted us to be reeducated, and we were in fact the best CCP-mentored generation, but in the end, when the university exams reopened, why did they refer to us as the lost generation? We were lost because our ideas—our understanding of truths and what that CCP system spewed out—were totally incompatible, because we were cheated. We were so cheated. Not just in ideal and beliefs but also in our lives. All this at the expense of millions of real lives. (I52, 10)

Based on these interviewees' conclusions, rustication for reeducation through exposure to the peasantry and rural life was not cost-effective and was quite possibly counterproductive in many cases. Had the program included a more substantial formal educational component rather than leaving reeducation in the rural villages primarily to osmosis through interaction with the peasants, the benefits might have been much more substantial.

"To Be Tempered into Steel in the Revolutionary Furnace"

Hard physical labor and harsh living conditions were a third component of socialist reeducation.[3] Physically and in terms of an ability to endure hardship, urban youth were less than the revolutionary ideal portrayed by propaganda posters, pictures, and CCP literature. Mao's longstanding belief that socialist thought reform could be achieved through labor was prominent in the Cultural Revolution. Some Red Guard units established "reformatories through labor" during the height of the so-called Red Terror in 1966 (Yan and Gao 1996, 82). As in the case of exposure to the peasantry and peasant life, tempering occurred but not necessarily with the intended effect.

Only two of my interviewees connected the hardships of being sent down with greater socialist consciousness. Yang did so indirectly in the sense that she believed her rustication experience made her a better cadre: "It definitely made me more capable as a person. Later, when I became an administrator and after I learned Mongol, the local dialect, my experience made me a better cadre because I was much more able to handle different kinds of situations and better communicate with different types of people. I was tempered into a better person" (I49, 7). Meng was more direct: "For our generation, it was definitely a reeducation because we really were reeducated in the countryside. Individually, we learned how to take care of ourselves; we developed ourselves with new capabilities, and learned how to completely dissolve ourselves into a total communitarian lifestyle, so it was just like the chairman had intended, we learned how to help each other, how to work and live with each other like members of a party" (I33, 9).

With one exception, the others associated tempering with being able to overcome hardships, to endure, and to deal with anything that comes their way. The following is a sampling of what tempering meant to them:

> **Song (I39, 15):** "For me, I am rather thankful for that experience because it really tempered me. It built the foundation of my character and made everything else possible for me. It really was a reeducation. I really think the kids today should have an educational experience like that because the youth today are so pampered and coddled that they can't take anything the least bit physically or psychologically challenging."
> **Tan (I42, 19):** "After that experience, you got a bottom line because you went through so much difficulty and hardship so you develop a certain confidence, that no matter what, you can face anything seemingly insurmountable and you can be persistent in your pursuit no matter what you wanted to do in life."
> **Tang (I43, 19):** "For the urban kids of our generation, it was such a difficult experience. It was an incredibly hard experience, because we were all kids from the city, so who would have done that kind of work? But it was precisely that kind of physical work that tempered you."
> **Wen (I47, 18):** "When the smoke and dust settled, I survived intact and not broken. Even though I had been wronged, bullied, abused, and beaten, I never ended up taking it out on my wife and child. I never lost it and kicked down the doors of those cadres who wronged me, and I never wasted my time being bitter because I refused to let my sent-down experience and my abusers affect the later years of my life in any way. I refused to let what they did to me physically and psychologically weaken me as a person so that I would end up taking it out on others and become what they were.
> **Zhao (I53, 8):** "Yes, I had this experience, and so if in the future am I to face any insurmountable difficulty maybe I am more prepared to deal with it. And, yes, the price was heavy but there's nothing you can do about it. You can't turn back time and you got no other choices and that's life."[4]

By contrast, Ding sounded beaten down by rustication:

> Once you are living at the very bottom of society, the lowest where you could not possibly get lower, there is no place for aspirations, ideals, or any wishful thinking about the future in your daily schedule. You go on one day at a time, and your only goal is to stay alive. Another day that you live on, another day that you go work in the field when the sun rises in the morning only to leave when the sun goes down at night. It's just this repeated process of physical labor every day, day after day, month after month, year

after year—and all this extensive hard work was just to satisfy your basic needs so that you won't perish. . . . I lost all faith in my future completely. (I6, 28–29)

Collectively, these accounts point to the failure of the rustication bureaucracy systematically to connect tempering to socialist reeducation or thought reform. For my interviewees, tempering was mostly surviving hardship and developing self-confidence in their ability to meet whatever challenges they might confront. However, in the countryside, tempering may perversely have been all the greater due to the rustication administrations' neglect of the sent-downs once they were settled in. By contrast, tempering was both intentionally and perhaps unintentionally built into administration on the military farms where the sent-downs faced a deliberately harsh daily regimen and could also be subject to brutal treatment at the whim of the individuals in charge.

Conclusion

The main objective of this study is to develop an understanding of the public administrative dimensions of the rustication program and to show how they were related to the Cultural Revolution. In so doing, one of its major contributions to our knowledge about the rustication program is exploring how varied the sent-downs' experiences were. This refines the extant scholarship on rustication, but it also cautions against overgeneralization. Overall, then, with this constraint in mind, what can be said of public administration, bureaucratization, and the Cultural Revolution? Several conclusions can be drawn.

First, as this research emphasizes, the Cultural Revolution was partly fomented as a result of a longstanding conflict between Maoist Marxians and Chinese Weberians over how to organize and promote Chinese socioeconomic development. This conflict was inextricably interwoven into a contest between Mao's charismatic authority and the Chinese Weberians' effort to trump, contain, or circumvent it with bureaucratically organized authority based on rationality, trained expertise, and technology. In this sense the Maoists rightly viewed bureaucratization as a threat to both their vision of China's socialist revolutionary future and their place in it. Mao attacked bureaucratic privilege and deviance from his socialist ideals, but bureaucratization based on technical expertise was itself a threat. As an authority structure, the CCP bureaucracy was clearly at odds with a socialist society based on the mass line and rooted in the peasantry and working class. Mao's solution within the framework of the Cultural Revolution was to topple the more senior cadres and create tremendous insecurity for those who replaced them or remained. The toppling acted as something of a spoils system. The Chinese Weberians, being viewed as opponents of the Maoist Marxists, were most vulnerable to being labeled "capitalist roaders" or purged simply due to bad family backgrounds. In public administrative terms, personnel administration became highly politicized in ways that favored the Maoist Marxians.

Second, the rustication program created multiple public administrative ironies for the Cultural Revolution. Rustication was perforce bureaucratized. What public administrative alternative is available for effectively transferring seventeen million urban teenagers from the cities to the countryside—often against their will and that of their parents? Based on my interviewees' accounts, it is useful to distinguish between two types of activities when considering administration of the rustication program: routine processing of cases and sociotherapeutic undertakings (see Mashaw 1983; Rosenbloom, Kravchuk, and Clerkin 2009, 378, 458). The rustication administration was reportedly excellent at organizing the recruitment and transfer of the sent-downs to the countryside. Interviewee after interviewee said the process of getting urban youth to sign up, voluntarily or otherwise, taking care of the necessary paperwork such as canceling *hukou*, and transporting the sent-downs to their destinations was highly efficient. It apparently was done with low ratios of administrative personnel to sent-downs, although if the street office employees, teachers and other school personnel, military escorts, and railroad and other transportation administrators are counted, the total number of administrators involved was considerably greater than those who were under the rustication program's hierarchical authority per se. Consequently, it is reasonable to conclude, from an administrative perspective, rustication was at odds with the Cultural Revolutionary objective of reining in bureaucracy if only because it required a large-scale, vertically and horizontally integrated effort at various levels reaching from the national government virtually to the front door of every urban household with a potential *zhiqing* in it.

For the most part, settling the *zhiqing* in rural villages, on military farms, and on the Inner Mongolian grasslands was also efficient, though some locations were unprepared for the youth when they first arrived, and there were cases of misuse of the settling fees provided by the central government (Duan I8, 29; Pan 2003, 141). Nonetheless, the overall coordination was reportedly excellent.

The rustication administration did less well at sociotherapeutic tasks—integrating the sent-downs into rural villages, military farms, and life on the Inner Mongolian grasslands; tending to their general welfare; protecting them against abuse; and promoting their socialist reeducation. The study's research design is not amenable to assessing the sent-downs' integration overall because it applies only to those who returned to the cities. Many of my interviewees indicated that they knew sent-downs who married locals and remained in the countryside. The proportion that did so is apparently unknown. However, the accounts of those who returned are mostly unflattering with respect to rural village life and service on the military farms. Those who were sent down to the grasslands apparently

Conclusion

had the best experience and were probably most integrated with the local population. This seems to have been due more to ethnic Mongolian culture than to efforts by the rustication bureaucracy. Administrators in the rural villages apparently made minimal efforts to integrate the sent-downs with the peasantry, perhaps believing or calculating that their work was mostly done once the youth were settled in with at least a modicum of food and shelter. Some interviewees reported that they were told or permitted to leave their rural villages to go back home in winter, when there was less farm work to do. This undercut integration with the peasantry as well as studying Mao's Thought and being tempered (e.g., Fan, Wan, and Yu). As discussed earlier, the rustication administration did little or nothing to prepare the sent-downs for life in the countryside. The sent-downs were integrated into military farms in a formal organizational sense. Psychologically, though, many were clearly alienated by the harsh treatment and arduous work assignments they often received.

It is safe to conclude that the rustication administration also performed inadequately in providing for the general welfare of the sent-downs. Many sent-downs suffered from constant hunger and exhaustion. Females were said to have developed gynecological problems due to the nature of required physical labor during menstruation. In many destinations, especially in rural villages, health care was inadequate, primitive, or wholly absent. Adequate medical treatment could be especially lacking for those requiring advanced treatment (e.g., Zhao, who lost the use of four fingers in an accident and had to take a long tractor ride to a clinic where he received unsanitary treatment that led to severe infection). All my interviewees survived, of course, but only a few thrived during their sent-down years.

The rustication administration's greatest failing was not doing enough to protect the sent-downs from abuse. Females who were subject to sexual harassment, predation, and rape—which was reportedly common on military farms—often had no effective recourse (see Pan 2003, 141; Liu 2009, 193). Some sent-downs were subject to sadistic treatment, beatings, and gratuitous physical danger (such as Wen, who was randomly beaten and could have frozen to death struggling through waist-high snow over a long distance to deliver a blank piece of paper). The survivors report having been tempered, but an unknown number of sent-downs did not survive. My interviewees knew of several suicides by sent-downs, and there were many, both reported and unreported. Particularly for females, marriage to locals, however reluctantly, provided another escape from both the grueling physical labor and the abusive local cadres. The overall number of lives shortened or irreversibly damaged either physically or mentally by rustication is unknowable, though certainly substantial as terming the sent-downs "the lost generation" strongly suggests.

The rustication administration also performed poorly with respect to socialist reeducation in the rural villages. As discussed, some sent-downs received no exposure to Mao's Thought, and for others it was pro forma and sometimes irreverent. Mao's Thought was a more prominent feature of daily life on the military farms, partly due to regimented scheduling. Judging from my interviewees, contact with the peasantry and tempering did not have the desired effects and, indeed, may have had opposite ones.

Third, as discussed in chapter 5, a substantial and continuing change in China's administrative culture was reportedly associated with the rustication administration. The post-1949 use of *guanxi*, including bribes, gifts, hospitality, and sexual favors appears to have become pronounced in conjunction with entering the military as an alternative to being sent down and in the processes involved in returning sent-downs to the cities. Administrative corruption is contagious (Rosenbloom 2009, xiv). Once it begins, it is difficult to stop and can become standard operating procedure. A digression into China's current problems with administrative corruption would be inappropriate. However, several of my interviewees' comparisons between cadre behavior pre– and post–Cultural Revolution and rustication are telling:

> **Lan (I24, 28–29):** "Prior to the Cultural Revolution, the cadres were extremely tightly controlled and disciplined. . . . After the military supervision phase began, which occurred across the country and in various institutions, this changed. . . . China's modern corruption problems as a result of privilege and authority really began after military supervision took place. . . . Prior to the Cultural Revolution, no cadres dared to do anything corrupt."
>
> **Sun (I41, 31):** "Not only did the Cultural Revolution change it [bureaucratic culture from clean to corrupt], but because the Cultural Revolution as a whole was officially negated, bureaucratic corruption today is much worse and more widespread. What was criticized back then became the right thing to do today—the now standard operating procedure and behavior."
>
> **Wang (I46, 22):** "Prior to the Cultural Revolution and the sent-down program, people absolutely did not doubt anything that the CCP did. It was an utmost honor to become a party member. Today, any party official's behavior is suspected by the people. It went from people believing in everything the CCP did to not much of anything anymore."
>
> **Yuan (I51, 9):** "Today if you want to be promoted into a leadership position, then you have to sleep with the higher-ups. No one thinks it's scandalous anymore. Women who do it just say that they're exploring their 'personal resources.' And if you are clean and uncorrupt today, there is no way you can survive being a cadre or an official because everyone else is so corrupt. . . . If honest people got promoted like the knowledgeable ones that were persecuted during the Cultural Revolution; if those people had not vanished but were instead promoted through the ranks into senior administrative positions, if that had happened, China would not be like this today."

Conclusion

Finally, from a public administrative perspective, rustication presented Mao with a great irony. Mao's disdain for rational, bureaucratized public administration notwithstanding, rustication—arguably the capstone of the Cultural Revolution—could probably have served that revolution more effectively if it had been better organized and administered on the receiving end and in the return process. In short, if rustication had had better public administration of precisely the rational type based on the technical expertise that Mao detested, Mao would have been closer to attaining the goals he sought for it.

Notes

1. As discussed in chapter 4, rural development was another stated goal of the rustication component of the Cultural Revolution. Pan (2003, 138–41) concludes that agricultural production on the military farms remained low throughout the rustication program and suggests that the countryside fared little better, if at all. Only a few of my interviewees expressed strong views on the matter, some saying their labor was useless and others believing that they made some contribution to rural development, though primarily in terms of social matters, such as improving health care and building friendships and understanding, rather than productivity per se. For instance, Sun (I41, 32) said "I still feel that the most important thing was the emotional bond that we established with the local pastoralists [Mongolians]." Lan (I24, 30) and Song (I39, 8) expressed a similar thought. Because agricultural productivity depends on a wide variety of factors, no overall conclusion can be drawn concerning sent-downs' contribution to rural development. As of 1973, 34 percent of the sent-downs were self-sufficient, indicating that they were not a net drain on the rural sector; 35 percent were self-sufficient in food but not other products; and the remaining 31 percent were not self-sufficient in food or other goods (see Liu 2009, 179). Self-sufficiency in food did not preclude constant hunger.

2. Several interviewees expressed a similar sentiment for the future. As mentioned in the preface, president Xi Jinping is among China's leaders who were rusticated.

3. "To Be Tempered into Steel in the Revolutionary Furnace" is a popular Cultural Revolutionary slogan (Pan 2003, 145).

4. Lan (I24, 30) and Lu (I30, 14) also said they were tempered and strengthened by their sent-down experiences.

Appendix A

Interviewee Profiles

Interviewee #1 (Control[1])

Pseudonym: Weimin BAI[2]
Age as of 2009: 64
Birth year: 1944
Gender: Male
Age when reeducated or sent down: 22
Formal education completed before receiving reeducation or being sent down: College student, fourth year of a five-year university in Shenyang majoring in engineering and science (prior to the Cultural Revolution, a bachelor's degree in science and technology required five years of study)
Family background and status of family background at time of reeducation: Urban poor, good[3]
Total length of years for reeducation received or being sent down: 1 year
Form of reeducation: Reeducation at a state farm prior to job assignment by the government
City of return: Assigned to the department of defense, weaponry design unit in Beijing
Current education level and employment status: BA, now retired (formerly a director of weaponry design and technology in defense)
Member of the Chinese Communist Party: Yes
Interview date, location, and time: June 22, 2009, in Shenzhen, 1:00 PM–5:15 PM

Interviewee #2 (Control)

Pseudonym: Yonglin CAI
Age as of 2009: 70
Birth year: 1939

Gender: Male
Age when reeducated or sent down: 29
Formal education completed before receiving reeducation or being sent down: BA, was already working as an administrator for several years in Shanghai
Family background and status of family background at time of reeducation: Administrative staff, neutral
Total length of years for reeducation received or being sent down: 1 year
Form of reeducation: Reeducation at a state farm, then returned to work
City of return: Back to original Shanghai workplace
Current education level and employment status: BA, now retired (formerly a government bureaucrat)
Member of the Chinese Communist Party: No
Interview date, location, and time: June 23, 2009, in Shenzhen, 12:00 PM–2:40 PM

Interviewee #3 (Control)

Pseudonym: Qiang CHEN
Age as of 2009: 64
Birth year: 1945
Gender: Male
Age when reeducated or sent down: 21
Formal education completed before receiving reeducation or being sent down: College student in Beijing, third year of a five-year university majoring in architecture
Family background and status of family background at time of reeducation: Urban poor, good
Total length of years for reeducation received or being sent down: 1 year
Form of reeducation: Reeducation in a state farm prior to job assignment by the government
City of return: Assigned to work in the bureau of cement and steel in Beijing
Current education level and employment status: BA, retired (formerly director of a state-owned enterprise of building material)
Member of the Chinese Communist Party: No
Interview date, location, and time: June 24, 2009, in Shenzhen, 12:30 PM–2:30 PM

Interviewee Profiles

Interviewee #4 (Control)

Pseudonym: Wei CHENG
Age as of 2009: 67
Birth year: 1942
Gender: Male
Age when reeducated or sent down: 23
Formal education completed before receiving reeducation or being sent down: College student in Wuhan, last year of a five-year university majoring in engineering
Family background and status of family background at time of reeducation: Poor peasant, good
Total length of years for reeducation received or being sent down: 2 years (first year as the general director of a propaganda performing arts troupe)
Form of reeducation: Reeducation in a factory workshop prior to job assignment by the government
City of return: Assigned to work as an engineer in Nanjing
Current education level and employment status: BA, retired (formerly an engineer)
Member of the Chinese Communist Party: No
Interview date, location, and time: June 21, 2009, in Shenzhen, 6:00 PM–8:00PM; and June 25, 2009, in Shenzhen, 4:00 PM–8:00 PM

Interviewee #5 (Control)

Pseudonym: Min DENG
Age as of 2009: 55
Birth year: 1954
Gender: Female
Age when reeducated or sent down: 16
Formal education completed before receiving reeducation or being sent down: Completed elementary school in Guangdong
Family background and status of family background at time of reeducation: Revolutionary cadre, bad
Total length of years for reeducation received or being sent down: Worked in the local town factory until 1993
Form of reeducation: Reeducation among workers in local factory in Guangdong county town
City of return: Stayed in the local Meixian county town in Guangdong until job transfer from the local factory to Shenzhen

Current education level and employment status: Vocational school, bookkeeper
Member of the Chinese Communist Party: Yes
Interview date, location, and time: June 26, 2009, in Shenzhen, 7:00 PM–10:00PM

Interviewee #6

Pseudonym: Bin DING
Age as of 2009: 61
Birth year: 1948
Gender: Male
Age when reeducated or sent down: 18
Formal education completed before receiving reeducation or being sent down: Twelfth grade, last year of high school
Family background and status of family background at time of reeducation: Revolutionary cadre, bad
Total length of years for reeducation received or being sent down: 8 years, 1968–75
Form of reeducation: Countryside rural village, Guangdong
City of return: Home city, Longchuan county town in Guangdong
Current education level and employment status: MA, retired (formerly a municipal government official)
Member of the Chinese Communist Party: Yes
Interview date, location, and time: June 27, 2009, in Shenzhen, 11:30 AM–5:30 PM

Interviewee #7 (Control)

Pseudonym: Fei DU
Age as of 2009: 63
Birth year: 1946
Gender: Female
Age when reeducated or sent down: 21
Formal education completed before receiving reeducation or being sent down: Graduated from a high school-level technical school in Beijing
Family background and status of family background at time of reeducation: Worker, good

Interviewee Profiles 185

Total length of years for reeducation received or being sent down: 18 years, 1967–85
Form of reeducation: Reeducation by working in weaponry assembly factory set up by the Department of Defense in a remote mountain region, Shanxi
City of return: Was never able to return back to home city, Beijing, job transfer to Shenzhen in 1985
Current education level and employment status: Technical school, retired (formerly director of a state-owned estate development enterprise)
Member of the Chinese Communist Party: Yes
Interview date, location, and time: July 3, 2009, in Shenzhen, 6:30 PM–11:00 PM

Interviewee #8

Pseudonym: Chao DUAN
Age as of 2009: 58
Birth year: 1951
Gender: Male
Age when reeducated or sent down: 17
Formal education completed before receiving reeducation or being sent down: Eighth grade, second year of middle school
Family background and status of family background at time of reeducation: Intellectual, neutral
Total length of years for reeducation received or being sent down: 4 years, 1968–72
Form of reeducation: Countryside rural village, Shanxi
City of return: Home city, Beijing
Current education level and employment status: Postgraduate, scholar and researcher in social science think tank
Member of the Chinese Communist Party: No
Interview date, location, and time: July 10, 2009, in Beijing, 4:00 PM–8:00 PM

Interviewee #9

Pseudonym: Tao FAN
Age as of 2009: 58
Birth year: 1951
Gender: Male
Age when reeducated or sent down: 17

Formal education completed before receiving reeducation or being sent down: Eighth grade, second year of middle school
Family background and status of family background at time of reeducation: Revolutionary cadre, bad
Total length of years for reeducation received or being sent down: 2 years, 1968–early 1971
Form of reeducation: Countryside rural village, Shanxi
City of return: Home city, Beijing
Current education level and employment status: BA, independent business owner
Member of the Chinese Communist Party: Yes
Interview date, location, and time: July 10, 2009, in Beijing, 4:30 PM–8:00 PM

Interviewee #10

Pseudonym: Mei FANG
Age as of 2009: 54
Birth year: 1955
Gender: Female
Age when reeducated or sent down: 14 (turned 15 while being sent down)
Formal education completed before receiving reeducation or being sent down: Fourth grade, elementary school
Family background and status of family background at time of reeducation: Revolutionary cadre, good
Total length of years for reeducation received or being sent down: 2 years, 1970–72
Form of reeducation: Countryside rural village on the outskirts of Beijing
City of return: Home city, Beijing
Current education level and employment status: BA, editor for a television station
Member of the Chinese Communist Party: No
Interview date, location, and time: July 13, 2009, in Beijing, 11:30 AM–2:00 PM

Interviewee #11 (Control)

Pseudonym: Dan FENG
Age as of 2009: 63

Interviewee Profiles

Birth year: 1946
Gender: Male
Age when reeducated or sent down: 18
Formal education completed before receiving reeducation or being sent down: Graduated from a high school–equivalent technical school in Beijing
Family background and status of family background at time of reeducation: Revolutionary cadre, bad
Total length of years for reeducation received or being sent down: 12 years, 1964–76
Form of reeducation: Among workers in a local factory in Beijing
City of return: Home city, Beijing
Current education level and employment status: AA, partner of an advertising agency
Member of the Chinese Communist Party: No
Interview date, location, and time: July 13, 2009, in Beijing, 2:00 PM–6:00 PM

Interviewee #12

Pseudonym: Ningli GAN
Age as of 2009: 59
Birth year: 1949
Gender: Female
Age when reeducated or sent down: 19
Formal education completed before receiving reeducation or being sent down: Ninth grade, last year of middle school
Family background and status of family background at time of reeducation: Administrative bureaucrat, bad (historical counterrevolutionary)
Total length of years for reeducation received or being sent down: 10 years, 1968–78
Form of reeducation: Countryside rural village, Inner Mongolia
City of return: Home city, Beijing, by divorcing her husband to qualify for the returning policy (later remarried her husband after ten years of separation waiting for a quota number allowing the work transfer of her husband to Beijing)
Current education level and employment status: BA, retired (formerly a bookkeeper)
Member of the Chinese Communist Party: No
Interview date, location, and time: July 14, 2009, in Beijing, 8:30 AM–12:30 PM

Interviewee #13

Pseudonym: Xiaolin GAO
Age as of 2009: 59
Birth year: 1950
Gender: Female
Age when reeducated or sent down: 19
Formal education completed before receiving reeducation or being sent down: Eighth grade, second year of middle school in Hangzhou, Zhejiang
Family background and status of family background at time of reeducation: Revolutionary cadre, bad
Total length of years for reeducation received or being sent down: 8 years, 1969–77
Form of reeducation: Military farm, Heilongjiang (northeast)
City of return: Harbin, Heilongjiang, to attend writers' training school
Current education level and employment status: Writers' training program, award-winning professional writer and novelist
Member of the Chinese Communist Party: Yes
Interview date, location, and time: July 14, 2009, in Beijing, 5:00 PM–7:00 PM

Interviewee #14

Pseudonym: Chengfei GU
Age as of 2009: 59
Birth year: 1950
Gender: Male
Age when reeducated or sent down: 18
Formal education completed before receiving reeducation or being sent down: Eighth grade, second year of middle school
Family background and status of family background at time of reeducation: Revolutionary cadre, bad
Total length of years for reeducation received or being sent down: 1 year, 1968–69
Form of reeducation: Military farm, Heilongjiang, left to join the PLA
City of return: Home city, Beijing
Current education level and employment status: Midlevel government bureaucrat in the CCP in Beijing
Member of the Chinese Communist Party: Yes
Interview date, location, and time: July 16, 2009, in Beijing, 9:30 AM–11:30 AM

Interviewee #15

Pseudonym: Haoyu GUAN
Age as of 2009: 55
Birth year: 1954
Gender: Male
Age when reeducated or sent down: 15
Formal education completed before receiving reeducation or being sent down: Ninth grade, third year of middle school
Family background and status of family background at time of reeducation: Intellectual, neutral
Total length of years for reeducation received or being sent down: 4 years, 1969–73
Form of reeducation: Military farm, Heilongjiang
City of return: Home city, Beijing, through admission to Beijing Foreign Studies University
Current education level and employment status: Postgraduate, deputy director of a research institute
Member of the Chinese Communist Party: Yes
Interview date, location, and time: July 16, 2009, in Beijing, 3:00 PM–6:00 PM

Interviewee #16 (Control)

Pseudonym: Zhiyong GUO
Age as of 2009: 61
Birth year: 1948
Gender: Male
Age when reeducated or sent down: 18
Formal education completed before receiving reeducation or being sent down: Twelfth grade, last year of high school
Family background and status of family background at time of reeducation: Rightist and bad element, bad
Total length of years for reeducation received or being sent down: 10 years, 1968–78
Form of reeducation: Returning youth, attending school in the Yongding county town and returned to ancestral rural village in Fujian
City of return: Shanghai, through admission to Fudan University
Current education level and employment status: BA, director of a writers' association

Member of the Chinese Communist Party: Yes
Interview date, location, and time: July 17, 2009, in Beijing, 10:00 AM–1:00 PM

Interviewee #17

Pseudonym: Haoran HAN
Age as of 2009: 61
Birth year: 1948
Gender: Male
Age when reeducated or sent down: 17
Formal education completed before receiving reeducation or being sent down: Eleventh grade, second year of high school
Family background and status of family background at time of reeducation: Petit bourgeois, bad
Total length of years for reeducation received or being sent down: 2 years, 1968–70
Form of reeducation: Countryside rural village, Shanxi
City of return: Taiyuan, through admission to Shanxi University
Current education level and employment status: BA, host of various radio station music programs
Member of the Chinese Communist Party: No
Interview date, location, and time: July 17, 2009, in Beijing, 3:00 PM–6:30 PM

Interviewee #18

Pseudonym: Yong HAO
Age as of 2009: 55
Birth year: 1954
Gender: Male
Age when reeducated or sent down: 15
Formal education completed before receiving reeducation or being sent down: Ninth grade, third year of middle school
Family background and status of family background at time of reeducation: Revolutionary cadre, good
Total length of years for reeducation received or being sent down: 2 years, 1969–71
Form of reeducation: Military farm, Yunnan, left to join the PLA
City of return: Home city, Beijing

Interviewee Profiles 191

Current education level and employment status: MA, general director of an international investment banking firm, China division
Member of the Chinese Communist Party: Yes
Interview date, location, and time: July 19, 2009, in Beijing, 10:00 AM–12:00 PM

Interviewee #19

Pseudonym: Hui HU
Age as of 2009: 59
Birth year: 1950
Gender: Female
Age when reeducated or sent down: 18
Formal education completed before receiving reeducation or being sent down: Ninth grade, third year of middle school in Heilongjiang
Family background and status of family background at time of reeducation: Urban poor, good
Total length of years for reeducation received or being sent down: 9 years, 1968–77
Form of reeducation: Military farm, Heilongjiang
City of return: Local county town, Heilongjiang
Current education level and employment status: BA, retired (formerly a high school teacher who taught politics)
Member of the Chinese Communist Party: No
Interview date, location, and time: July 19, 2009, in Beijing, 5:40 PM–7:00 PM

Interviewee #20

Pseudonym: Yishan HUANG
Age as of 2009: 58
Birth year: 1951
Gender: Female
Age when reeducated or sent down: 18
Formal education completed before receiving reeducation or being sent down: Seventh grade, second year of middle school
Family background and status of family background at time of reeducation: Revolutionary cadre, bad
Total length of years for reeducation received or being sent down: 4 years, 1969–early 1974
Form of reeducation: Countryside rural village, Shanxi

City of return: Home city, Beijing, through labor recruitment to work in a local factory in Beijing
Current education level and employment status: BA, director of a foreign-based company in steel technology
Member of the Chinese Communist Party: Yes
Interview date, location, and time: July 20, 2009, in Beijing, 9:30 AM–12:00 PM

Interviewee #21

Pseudonym: Jianhua JIANG
Age as of 2009: 62
Birth year: 1947
Gender: Male
Age when reeducated or sent down: 18
Formal education completed before receiving reeducation or being sent down: Twelfth grade, last year of high school
Family background and status of family background at time of reeducation: Revolutionary martyr, good
Total length of years for reeducation received or being sent down: 4 years, 1968–72
Form of reeducation: Military farm, Heilongjiang, left to join the PLA
City of return: Home city, Beijing
Current education level and employment status: BA, director and producer of TV military programs
Member of the Chinese Communist Party: Yes
Interview date, location, and time: July 20, 2009, in Beijing, 4:00 PM–6:00 PM

Interviewee #22

Pseudonym: Wanxin JIN
Age as of 2009: 56
Birth year: 1953
Gender: Male
Age when reeducated or sent down: 15
Formal education completed before receiving reeducation or being sent down: Sixth grade, finished elementary school
Family background and status of family background at time of reeducation: Revolutionary cadre, good

Interviewee Profiles

Total length of years for reeducation received or being sent down: 10 years, 1968–78
Form of reeducation: Military farm, Yunnan
City of return: Home city, Beijing
Current education level and employment status: BA, retired (formerly a government bureaucrat)
Member of the Chinese Communist Party: No
Interview date, location, and time: July 21, 2009, in Beijing, 1:00 PM–5:00 PM

Interviewee #23

Pseudonym: Zhi KONG
Age as of 2009: 61
Birth year: 1948
Gender: Male
Age when reeducated or sent down: 18
Formal education completed before receiving reeducation or being sent down: Twelfth grade, last year of high school
Family background and status of family background at time of reeducation: Revolutionary cadre, good
Total length of years for reeducation received or being sent down: 5 years, 1968–73
Form of reeducation: Military farm, Heilongjiang
City of return: Home city, Beijing
Current education level and employment status: Postgraduate, head of a financial investment firm
Member of the Chinese Communist Party: Yes
Interview date, location, and time: July 22, 2009, in Beijing, 3:00 PM–7:00 PM

Interviewee #24

Pseudonym: Ning LAN
Age as of 2009: 60
Birth year: 1949
Gender: Male
Age when reeducated or sent down: 18
Formal education completed before receiving reeducation or being sent down: Tenth grade, high school

Family background and status of family background at time of reeducation: Revolutionary cadre, good
Total length of years for reeducation received or being sent down: 10 years, 1967–77
Form of reeducation: Pastoral grasslands, Inner Mongolia
City of return: Home city, Beijing
Current education level and employment status: Postgraduate, professor at a university
Member of the Chinese Communist Party: Yes
Interview date, location, and time: July 23, 2009, in Beijing, 9:00 AM–1:00 PM

Interviewee #25

Pseudonym: Jia LI
Age as of 2009: 56
Birth year: 1953
Gender: Female
Age when reeducated or sent down: 15
Formal education completed before receiving reeducation or being sent down: Sixth grade, elementary school
Family background and status of family background at time of reeducation: Administrative bureaucrat, bad
Total length of years for reeducation received or being sent down: 9 years, 1969–78
Form of reeducation: Military farm, Yunnan
City of return: Kunming, Yunnan, through admission to Yunnan University, returned to home city, Beijing, through admission to graduate school in Beijing, returned to home city, Beijing
Current education level and employment status: Postgraduate, scholar, and researcher at a think tank
Member of the Chinese Communist Party: Yes
Interview date, location, and time: July 24, 2009, in Beijing, 9:30 AM–11:30 AM

Interviewee #26

Pseudonym: Jun LIANG
Age as of 2009: 55
Birth year: 1954
Gender: Male

Interviewee Profiles 195

Age when reeducated or sent down: 14 (turned 15 while being sent down)
Formal education completed before receiving reeducation or being sent down: Eighth grade, second year of middle school
Family background and status of family background at time of reeducation: Revolutionary cadre, bad
Total length of years for reeducation received or being sent down: 4 years, 1968–early 1973
Form of reeducation: Countryside rural village, Heilongjiang
City of return: Jilin, Heilongjiang
Current education level and employment status: Postgraduate, professor of international relations at an elite university
Member of the Chinese Communist Party: Yes
Interview date, location, and time: July 24, 2009, in Beijing, 2:50 PM–5:10 PM

Interviewee #27

Pseudonym: Liangyu LIAO
Age as of 2009: 59
Birth year: 1950
Gender: Male
Age when reeducated or sent down: 18
Formal education completed before receiving reeducation or being sent down: Ninth grade, third year of middle school
Family background and status of family background at time of reeducation: Revolutionary cadre, good
Total length of years for reeducation received or being sent down: 9 years, 1968–77
Form of reeducation: Military farm, Heilongjiang
City of return: Home city, Beijing
Current education level and employment status: BA, host of radio station current affairs and news programs
Member of the Chinese Communist Party: Yes
Interview date, location, and time: July 25, 2009, in Beijing, 3:00 PM–7:00 PM

Interviewee #28 (Control)

Pseudonym: Kang LIN
Age as of 2009: 60

Birth year: 1950
Gender: Male
Age when reeducated or sent down: 9
Formal education completed before receiving reeducation or being sent down: Third grade, elementary school
Family background and status of family background at time of reeducation: Revolutionary cadre, bad
Total length of years for reeducation received or being sent down: 9 years, 1968–77
Form of reeducation: Returning youth, went to live in a rural village with his grandfather, outskirts of Beijing
City of return: Beijing, through admission to University of Agronomy in Beijing
Current education level and employment status: BA, director of publications at a daily newspaper
Member of the Chinese Communist Party: Yes
Interview date, location, and time: July 26, 2009, in Beijing, 5:30 PM–8:30 PM (declined to be on tape, interview recorded by extensive notes)

Interviewee #29

Pseudonym: Lina LIU
Age as of 2009: 60
Birth year: 1949
Gender: Female
Age when reeducated or sent down: 18
Formal education completed before receiving reeducation or being sent down: Ninth grade, last year of middle school
Family background and status of family background at time of reeducation: Administrative bureaucrat, bad (historical counterrevolutionary)
Total length of years for reeducation received or being sent down: 8 years, 1968–76
Form of reeducation: Countryside rural village, Shanxi
City of return: Home city, Beijing
Current education level and employment status: Vocational school, retired (formerly a cashier at a state-run cookie shop)
Member of the Chinese Communist Party: No
Interview date, location, and time: July 27, 2009, in Beijing, 9:30 AM–12:30 PM

Interviewee #30

Pseudonym: Yan LU
Age as of 2009: 58
Birth year: 1951
Gender: Female
Age when reeducated or sent down: 17
Formal education completed before receiving reeducation or being sent down: Eighth grade, second year of middle school
Family background and status of family background at time of reeducation: Intellectual, bad
Total length of years for reeducation received or being sent down: 10 years, 1968–78
Form of reeducation: Countryside rural village, Shanxi
City of return: Home city, Beijing
Current education level and employment status: Vocational school, retired (formerly an administrative assistant)
Member of the Chinese Communist Party: No
Interview date, location, and time: July 28, 2009, in Beijing, 10:00 AM–12:00 PM

Interviewee #31

Pseudonym: Cheng LUO
Age as of 2009: 58
Birth year: 1951
Gender: Male
Age when reeducated or sent down: 18
Formal education completed before receiving reeducation or being sent down: Eighth grade, second year of middle school in Harbin, Heilongjiang
Family background and status of family background at time of reeducation: Worker, good
Total length of years for reeducation received or being sent down: 10 years, 1969–79
Form of reeducation: Military farm, Heilongjiang
City of return: Home city, Harbin
Current education level and employment status: Vocational school, retired (formerly a factory worker)
Member of the Chinese Communist Party: Yes
Interview date, location, and time: July 28, 2009, in Beijing, 2:00 PM–4:30 PM

Interviewee #32

Pseudonym: Linfen MA
Age as of 2009: 58
Birth year: 1951
Gender: Female
Age when reeducated or sent down: 18
Formal education completed before receiving reeducation or being sent down: Eighth grade, second year of middle school
Family background and status of family background at time of reeducation: Bad element (counterrevolutionary)
Total length of years for reeducation received or being sent down: 10 years, 1969–79
Form of reeducation: Military farm, Heilongjiang
City of return: Home city, Beijing
Current education level and employment status: Vocational school, retired (formerly a bus ticket seller)
Member of the Chinese Communist Party: Yes
Interview date, location, and time: July 28, 2009, in Beijing, 2:00 PM–4:30 PM

Interviewee #33

Pseudonym: Zhiyun MENG
Age as of 2009: 59
Birth year: 1950
Gender: Male
Age when reeducated or sent down: 18
Formal education completed before receiving reeducation or being sent down: Ninth grade, last year of middle school
Family background and status of family background at time of reeducation: Capitalist, bad
Total length of years for reeducation received or being sent down: 10 years, 1968–78
Form of reeducation: Military farm, Heilongjiang
City of return: Home city, Beijing
Current education level and employment status: BA, retired (formerly a government bureaucrat)
Member of the Chinese Communist Party: Yes
Interview date, location, and time: July 28, 2009, in Beijing, 6:00 PM–7:30 PM

Interviewee Profiles

Interviewee #34

Pseudonym: Wenbin MO
Age as of 2009: 61
Birth year: 1948
Gender: Male
Age when reeducated or sent down: 20
Formal education completed before receiving reeducation or being sent down: Eleventh grade, second year of high school
Family background and status of family background at time of reeducation: High intellectual, bad
Total length of years for reeducation received or being sent down: 7 years, 1968–75
Form of reeducation: Countryside rural village, Shanxi
City of return: Home city, Beijing
Current education level and employment status: Postgraduate, professor at an elite university
Member of the Chinese Communist Party: No
Interview date, location, and time: July 29, 2009, in Beijing, 3:00 PM–7:00 PM

Interviewee #35

Pseudonym: Yuxin PENG
Age as of 2009: 58
Birth year: 1951
Gender: Male
Age when reeducated or sent down: 17
Formal education completed before receiving reeducation or being sent down: Eighth grade, second year of middle school
Family background and status of family background at time of reeducation: High intellectual, bad
Total length of years for reeducation received or being sent down: 4 years, 1969–73
Form of reeducation: Countryside rural village, Shanxi
City of return: Settled in several other cities, unable to return to home city, Beijing, until 1990
Current education level and employment status: BA, director of a real estate company
Member of the Chinese Communist Party: Yes
Interview date, location, and time: July 30, 2009, in Beijing, 10:00 AM–12:00 PM

Interviewee #36

Pseudonym: Ling REN
Age as of 2009: 57
Birth year: 1952
Gender: Female
Age when reeducated or sent down: 16
Formal education completed before receiving reeducation or being sent down: Seventh grade, first year of middle school
Family background and status of family background at time of reeducation: Worker, good
Total length of years for reeducation received or being sent down: 7 years, 1968–75
Form of reeducation: Military farm, Heilongjiang
City of return: Home city, Beijing
Current education level and employment status: Vocational school, retired (formerly a factory bookkeeper)
Member of the Chinese Communist Party: No
Interview date, location, and time: July 30, 2009, in Beijing, 3:00 PM–5:00 PM

Interviewee #37

Pseudonym: Lei SHEN
Age as of 2009: 58
Birth year: 1951
Gender: Male
Age when reeducated or sent down: 18
Formal education completed before receiving reeducation or being sent down: Eighth grade, second year of middle school
Family background and status of family background at time of reeducation: Revolutionary soldier, good
Total length of years for reeducation received or being sent down: 9 years, 1969–78
Form of reeducation: Military farm, Heilongjiang
City of return: Home city, Beijing
Current education level and employment status: BA, staff in proofreading department of a daily newspaper
Member of the Chinese Communist Party: Yes
Interview date, location, and time: July 30, 2009, in Beijing, 3:00 PM–5:00 PM

Interviewee Profiles

Interviewee #38

Pseudonym: Chaowei SHI
Age as of 2009: 56
Birth year: 1953
Gender: Male
Age when reeducated or sent down: 16
Formal education completed before receiving reeducation or being sent down: Sixth grade, elementary school
Family background and status of family background at time of reeducation: High intellectual, neutral
Total length of years for reeducation received or being sent down: 8 years, 1969–77
Form of reeducation: Military farm, Heilongjiang
City of return: Home city, Beijing
Current education level and employment status: Actors' training; film, TV, and stage actor
Member of the Chinese Communist Party: Yes
Interview date, location, and time: July 30, 2009, in Beijing, 11:30 PM–1:30 AM

Interviewee #39

Pseudonym: Liya SONG
Age as of 2009: 56
Birth year: 1953
Gender: Female
Age when reeducated or sent down: 15
Formal education completed before receiving reeducation or being sent down: Eighth grade, second year of middle school
Family background and status of family background at time of reeducation: Revolutionary cadre, bad
Total length of years for reeducation received or being sent down: 8 years, 1968–75
Form of reeducation: Military farm, Heilongjiang
City of return: Xi'an, Shaanxi, later was able to return to home city, Beijing
Current education level and employment status: Vocational school, president of a travel agency
Member of the Chinese Communist Party: No
Interview date, location, and time: August 3, 2009, in Beijing, 11:00 AM–2:30 PM

Interviewee #40

Pseudonym: Tingyu SU
Age as of 2009: 57
Birth year: 1952
Gender: Female
Age when reeducated or sent down: 17
Formal education completed before receiving reeducation or being sent down: Eighth grade, second year of middle school
Family background and status of family background at time of reeducation: Intellectual, bad
Total length of years for reeducation received or being sent down: 5 years, 1969–73
Form of reeducation: (Pure) military farm, Inner Mongolia
City of return: Local small town, Inner Mongolia, to attend a technical school, returned to home city, Beijing, through job transfer 20 years later
Current education level and employment status: BA, retired (formerly an administrator at a science institute)
Member of the Chinese Communist Party: Yes
Interview date, location, and time: August 3, 2009, in Beijing, 11:00 AM–2:30 PM

Interviewee #41

Pseudonym: Hong SUN
Age as of 2009: 60
Birth year: 1949
Gender: Male
Age when reeducated or sent down: 18
Formal education completed before receiving reeducation or being sent down: Twelfth grade, last year of high school
Family background and status of family background at time of reeducation: Worker, good
Total length of years for reeducation received or being sent down: 4 years, 1967–71
Form of reeducation: Pastoral grasslands, Inner Mongolia
City of return: Xilinhot, Inner Mongolia, returned to home city, Beijing in 1983
Current education level and employment status: BA, market researcher and analyst for a foreign-based company in China

Member of the Chinese Communist Party: Yes
Interview date, location, and time: August 3, 2009, in Beijing, 3:30 PM–6:00 PM

Interviewee #42

Pseudonym: Jing TAN
Age as of 2009: 51
Birth year: 1958
Gender: Female
Age when reeducated or sent down: 18
Formal education completed before receiving reeducation or being sent down: Twelfth grade, completed high school
Family background and status of family background at time of reeducation: High intellectual, neutral
Total length of years for reeducation received or being sent down: 2 years, 1976–78
Form of reeducation: Countryside rural village, outskirts of Beijing
City of return: Home city, Beijing
Current education level and employment status: Postgraduate, licensed medical doctor in the United States
Member of the Chinese Communist Party: No
Interview date, location, and time: August 4, 2009, in Beijing, 8:00 AM–9:30 AM

Interviewee #43

Pseudonym: Bo TANG
Age as of 2009: 51
Birth year: 1958
Gender: Male
Age when reeducated or sent down: 18
Formal education completed before receiving reeducation or being sent down: Twelfth grade, completed high school
Family background and status of family background at time of reeducation: Capitalist, bad
Total length of years for reeducation received or being sent down: 1 year, 1976–77
Form of reeducation: Countryside rural village, outskirts of Beijing
City of return: Home city, Beijing

Current education level and employment status: MA, vice president of a large bank in the United States
Member of the Chinese Communist Party: No
Interview date, location, and time: August 4, 2009, in Beijing, 8:00 AM–9:30 AM

Interviewee #44

Pseudonym: Jie TIAN
Age as of 2009: 58
Birth year: 1951
Gender: Female
Age when reeducated or sent down: 17
Formal education completed before receiving reeducation or being sent down: Eighth grade, second year of middle school
Family background and status of family background at time of reeducation: Landlord, bad
Total length of years for reeducation received or being sent down: 8 years, 1968–76
Form of reeducation: Countryside rural village, Shanxi
City of return: Home city, Beijing
Current education level and employment status: Same education level as when sent down, retired (formerly a worker at a lock factory)
Member of the Chinese Communist Party: No
Interview date, location, and time: August 4, 2009, in Beijing, 3:30 PM–6:30 PM

Interviewee #45

Pseudonym: Yanli WAN
Age as of 2009: 59
Birth year: 1950
Gender: Female
Age when reeducated or sent down: 18
Formal education completed before receiving reeducation or being sent down: Ninth grade, third year of middle school
Family background and status of family background at time of reeducation: Intellectual, bad

Total length of years for reeducation received or being sent down: 3 years, 1968–71
Form of reeducation: Countryside rural village, Shanxi
City of return: Taiyuan, Shanxi, through admission to Shanxi University. Never returned to the home city, Beijing; later resettled in Shenzhen
Current education level and employment status: BA, retired (formerly a manager and director of personnel and human resources at a state-owned enterprise)
Member of the Chinese Communist Party: Yes
Interview date, location, and time: August 4, 2009, in Beijing, 3:30 PM–6:30 PM

Interviewee #46

Pseudonym: Ting WANG
Age as of 2009: 59
Birth year: 1950
Gender: Female
Age when reeducated or sent down: 18
Formal education completed before receiving reeducation or being sent down: Ninth grade, last year of middle school
Family background and status of family background at time of reeducation: Capitalist, bad
Total length of years for reeducation received or being sent down: 6 years, 1968–74
Form of reeducation: Military farm, Heilongjiang
City of return: Small town near the military farm, returned to Beijing, home city, after 1979 by divorcing her husband to qualify for the returning policy (remarried her husband after 8 years of separation)
Current education level and employment status: Vocational school, retired (formerly a bookkeeper)
Member of the Chinese Communist Party: No
Interview date, location, and time: August 5, 2009, in Beijing, 9:30 AM–12:30 PM

Interviewee #47

Pseudonym: Kai WEN
Age as of 2009: 60

Birth year: 1949
Gender: Male
Age when reeducated or sent down: 19
Formal education completed before receiving reeducation or being sent down: Ninth grade, last year of middle school
Family background and status of family background at time of reeducation: Revolutionary cadre, bad
Total length of years for reeducation received or being sent down: 12 years, 1968–late 1979
Form of reeducation: Military farm, Heilongjiang
City of return: Home city, Beijing
Current education level and employment status: AA, retired (formerly an administrator at a science institute)
Member of the Chinese Communist Party: No
Interview date, location, and time: August 5, 2009, in Beijing, 3:40 PM–7:40 PM

Interviewee #48

Pseudonym: Yun WU
Age as of 2009: 57
Birth year: 1952
Gender: Male
Age when reeducated or sent down: 17
Formal education completed before receiving reeducation or being sent down: Eighth grade, second year of middle school
Family background and status of family background at time of reeducation: Revolutionary cadre, bad
Total length of years for reeducation received or being sent down: 3 years, 1969–71
Form of reeducation: Military farm, Heilongjiang, then transferred to his father's Hebei ancestral rural village by "depending on family and relying on friends" as permitted under the policy
City of return: Shijiazhuang, Hebei; returned to home city, Beijing, in 1984 qualified under the "older in age still single and unmarried" policy amendment
Current education level and employment status: BA, administrator in an organization for athletics and sports
Member of the Chinese Communist Party: Yes
Interview date, location, and time: August 6, 2009, in Beijing, 3:30 PM–5:30 PM

Interviewee #49

Pseudonym: Lijun YANG
Age as of 2009: 62
Birth year: 1947
Gender: Female
Age when reeducated or sent down: 20
Formal education completed before receiving reeducation or being sent down: Twelfth grade, last year of high school
Family background and status of family background at time of reeducation: Revolutionary cadre, bad
Total length of years for reeducation received or being sent down: 3 years, 1967–70
Form of reeducation: Pastoral grasslands, Inner Mongolia
City of return: Local city through job transfer to work in the municipal government in Inner Mongolia; returned to home city, Beijing, under "family difficulty" as permitted by the policy qualifying under "no child in the family was residing close by to take care of aging parents" in 1978
Current education level and employment status: BA, director of a senior bureaucrats training center
Member of the Chinese Communist Party: Yes
Interview date, location, and time: August 7, 2009, in Beijing, 12 PM–1:00 PM on the phone (declined to be on tape, interview recorded by extensive notes)

Interviewee #50

Pseudonym: Kelin YU
Age as of 2009: 57
Birth year: 1952
Gender: Male
Age when reeducated or sent down: 14 (turned 15 while sent down)
Formal education completed before receiving reeducation or being sent down: Seventh grade, first year of middle school
Family background and status of family background at time of reeducation: Revolutionary cadre, good
Total length of years for reeducation received or being sent down: 4 years, 1968–72
Form of reeducation: Countryside rural village, Shaanxi
City of return: Home city, Beijing, through admission to a university in Beijing

Current education level and employment status: BA, owner of a trading company
Member of the Chinese Communist Party: Yes
Interview date, location, and time: August 7, 2009, in Beijing, 3:30 PM–5:30 PM

Interviewee #51

Pseudonym: Ying YUAN
Age as of 2009: 60
Birth year: 1949
Gender: Female
Age when reeducated or sent down: 19
Formal education completed before receiving reeducation or being sent down: Ninth grade, last year of middle school
Family background and status of family background at time of reeducation: Administrative bureaucrat, bad
Total length of years for reeducation received or being sent down: 17 years in a factory, Taiyuan, Shanxi, 1968–85
Form of reeducation: Although she was supposed to be sent down to a rural village in Shanxi, she was immediately recruited into a local factory in Taiyuan city and received reeducation in a factory among workers instead
City of return: Was unable to return to home city, Beijing; finally returned after she retired
Current education level and employment status: AA, retired (formerly a personnel administrator at a municipal government)
Member of the Chinese Communist Party: Yes
Interview date, location, and time: August 10, 2009, in Beijing, 1:30 PM–5:00 PM

Interviewee #52

Pseudonym: Jian ZHANG
Age as of 2009: 57
Birth year: 1952
Gender: Male
Age when reeducated or sent down: 16
Formal education completed before receiving reeducation or being sent down: Seventh grade, first year of middle school

Interviewee Profiles

Family background and status of family background at time of reeducation: Intellectual, bad
Total length of years for reeducation received or being sent down: 5 years, 1968–73
Form of reeducation: Pastoral grasslands, Inner Mongolia
City of return: Local city, Inner Mongolia, to attend a technical school; returned to home city, Beijing, through admission to graduate school
Current education level and employment status: PhD, scholar and researcher at a public policy research institute
Member of the Chinese Communist Party: No
Interview date, location, and time: August 11, 2009, in Beijing, 11:40 AM–2:05 PM

Interviewee #53

Pseudonym: Ming ZHAO
Age as of 2009: 58
Birth year: 1951
Gender: Male
Age when reeducated or sent down: 17
Formal education completed before receiving reeducation or being sent down: Eighth grade, last year of middle school
Family background and status of family background at time of reeducation: Intellectual, bad
Total length of years for reeducation received or being sent down: 7 years, 1968–75
Form of reeducation: Military farm, Yunnan
City of return: Home city, Beijing, through sick leave as permitted under the policy
Current education level and employment status: Same education level as when sent down, retired (formerly a worker in automobile parts factory)
Member of the Chinese Communist Party: No
Interview date, location, and time: August 11, 2009, in Beijing, 3:34 PM–5:00 PM

Interviewee #54 (Military Representative)

Pseudonym: Zhixin ZHOU
Age as of 2009: 66

Birth year: 1943
Gender: Male
Age when reeducated or sent down: 24, when he was sent into an all-girls high school in the fall of 1967 to reclaim the school administration prior to the implementation of the sent-down policy; essentially worked as a school administrator
Formal education completed before receiving reeducation or being sent down: Completed his high school education when enlisted in the military at 21
Family background and status of family background at time of reeducation: Poor peasant, good (his family background was impeccable when he enlisted in 1964, as one had to pass "political assessment" before being selected for military service)
Total length of years for reeducation received or being sent down: 2 years of service as a military rep (frontline training); he worked as a military rep for the all-girls' high school for 1 year from 1967 to 1968 and assumed the role of the principal administrator for an elementary school the following year
Form of reeducation: Both schools where he served were located in Beijing City
City of return: N/A
Current education level and employment status: Same education level, retired (formerly a chauffeur in a state-owned enterprise, a job assigned to him after he was discharged from the military when his tour ended)
Member of the Chinese Communist Party: Yes
Interview date, location, and time: August 20, 2009, in Shenzhen, 11:00 AM–12:45 PM

Notes

1. Those in the "control" group were under parallel policies for socialist reeducation that were administered through other programs.

2. The interviewees' last names are capitalized.

3. The interviewees came from the full variety of the family class designations used during the Cultural Revolution, ranging from the top (revolutionary martyr, revolutionary soldier [military personnel], revolutionary cadre [military officer], worker, and poor and middle peasant) to the bottom five bad classes (landlord, rich peasant, counterrevolutionary, bad element, and rightist) to which capitalist roader and reactionary academic authority were added. Family background status was subject to change during the Cultural Revolution as individuals were targeted or persecuted for various reasons. For instance, this happened to Lijun Yang (I49), whose family was originally of revolutionary cadre background but later became bad because her father was labeled as a counterrevolutionary.

Appendix B

Interview Schedule

Opening Statement

[In Chinese] Thank you very much for agreeing to talk with me about your experiences during the Cultural Revolution for my research. I am primarily interested in the rustication program of the Cultural Revolution, especially the administrative organization involved in sending seventeen million urban youth up to the mountains and down to the countryside and subsequently arranging their return to the cities. Please feel free to decline to answer questions as you may wish. Your anonymity will be protected and nothing from the interview will be used that could identify you or others personally. Please be as expansive in answering the questions as you like.

General background questions

1. When were you born? Where?
2. Did you participate in the Cultural Revolution (CR)?
   a. How? Were you in the Red Guard?
3. How was your family affected by the CR?
4. Did you support the CR?
5. How? Why? Why not?
6. The CR was very disruptive of the Chinese society and economy. Why do you suppose people supported it?
7. Was China egalitarian when you were growing up?

Rustication Questions

1. Do you remember your reaction when Mao first called on students to rusticate?
   a. What was it?

2. What do you remember about the *administrative processes* of being sent down to the countryside?
    a. Did you volunteer? Why? Why not?
    b. How were you selected?
    c. Was there pressure? From whom?
    d. How old were you when you were sent down? What was your school/education level at the time?
    e. Could you refuse to be sent down? Evade being sent down? Do you know anyone who avoided being sent down? How? What were the consequences?
    f. What did your parents think about having a child sent down? Did they take any action to try to prevent it? What did they do?
    g. How many children in your family were sent down?
    h. What was the effect of the rustication policy on your family?
3. Please describe your sent-down experience from start to finish.
    a. Prompts: who selected you, how, determined where you went; on what basis; canceled *hukou*, transportation, treatment on arrival, work assignments, hierarchy, work points, daily life, health care, socialist (re)education in countryside;
    b. Institutional coordination; returning home—when, how, what was the process;
    c. Overall experience.
4. Would you say your experience was representative or atypical? Why or why not?
5. How long did you remain in the countryside?
6. What was life like there in terms of procedures for marriage, housing, food rationing, returning home for a visit?
7. Did you think about remaining in the countryside? Why? Why not?

Bureaucratic Questions

From an administrative (bureaucratic) perspective, how was rustication organized?
1. How many cadres were involved on the sending side and receiving end?
2. Did they follow rules strictly or use discretion?
3. Were they influenced by *guanxi* (connections, relationships)? How?
4. Some sent-downs went to better places. Why? Did they receive favorable treatment? How?
5. Overall, can you estimate the number of bureaucrats you encountered or knew who were involved in your personal sent-down experience?

6. How well organized was your daily life? By whom? Was it regimented? Did you have any free time?
7. What was the attitude of the bureaucrats involved in your entire sent-down experience? Would you say they were caring, impersonal, rigid, flexible, committed to the program, mostly interested in maintaining their own positions, making the program work?
8. When a sent-down had a grievance, how was it handled (what was the process)?
9. What were the main differences between state farms and military farms?
10. Overall, do you think that the cadres' children were sent to better locations? Received better treatment? Returned to their homes sooner?
    a. If so, why did that happen? What was the process?
11. Please describe how you returned.
    a. Prompts: permission, paperwork, transportation, *hukou* registration, housing, job, health care, marriage, family, role of bureaucrats.

Final Comments

This interview has been very helpful. I appreciate your willingness to talk with me. Is there anything we haven't covered that you would like to mention or explain?

Glossary

Anti-Confucius Campaign (1973–74): Campaign to discredit Confucian thought and its influence on Chinese culture.
Anti-Interference Campaign (1966): The Chinese Communist Party's campaign against rebelling students on university campuses.
Antirightist Campaign (1957): Campaign to purge rightists from the Chinese Communist Party.
barefoot doctor: A backpack medic who makes rounds in rural areas.
Bitter Years of Great Famine (1959–61): Famine following the Great Leap Forward.
Counterrevolutionary: Interchangeable with "revisionist" and "capitalist roader"; refers to those who dissented from Mao's vision for Communist China.
Cultural Revolution: Mao Zedong's attempt, beginning in 1965, to reassert his leadership and imbue China with revolutionary socialism. Variously dated to 1968 or 1976, when Mao died.
danwei: A work unit organization or institution.
Four Olds: Old ideas, cultures, habits, and customs.
Great Leap Forward (1958–60): Mao's effort to rapidly modernize China.
hukou: Residential permit.
Hundred Flowers Campaign (1957): Mao Zedong's campaign to "Let a hundred flowers bloom together, let the hundred schools of thought contend."
May Seventh Cadre School: Farms called cadre schools across China where cadres and intellectuals were sent down from the cities to engage in socialist reeducation and manual labor; established in 1968 in response to Mao Zedong's earlier call on May 7, 1966, for such schools.
Red Army: Communist Party military prior to the founding of the People's Liberation Army.
Sanfan (1951): The three antis—anticorruption, antiwaste, and antibureaucratic spirit.
sanzi yibao: Three-freedom policy permitting the personal use of small plots of land, small-scale commerce in nongrain produce, and cooking in individual homes.
shanghen wenxue: Variously translated as "scar" or "wound" literature; based on a short story titled "The Wound."
shangshan xiaxiang: Up to the mountains and down to the countryside.

Siqing (1962): Also known as the "Socialist Education Movement," the four cleansings of politics, economics, organization, and ideology.

Sufan (1955): Campaign to wipe out hidden counterrevolutionaries.

Weberian: Referring to the work of Max Weber (1864–1920), a German social scientist who is known for his analysis of bureaucracy, among other phenomena.

work team: Task force teams sent to take over the leadership of a given institution.

Wufan (1952): Five antis—antibribery, antitax evasion, antifraud, antitheft of government property, and antistealing of state economic secrets.

xiafang: Exiled or sent away for socialist reeducation.

zhiqing: Contraction of *zhishi qingnian*, meaning "knowledgeable youth" in Chinese, which is the Chinese term for sent-downs.

References

Ake, Claude. 1987. "The African Context of Human Rights" *Africa Today* 34, nos. 1 & 2: 83–89.

Bernstein, Thomas P. 1977a. *Up to the Mountains and Down to the Villages: The Transfer of Youth from Urban to Rural China*. New Haven, CT: Yale University Press.

———. 1977b. "Urban Youth in the Countryside: Problems of Adaptation and Remedies," *China Quarterly* 69 (March): 75–108.

———. 1984. "Stalinism, Famine, and Chinese Peasants: Grain Procurements during the Great Leap Forward," *Theory and Society* 13, no. 3: 339–77.

Borcherding, Thomas, ed. 1977. *Budgets and Bureaucrats*. Durham, NC: Duke University Press.

CCP. 2006. "News of the Communist Party of China: Comments and Historical Resolution," *Communist Party of China*, June 14. Accessed March 10, 2009, http://english.cpc.people.com.cn/66095/4471924.html.

Chan, Hon. 2004. "Cadre Personnel Management in China: The Nomenklatura System, 1990–1998," *China Quarterly* 179:703–34.

Chan, Kam Wing, and Li Zhang. 1999. "The Hukou System and Rural-Urban Migration in China: Processes and Changes," *China Quarterly* 160 (December): 818–55.

Chang, Jung, and Jon Halliday. 2005. *Mao: The Unknown Story*. London: Jonathan Cape.

Chen, Pi-chao. 1972. "Overurbanization, Rustication of Urban-Educated Youths, and Politics of Rural Transformation: The Case of China," *Comparative Politics* 4, no. 3: 361–86.

Clark, Paul. 2008. *The Chinese Cultural Revolution: A History*. New York: Cambridge University Press.

Danet, Brenda. 1989. *Pulling Strings: Biculturalism in Israeli Bureaucracy*. Albany: State University of New York Press.

Deng, Zhou, and Donald J. Treiman. 1997. "The Impact of the Cultural Revolution on Trends in Educational Attainment in the People's Republic of China," *American Journal of Sociology* 103, no. 2: 391–428.

Djilas, Milovan. 1957. *The New Class*. New York: Praeger.

Downs, Anthony. 1967. *Inside Bureaucracy*. Boston: Little, Brown.

Fairbank, John King, and Merle Goldman. 1992. *China: A New History*, 2nd ed. Cambridge, MA: Harvard University Press.

———. 2006. *China: A New History*, 2nd enlarged ed. Cambridge, MA: Harvard University Press.

FAO. 2006. *The State of World Fisheries and Aquaculture 2006*. Rome, Italy: Food and Agriculture Organization of the United Nations.

Feng, Jicai. 1996. *Ten Years of Madness: Oral Histories of China's Cultural Revolution*. San Francisco: China Books & Periodicals, Inc.

Gong, Ting, and Steven Ma, eds. 2009. *Preventing Corruption in Asia*. New York: Routledge.

Gregor, A. James, and Maria Hsia Chang. 1979. "Anti-Confucianism: Mao's Last Campaign," *Asian Survey* 19, no. 11: 1073–92.

Heidenheimer, Arnold. 1989. "Perspectives on the Perception of Corruption." In *Political Corruption: A Handbook*, edited by Arnold Heidenheimer, Michael Johnston, and Victor Levine, 149–63. New Brunswick, NJ: Transaction Books.

Hummel, Ralph. 1994. *The Bureaucratic Experience*, 4th ed. New York: St. Martin's Press.

Hung, Eva P. W., and Stephen W. K. Chiu. 2003. "The Lost Generation: Life Course Dynamics and Xiagang in China," *Modern China* 29, no. 2: 204–36.

Jacoby, Henry. 1973. *The Bureaucratization of the World*. Berkeley: University of California Press.

Jowett, A. J. 1984. "The Growth of China's Population, 1949–1982," *Geographic Journal* 150, no. 2: 155–70.

Jreisat, Jamil. 2012. *Globalization and Comparative Administration*. Boca Raton, FL: CRC Press.

Kalberg. Stephen. 2003. "Max Weber." In *The Blackwell Companion to Major Classical Social Theorists*, edited by George Ritzer, 144–204. Malden, MA: Blackwell.

Laliberté, André, and Marc Lanteigne. 2008. *The Chinese Party-State in the 21st Century*. New York: Routledge.

Latham, Kevin. 2007. *Pop Culture China! Media, Arts and Lifestyle*. Santa Barbara, CA: ABC-CLIO.

Lee, Hong Yung. 1978. *The Politics of the Chinese Cultural Revolution: A Case Study*. Berkeley: University of California Press.

———. 1991. *From Revolutionary Cadres to Party Technocrats in Socialist China*. Berkeley: University of California Press.

Leung, Laifong. 1994. *Morning Sun: Interviews with Chinese Writers of the Lost Generation*. Armonk, NY: M. E. Sharpe.

Li, Kwok-sing. 1995. *A Glossary of Political Terms of the People's Republic of China*, translated by Mary Lok. Shatin, NT, Hong Kong: Chinese University Press.

Lipsky, Michael. 1980. *Street-Level Bureaucracy: Dilemmas of the Individual in Public Services*. New York: Russell Sage Foundation.

Liu, Xiaomeng. 2009. *Zhongguo Zhiqing Shi: Dachao (1966–1980)* [*Chinese Zhiqing History*], 2nd ed. Beijing: Contemporary China Publishing House.

MacFarquhar, Roderick, and Michael Schoenhals. 2006. *Mao's Last Revolution*. Cambridge, MA: Harvard University Press.

Manning, Kimberly. 2005. "Marxist Maternalism, Memory, and Mobilization of Women in the Great Leap Forward," *China Review* 5, no. 1: 83–110.

———. 2008. "Communes, Canteens, and Crèches: The Gendered Politics of Remembering the Great Leap Forward." In *Re-envisioning the Cultural Revolution*, edited by Ching Kwan Lee and Goubin Yang, 93–118. Stanford, CA: Stanford University Press.

Mao, Tse Tung. 1939. "The Orientation of the Youth Movement," *Selected Works of Mao Tse-tung* (May 4), www.marxists.org/reference/archive/mao/selected-works/volume-2/mswv2_14.htm (accessed January 11, 2010).

———. 1965. "Directive on Public Health," *Selected Works of Mao Tse-Tung*, www.marxists.org/reference/archive/mao/selected-works/volume-9/mswv9_41.htm (accessed January 11, 2010).

———. 1966. *Quotations from Mao Tse-Tung*. Peking: Foreign Languages Press. Accessed January 11, 2010, www.marxists.org/reference/archive/mao/works/red-book/.

———. 1967. "Problems of War and Strategy." From the *Selected Works of Mao Tse-tung*, vol. II, 219–35. Peking: Foreign Languages Press. Accessed January 11, 2010, www.marx2mao.com/Mao/PWS38.html.

———. 1968. "We too Have Two Hands, Let Us not Laze about in the City." *People's Daily*, December 12.

Marx, Karl. 1845. *The German Ideology*. Part I: Feuerbach. Opposition of the Materialist and Idealist Outlook A. Idealism and Materialism. Private Property and Communism. Accessed December 10, 2009, www.marxists.org/archive/marx/works/1845/german-ideology/ch01a.htm#4.

———. 1875. *Critique of the Gotha Programme*. Section I. Accessed December 10, 2009, www.marxists.org/archive/marx/works/1875/gotha/index.htm.

Marx, Karl, and Frederick Engels. 1847. *Manifesto of the Communist Party*. Proletarians and Communists. Accessed December 10, 2009, www.marxists.org/archive/marx/works/1848/communist-manifesto/.

Mashaw, Jerry. 1983. *Bureaucratic Justice: Managing Social Security Disability Claims*. New Haven, CT: Yale University Press.

Maynard-Moody, Steven, and Michael Musheno, 2003. *Cops, Teachers, Counselors*. Ann Arbor: University of Michigan Press.

Mayo, Elton. 1945. *The Social Problems of an Industrial Civilization*. Boston: Graduate School of Business, Harvard University.

Meisner, Maurice. 1971a. "Leninism and Maoism: Some Populist Perspectives on Marxism-Leninism in China," *China Quarterly* 45 (January–March): 2–36.

———. 1971b. "Images of the Paris Commune in Contemporary Chinese Marxist Thought," *The Massachusetts Review* 12, no. 3: 479–97.

———. 1977. "The Maoist Legacy and Chinese Socialism," *Asian Survey* 17, no. 11: 1016–27.

———. 1999. *Mao's China and After: A History of the People's Republic*, 3rd ed. New York: Free Press.

Michels, Robert. *Political Parties: A Sociological Study of the Oligarchical Tendencies of Modern Democracy*. Glenco, IL: Free Press, 1949.

Milner, Graham. No date. "China Youth and the Cultural Revolution," *Links International Journal of Socialist Renewal*. Accessed December 10, 2009, http://links.org.au/node/1326.

Myrdal, Jan. 1965. *Report from a Chinese Village*. New York: Pantheon/Random House.

Nachmias, David, and David H. Rosenbloom. 1978. *Bureaucratic Culture: Citizens and Administrators in Israel*. New York: St. Martin's Press.

Nanchu. 2001. *Red Sorrow*. New York: Arcade Publishing.

Niskanen, William, Jr. 1971. *Bureaucracy and Representative Government*. Chicago: Aldine Atherton.

Pan, Yihong. 2003. *Tempered in the Revolutionary Furnace: China's Youth in the Rustication Movement*. Lanham, MD: Lexington Books.

Peng, Xizhe. 1987. "Demographic Consequences of the Great Leap Forward in China's Provinces." *Population and Development Review* 13, no. 4: 639–70.

Poon, Leon. No date. "The People's Republic of China: III, The Cultural Revolution Decade, 1966–76." Accessed December 10, 2009, www.chaos.umd.edu./history/prc3.html.

Rondinelli, Dennis. 1993. *An Adaptive Approach to Development Administration*, 2nd ed. London: Routledge.

Rosen, Stanley. 1981. *The Role of Sent-Down Youth in the Chinese Cultural Revolution: The Case of Guangzhou*. China Research Monograph No. 19. Berkeley: University of California Center for Chinese Studies.

Rosenbloom, David H. 2009. "Foreword." In *Preventing Corruption in Asia*, edited by Ting Gong and Steven Ma, xiv–xvii. New York: Routledge.

Rosenbloom, David H., Robert Kravchuk, and Richard Clerkin. 2009. *Public Administration: Understanding Management, Politics, and Law in the Public Sector*, 7th ed. New York: McGraw-Hill Higher Education.

Seybolt, Peter J. 1977. *The Rustication of Urban Youth in China*. White Plains, NY: M. E. Sharpe.

Shapiro, Judith. 2001. *Mao's War against Nature: Politics and the Environment in Revolutionary China*. New York: Cambridge University Press.

Shirk, Susan. 1978. "Book Review," *Journal of Asian Studies* 38, no. 1: 148–52.

Singer, Martin. 1971. *Educated Youth and the Cultural Revolution in China*. Ann Arbor: University of Michigan Center for Chinese Studies.

Snow, Edgar. 1973. *The Long Revolution*. New York: Vintage Press.

Teiwes, Frederick. 1993. *Politics and Purges in China: Rectification and the Decline of Party Norms, 1950–1965*, 2nd ed. Armonk, NY: M. E. Sharpe.

Thaxton, Ralph, Jr. 2008. *Catastrophe and Contention in Rural China: Mao's Great Leap Forward Famine*. New York: Cambridge University Press.

Thompson, Victor. 1961. *Modern Organization*. New York: Alfred A. Knopf.

Tyler, Patrick E. 1997. "Deng Xiaoping: A Political Wizard Who Put China on the Capitalist Road," *New York Times*, February 20.

Unger, Jonathan. 1979. "China's Troubled Down-to-the-Countryside Campaign," *Contemporary China* 3:79–92. Accessed December 10, 2009, http://ips.cap.anu.edu.au/psc/ccc/publications/papers/JU_Troubled_Campaign.pdf.

Vogel, Ezra. 1967. "Revolutionary to Semi-Bureaucrat: The 'Regularisation' of Cadres," *China Quarterly* 29 (January–March): 36–60.

Vohra, Ranbir. 2000. *China's Path to Modernization: A Historical Review from 1800 to the Present*, 3rd ed. Upper Saddle River, NJ: Prentice-Hall.

Weber, Max. 1958. *From Max Weber: Essays in Sociology*. Edited and translated by H. H. Gerth and C. W. Mills. New York: Oxford University Press.

———. 1964. *The Theory of Social and Economic Organization*. Edited and translated by Talcott Parsons. New York: Free Press.

———. 1994. *Max Weber: Political Writings*. Edited and translated by Peter Lassman and Ronald Speirs. New York: Cambridge University Press.

Whyte, Martin King. 1980. "Bureaucracy and Antibureaucracy in the People's Republic of China." In *Hierarchy & Society*, edited by Gerald Britan and Ronald Cohen, 123–41. Philadelphia: Institute for the Study of Human Issues.

Yan, Jiaqi, and Gao Gao. 1996. *Turbulent Decade: A History of the Cultural Revolution*. Edited and translated by D. W. Y. Kwok. Honolulu: SHAPS Library of Translation, University of Hawai'i Press.

Yu, Shicun, and Francesco Sisci. 2002. "China's Numbers Game." *Asia Times Online*, May 3. www.atimes.com/china/DD03Ad02.html (accessed January 11, 2010).

Zhou, Qingjun. 1994. "Mao Zedong (1893–1976): The Educational Doctrine of Mao Zedong," *Quarterly Review of Comparative Education* 24, no. 1/2: 93–106.

Zhou, Xueguang. 2004. *The State and Life Chances in Urban China: Redistribution and Stratification, 1949–1994*. Cambridge: Cambridge University Press.

Zhou, Xueguang, and Liren Hou. 1999. "Children of the Cultural Revolution: The State and the Life Course in the People's Republic of China," *American Sociological Review* 64:12–36.

Index

administration of the rustication program, 81–82
  bureaucratic control exercised through, 159–60
  bureaucratic impersonality in, 112–13
  efficiency and effectiveness of, xi–xiii, 1–4, 104, 111–17
  failings of, 176–79
  implementation at the receiving end, 85–88, 169
  ironies created by, 160–61, 176
  military and state farms, 82–84, 139–45, 153–56
  overall structure and operation, 104–11
  personnel involved in, number of, 117–18
  the receiving end, efficiency on, 116–17
  return to cities, process of, 150–52
  rural villages and Inner Mongolian grasslands, 84–85, 131–37, 145–48, 156–59
  street-level administrative behavior, 152–59
  transporting sent-downs to their destinations, 128–31
administrative culture, impact of rustication on, 118
  discretion and power, 121–23, 151–52
  guanxi and corruption, 123–28, 150, 164, 178
  privileges of bureaucrats, 119–21
agrarian socialism, 26
Anti-Confucius Campaign, 91–92
Anti-Interference Campaign, 44
Antirightist Campaign, 28

Bai, Weimin, 181
Bernstein, Thomas, 7, 86–87, 95–96
Bitter Years of Great Famine, 30–31, 34–35
Bo Yibo, 45
bureaucracy
  the army and Weberian, 61–63, 68–69
  conceptual framework for analyzing, 4–6
  continuity of despite the Cultural Revolution, 52–54, 69–71
  the First Five-Year Plan and, 19–21, 55
  the "iron cage" consequences of, 23–24
  Maoist Marxian *vs.* Chinese Weberian (*see* Maoist Marxians *vs.* Chinese Weberians)
  Mao's struggle with, xii, 1–6, 18, 22, 25–35 (*see also* politics of the Cultural Revolution)
  the new elite, rise of, 22
  revolution committees, 70–71
  routinization of CCP, the Cultural Revolution and, 51–52
  rustication program and, 79, 88, 100–101 (*see also* rustication program)
  war on, the Cultural Revolution as, 38 (*see also* Cultural Revolution; politics of the Cultural Revolution)
  Weber's theory of and Chinese economic development, 19–21
  See also public administration

"cadre," 35n.1
Cai, Yonglin, 181–82
Cao Yiou, 42
CCP. *See* Chinese Communist Party

Chen, Qiang, 182
Chen Boda, 41, 54
Cheng, Wei, 183
Chen Jiangong, 37
Chen Zaidao, 66
China, People's Republic of (PRC)
  as party-state, 13n.7, 15
  timeline, 1949–1962, 17
Chinese Communist Party (CCP)
  Antirightist Campaign of, 28
  bureaucratic power and privileged elites in, 4–6
  Mao's conflicts with the elite bureaucrats of, 26–31, 38 (see also Cultural Revolution; Maoist Marxians vs. Chinese Weberians)
  "mass line," definition of, 15–16
  party-state, role in, 15
  Red Guards and privileged elites in, 48–49
  Weberian bureaucratization of (see Chinese Weberians)
Chinese Weberians
  Maoist Marxians vs. (See Maoist Marxians vs. Chinese Weberians; politics of the Cultural Revolution)
  pragmatic trade-off of freedom for economic development, 24
  restoration of, 32
  rise of, 18–24
Chu-Chou model, 86
class divisions, 46–51
Confucianism, 46
Confucius, 91–92
Cultural Revolution
  Anti-Interference Campaign, 44
  armed struggle as official policy of, 68–69
  beginnings of, 40–43
  bureaucracy, failure to achieve goals regarding, 163–64
  deescalation of, Mao's strategic plan for, 69–71
  the February countercurrent, 62–65
  framework for understanding, 4–6
  guanxi and, 124–28
  interviewees' perceptions of bureaucratic administration during, 71–72
  the January seizure of power, 56, 59–62
  June 18 incident, 44
  Mao's goals in, 2, 4, 69
  May 16 Notice, 41
  politics of (see politics of the Cultural Revolution)
  public administration, continued functioning of, 2–3
  the Red Guards (see Red Guards)
  rustication program as culmination of, 75–76 (see also rustication program)
  timeline of, 39
  the Up to the Mountains and Down to the Countryside campaign (see rustication program)
  the Wuhan Incident, 65–68
Cultural Revolution Small Group, 41–43, 51–52, 54, 56, 61–63, 65–70

Deng, Min, 154, 162n.17, 183–84
Deng, Zhou, 94
Deng Tuo, 41
Deng Xiaoping, 27–28, 31–33, 41, 43–45, 51–52, 54–57, 73n.8, 91–92, 163
Ding, Bin, 3, 20, 34–35, 53, 72, 106–7, 111, 114, 117–18, 122–24, 128–36, 139, 148–51, 157–59, 162n.15, 162n.18, 163, 165, 169, 174–75, 184
Downs, Anthony, 63
Du, Fei, 184–85
Duan, Chao, 53, 102n.5, 112, 114, 117, 120, 124, 137, 148, 157, 162n.14, 172, 185

economic development
  agrarian socialism, 26
  Bitter Years of Great Famine, 30–31, 34–35
  communalization as Mao's antibureaucratic approach to, 24–25
  First Five-Year Plan, 18–23, 55, 76
  Great Leap Forward, 25, 28–32, 34–35
  mass line vs. rational public administration and, 16, 18
  public administration and, 33–35
  Second Five-Year Plan, 26–29
  Third Five-Year Plan, 44
  timeline of pre-Cultural Revolution administration and, 17

Index

education/reeducation for socialism, 92–94, 164–75
  hard labor, tempering and socialist thought reform through, 173–75
  Mao's Thought, study of, 165–68
  peasantry and peasant life, connecting with, 165–68, 168–73

family structure, 90–92
Fan, Tao, 102n.13, 107–8, 113–14, 120, 122, 124, 137–39, 148, 155–56, 159, 162n.14, 166–67, 169–70, 172, 185–86
Fang, Mei, 148, 150, 186
Feng, Dan, 186–87
First Five-Year Plan, 18–23, 55, 76
freedom, trade-off between bureaucracy and, 23–24

Gan, Ningli, 20, 110–11, 112, 115, 118, 121, 124, 130–31, 147–49, 157, 162n.20, 171–72, 187
Gao, Gao, 96–97
Gao, Xiaolin, 149, 188
Gao Gang, 25
gender
  female sent-downs, particular difficulties faced by, 152–53
  military farms, sexual predation at, 153–56
  rural villages, differential treatment and sexual predation in, 156–59
  in rustication program implementation, 112, 177
Great Exchange of Revolutionary Experience program, 78
Great Leap Forward, 25, 28–32, 34–35
Great Proletarian Cultural Revolution. *See* Cultural Revolution
Gu, Chengfei, 149, 188
Guan, Haoyu, 149, 189
Guan Feng, 41
guanxi (personal networks), 6–7, 87–88, 123–28, 150, 164, 178
Guo, Zhiyong, 189–90

Hai Rui, 40
Han, Haoran, 148, 190

Hao, Yong, 149, 190–91
Hou, Liren, 161n.5, 162n.13
Hu, Hui, 149, 191
Hua Guofeng, 73n.8
Huang, Yishan, 148–49, 191–92
hukou (residential permit) system, 23, 81–82
Hummel, Ralph, 23–24
Hundred Flowers Campaign, 26–28
Hu Ping, 46

insertion system, 84–85
interviewees
  family background status of, 8, 210n.3
  information, as source of, 6–7
  procedures and sample, 7–12
  profiles of, 181–210
iron rice bowl, policy of, 55
Israel, bureaucratic and administrative culture, 123

Jiang, Jianhua, 149, 192
Jiang Nanxiang, 42
Jiang Qing, 40–41, 63, 68, 73n.8
Jin, Wanxin, 149, 192–93
Jreisat, Jamil, 34
June 18 incident, 44

Kang Sheng, 41–42, 62
Knowledgeable Youth Resettlement Office, 104–5
Knowledgeable Youth Up to the Mountains and Down to the Countryside committee, 104
Kong, Zhi, 149, 193
Kuan Feng, 70

Lan, Ning, 1, 37, 71, 103, 147–49, 155, 168, 178, 179n.1, 179n.4, 193–94
Lee, Hong Yung, 4, 23, 49
Lenin, Vladimir Illyich, 5
Leung, Laifong, 37
Li, Jia, 2–3, 108, 113, 115, 117, 143, 149, 151–53, 155, 161n.10, 166, 172, 194
Liang, Jun, 20, 105–6, 109, 115, 118, 121, 133, 139, 149, 157, 161n.10, 167–69, 194–95
Liao, Liangyu, 149, 195

Li Fuchun, 62
Li Keqiang, xi
Lin, Kang, 14n.10, 71–72, 108–9, 112–13, 117, 124–27, 137–38, 195–96
Lin Biao, 30, 32–33, 52, 54, 64, 67–68, 73–74n.11, 73n.8
Liu, Lina, 103, 149, 196
Liu Shaoqi, 27–34, 40–41, 43–45, 47, 51–52, 54–57, 73n.8, 96
Liu Zhijian, 45
Li Xiannan, 63
Long March, the, 36n.6
"lost generation," xi, 73. See also sent-downs
Lu, Yan, 113–14, 127, 137, 149, 159, 179n.4, 197
Lu Dingyi, 40–41
Luo, Cheng, 149, 197
Luo Ruiqing, 64
Lushan Plenum, 30
Lu Xinhua, 36n.13

Ma, Linfen, 149, 198
Maoist Marxians
 the army and, 62–63
 socialism, interpretation of, 15
 See also Mao Zedong
Maoist Marxians vs. Chinese Weberians
 extension into conflicts throughout society, 47–48
 the politics of the Cultural Revolution and, 37–38, 45, 47, 56, 62–68 (see also politics of the Cultural Revolution)
 pre-Cultural Revolution administration of economic development and, 16–35
 the rustication program and, 75–76
 victory of the Chinese Weberians, 163
 the Wuhan Incident, 67–68
Mao's Thought, study of, 165–68
Mao Zedong
 agrarian socialism of, 26
 bureaucracy and the CCP elite, struggle with, xii, 1–6, 18, 22, 25–35 (see also Cultural Revolution; Maoist Marxians vs. Chinese Weberians; politics of the Cultural Revolution)
 class divisions, rejection of, 47
 communalization, vision of, 24–25
 Confucius, rejection of, 92
 Deng and, 73n.8
 deescalation of the Cultural Revolution, 69–71
 education, socialist vision of, 92–94, 164
 end of Cultural Revolution, declaration of, 13n.6
 the Great Leap Forward as economic plan of, 28–32
 the interviewees' perception of, 20
 Peng Dehuai, confrontation with, 30
 politics of the Cultural Revolution and, 37–38, 40–49, 51–52, 60–61, 64
 principles and goals of, 15–16
 on the rustication program, 75–76
 rustication program, purposes of, 89–96, 164, 168, 173 (see also purposes of the rustication program)
 urbanization, shifting position regarding, 18–19
 withdrawal from the CCP administration, 31
Marx, Karl, 31, 91–92, 102n.9
mass line
 administrative implementation and, 16–17
 Mao's theory of, 15–16
Maynard-Moody, Steven, 10
May 16 Notice, 41
May Seventh Cadre Schools, 164
media, the
 control of by the Cultural Revolution Small Group, 52
 Mao's takeover of the official CCP, 41
 mass line public administration and, 16
Meisner, Maurice, 4, 20–21, 53–54, 74n.13, 76, 88, 101
Meng, Zhiyun, 121, 140, 142–43, 149, 153, 165, 173–74, 198
methodology
 conceptual framework, 4–6
 interviews, 6–12
Michels, Robert, 5
Million Heroes, 66–67

Index

Mo, Wenbin, 149, 199
Musheno, Michael, 10
Mu Xin, 41
Myrdal, Jan, 11

Nie Rongzhen, 62
Nie Yuanzi, 42, 44
Niskanen, William, Jr., 63

Pan, Yihong, 14n.11, 80, 99, 162n.13, 179n.1
Paris Commune, 89
Peng, Yuxin, 149, 199
Peng Dehuai, 30, 33, 35, 40, 64
Peng Zhen, 40–41, 60
People's Liberation Army (PLA)
   the Cultural Revolution and, 52, 54, 60–64, 66–71
   Lin Biao as head of, 30
   Mao and ideological reeducation of, 33
   post-Cultural Revolution restoration of bureaucratic administration, 71
PLA. *See* People's Liberation Army
politics of the Cultural Revolution, 37–38
   the army and, 52, 54, 60–65
   conception of, 40–56
   deposing the Chinese Weberians, 51–52
   factionalism, 47–51, 54–56, 59–61, 65–66, 68–70
   ideology and class origins, 46–47
   Maoist Marxians *vs.* Chinese Weberians, 37–38, 45, 47, 56, 62–68, 175–76
   Maoist offensives and bureaucratic defenses, 42–45
   radicals, rise of the, 51–56
   the Red Guards (*see* Red Guards)
   workers, political divisions within, 54–56
PRC. *See* China, People's Republic of
public administration
   administrative culture, impact of rustication on (*see* administrative culture, impact of rustication on)
   charismatic *vs.* rational, the Cultural Revolution as, 71
   Leninist public management and Weberian bureaucracy, comparison of, 5
   Maoist Marxian *vs.* Chinese Weberian approach to (*see* Maoist Marxians *vs.* Chinese Weberians)
   mass line, 17–18
   of the rustication program (*see* administration of the rustication program)
   See also bureaucracy
purges
   of bureaucrats by 1966, 56–59
   of Gao Gang, 25
   of Liu Shaoqi and Deng Xiaoping, 54, 56, 73n.8
   of Peng Dehuai, 30
purposes of the rustication program
   alternative explanations for, 95–101
   bureaucratization, eliminating perceived ills of, 88, 100–101
   education/reeducation for socialism, 92–94, 164–75
   emancipation of mankind, 89–90
   family structure, transforming, 90–92
   hard labor, tempering and socialist thought reform through, 173–75
   liberation, 89–94
   as part of permanent revolution and perpetual class struggle, 90
   peasantry and peasant life, connecting with, 168–73
   rural development, 98–100, 179n.1
   urban unemployment, 95–97
   youthful unrest, 97–98

Qi Benyu, 41

Rao Shushi, 36n.7
Red Guards, 38, 74n.15
   conservative faction of, 48–49
   family structure, impact on, 92
   radical faction of, 49–51
   "reformatories through labor" established by, 173
   violence of the radical, 54
   as weapon against the intelligentsia and bureaucrats, 76
   workers and, 54–55, 59
Ren, Ling, 149, 200
revolutionary tourism, 78–79

revolution committees, 70–71
Rosen, Stanley, 95
rustication literature, 36n.13
rustication program, xi, 72–73, 76
    administrative culture, impact on (see administrative culture, impact of rustication on)
    administrative organization of (see administration of the rustication program)
    bureaucratic growth as unintended consequence of, 79, 88, 101, 160, 163
    compliance with, 113–16, 160
    conceptual framework for analyzing, 4–6
    the Cultural Revolution and, 3–4 (see also Cultural Revolution)
    dissatisfaction with, 87–88
    existence of despite lack of supportive constituencies, reasons for, 159–60
    goals of/explanations for (see purposes of the rustication program)
    interviewing survivors of, 6–12
    location as differentiator of experiences, 148–50
    origins of, 78–80
    the peasants' response to the sent-downs, 137–39
    percentage of the population effected by, 2
    politics of, 75–76
    puzzle of, 1–4
    settling into the countryside, interviewees' experience with, 131–48
    timeline of, 77

Sanfan (the three antis) campaign, 18
sanzi yibao ("three freedom" policy), 29
Second Five-Year Plan, 26–29
sent-downs, xi. See also interviewees; rustication program
Shanghai Commune, 60
Shen, Lei, 149, 200
Shi, Chaowei, 149, 201
Shirk, Susan, xi, 1, 159
Sixteen-Point Program of the Cultural Revolution, 93
Snow, Edgar, 45, 47

Social Education Movement (Siqing, or "four cleansings" movement), 32–33
socialist reeducation. See education/reeducation for socialism
Song, Liya, 113, 115, 143, 149, 151, 156, 174, 179n.1, 201
Steel-Tempered Second Headquarters, 65
Steel-Tempered September 13, 65
Steel-Tempered Workers' General, 65–66
Su, Tingyu, 113, 120, 125, 140, 143, 149, 153, 166, 202
Sufan campaign ("Campaign to Wipe Out Hidden Counterrevolutionaries"), 25
Sun, Hong, 103, 106, 119, 125, 147, 149, 166, 178, 179n.1, 202–3

Tan, Jing, 37–38, 112, 119, 125, 127–28, 131, 133, 149, 157, 169, 174, 203
Tang, Bo, 112, 119–20, 125–27, 131, 133, 149–50, 168, 172, 174, 203–4
Tan Zhenlin, 63–64, 78
Third Five-Year Plan, 44
Tian, Jie, 115, 127, 134, 137, 139, 149, 157, 167–68, 172, 204
Treiman, Donald J., 94

Unger, Jonathan, 87–88, 96, 98–99
Up to the Mountains and Down to the Countryside campaign, xi, 78. See also rustication program
urbanization, 18–19, 21
urban unemployment, 95–97

Vogel, Ezra, 4, 15

Wan, Yanli, 112–13, 115, 126, 134, 137, 139, 148–49, 157, 161n.8, 204–5
Wang, Ting, 109–10, 110, 112, 114, 140, 143–45, 149, 154–55, 165–66, 178, 205
Wang Kewen, 67
Wang Li, 41, 66–68, 70
Wang Zhaojun, 31
Weber, Max, 5, 19–21, 23–24, 63
Wen, Kai, 114–15, 118, 127–28, 140–42, 149, 153–54, 161n.8, 163, 174, 205–6
Whyte, Martin, 22–23
Workers' General Headquarters of Wuhan, 66

Index

Wu, Yun, 1–2, 52–53, 113–14, 116–17, 121–22, 140, 149, 153–55, 206
Wufan (the five antis) campaign, 18
Wu Han, 40–41
Wuhan Incident, 65–68
Wuhan Revolutionary Rebel General Headquarters, 65
Wuhan Steel-Tempered Three, 65

xiafang, 28, 36n.12
Xie Fuzhi, 66–67
Xi Jinping, xi, 179n.2
Xin Fu, 67
Xu Xiangqian, 62

Yan, Jiaqi, 96–97
Yang, Lijun, 14n.10, 120–21, 145–46, 149, 173, 207, 210n.3
Yao Wenyuan, 40–41
Ye Jianying, 45, 62
Yu, Kelin, 53, 72, 102n.5, 112, 114–15, 126–27, 136, 148–49, 157, 167, 170–71, 207–8
Yuan, Ying, 103, 115–16, 118, 126, 149, 163, 178, 208

Zhang, Jian, 2, 13n.8, 20, 104, 116, 126–27, 130, 140, 145, 149, 153, 158, 161n.1, 172–73, 208–9
Zhang Chunqiao, 40–41, 63, 68
Zhao, Ming, 110, 112, 116, 120, 122, 126, 130, 144, 149, 156, 174, 209
Zhou, Xueguang, 35n.1, 161n.5, 162n.13
Zhou, Zhixin, 209–10
Zhou Enlai, 42, 63, 67
Zhou Yang, 40